George Skipper

NORWICH·UNION·LIFE·INSURANCE·SOCIETY

GEORGE SKIPPER

THE ARCHITECT'S LIFE AND WORKS

Richard Barnes

FRONTIER

GEORGE SKIPPER – *The Architect's Life and Works*
First published 2020

Frontier Publishing
Kirstead
Norfolk
NR15 1EG

Text and Compilation © Richard Barnes 2021
All Rights Reserved

British Library Cataloguing in Publication Data:
A catalogue record for this publication is available from
The British Library Bibliographic database.

2nd (paperback) edition 2021

ISBN(13): 978-1-872914-47-3

For permission to reproduce any part of
this book, please contact the Publishers.

Photographs of drawings in George Skipper's pocket sketchbooks
(Half-title page and Plates 5, 6, 7, 7A, 19, 21, 30, 37, 71, 109,
158) are all ©RIBA Collections, (RIBA SKB 322 onwards) and
may not be reproduced. Taken by the architect's grandson, the
drawings were to be professionally photographed by RIBA staff.
In the exceptional circumstances of the Coronavirus pandemic
throughout 2020, this was not possible.

Design frontier
www.frontierpublishing.co.uk

PRINTED IN GREAT BRITAIN
Swallowtail Print, Norwich

CONTENTS

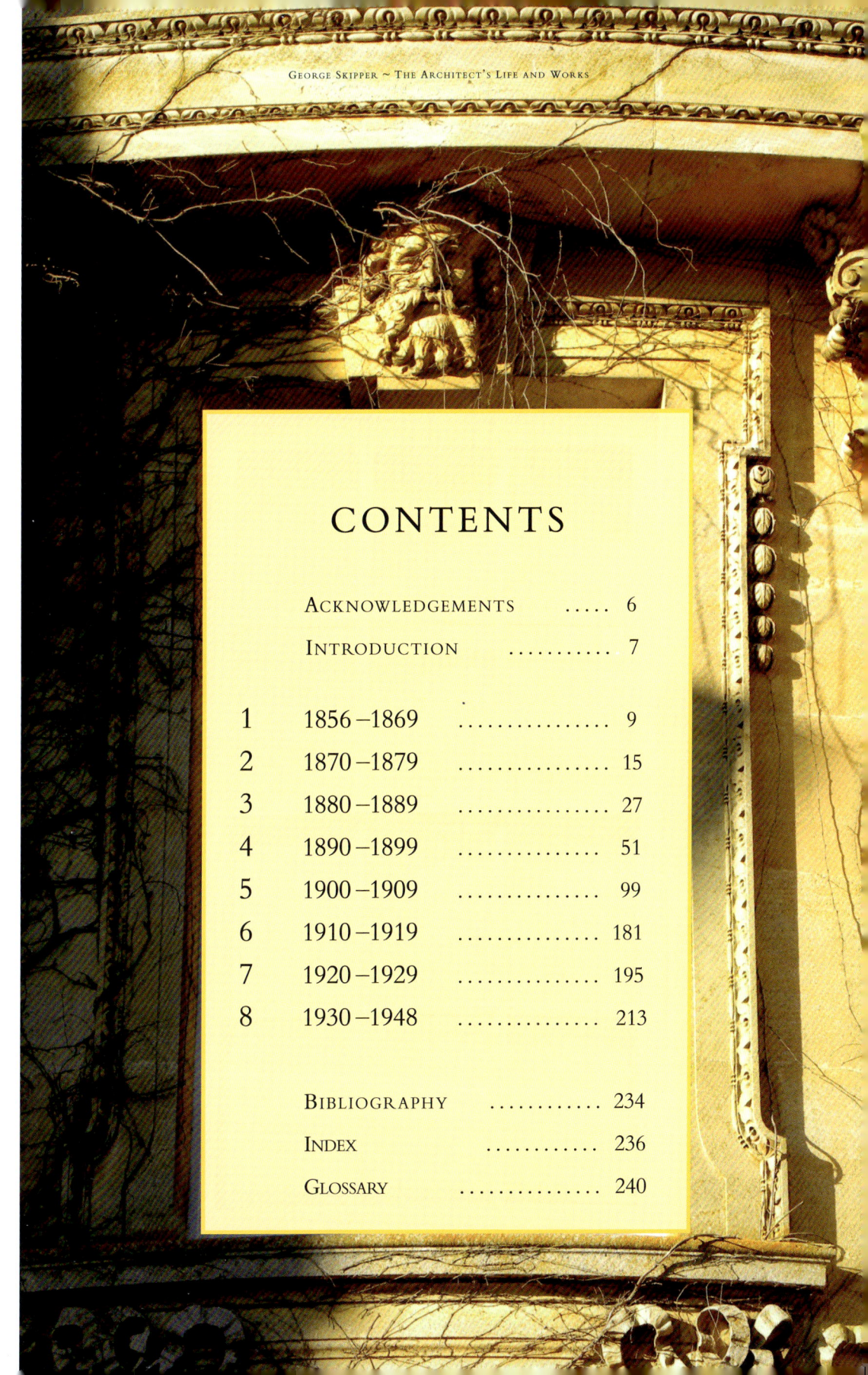

	ACKNOWLEDGEMENTS	.....	6
	INTRODUCTION	....	7
1	1856–1869	....	9
2	1870–1879	....	15
3	1880–1889	....	27
4	1890–1899	....	51
5	1900–1909	....	99
6	1910–1919	....	181
7	1920–1929	....	195
8	1930–1948	....	213
	BIBLIOGRAPHY	....	234
	INDEX	....	236
	GLOSSARY	....	240

ACKNOWLEDGEMENTS

For their valuable assistance and kindness, the author and publishers wish to thank:

George Skipper's family and descendants, Elizabeth Staunton, Rev Philip Foster, Betty Skipper, Jonathan Skipper, Colin Skipper — all of whom generously provided material, images and information; most especially, Stephen Thomas, for permission to access his 2005 dissertation on GJS, without which this publication could not have taken place; Faith Shaw, of whom very little is known, but whose early 1970s research into GJS was the first recorded work, and which inspired David Jolley of Norwich School of Art and George's son, the architect Edward Skipper, to take 'Skipper Studies' further in the 1970s and 80s; Charles Hind, FSA, Chief Curator and H.J. Heinz Curator of Drawings, RIBA British Architectural Library; Tom Barnes, Assistant Archivist at Surrey House (Aviva PLC), for guidance over Skipper's work at the former Norwich Union Insurance HQ; Caroline Jarrold and Peter Goodrum for clarification regarding Skipper's work to Jarrolds' building; Richard Cocke, Sarah Cocke, and David Bussey for initial advice and image references; Edward Back and Charles Temple-Richards for generous permission to visit and photograph Skipper buildings; *Country Life* Magazine for access to Clive Aslet's two part feature about Sennowe Park; the Royal Norfolk and Suffolk Yacht Club for permission to view the interior of the clubhouse; the former Cromer Preservation Society and Dereham Heritage Trust for information; Fakenham and District Community Archive for permission to reproduce their photograph of Wyman's former office; Mark Oakland for directions in Cromer, to Glenys Hitchings for her Skipper research in Cromer; Museum Holdings at R.G Carter Construction on behalf of J. Youngs Ltd, Builders.

INTRODUCTION

I knew very little about George Skipper before preparing this text. I do recall, however, that when I arrived in Norwich in the 1970s, I noticed three or four buildings that added to the atmosphere of the Market Place and the area around it. Of course this included the ancient Guildhall, but also the Royal Arcade, Haymarket Chambers, and what is now St Giles House. For at least ten years I had not realized that these buildings had been designed by one man, and that his name was George John Skipper.

My own interest is in British sculpture, and I wrote a book about a 19th century ancestor, the sculptor John Bell (1811–1895) who came from Norfolk and conducted a successful career in London. In doing so I chose the simplest structure, that of starting at the beginning of the subject's life, and going on until the end. Applying the same methodology with George Skipper came naturally.

Help was given at every turn. Other writers, especially Steven Thomas, in his 2005 dissertation, had already set out the frame of Skipper's chronology. It was noted that the First World War was a watershed in Skipper's life. From the beginning of the war, when work dried up, he was suddenly let down by bad investments and, at the same time, newly married to his wife Alice, and soon with young children to support. So there is a 'young architect' and 'older architect' aspect. While writing I became fond of my subject, and admired the way Skipper dealt with adversity in this post-WW1 phase of his life. It is hard to believe that he went back to work in London at the age of seventy.

This is not a complete biography: there are blank areas on the map of his life, but it brings together all that is presently known of the man. There are surprises, for instance George's joining with an evangelical movement, and later separating from it during the First World War because his son was not a Conscientious Objector. Initially the subject of George's evangelical Christianity seemed daunting. I imagined that it would have inhibited his architectural approach, but in practice Skipper was unrestrained in his architecture, adding verve with coloured tiles, turrets, statues and urns. One senses that he was different character whenever he picked up his pencil and started to draw. He has been described as an artist-architect.

I hope this book will explain George Skipper and his place in English architecture. With many others I believe he should be held in high regard.

Richard Barnes / Norfolk, July 2020

Pl.1
Dereham Market Place, 1867.
Print published by W.F Austin, Architect and Surveyor.

Half-title page illustration
George Skipper, Architect, pencil on paper.
Sketch of an urn, or vase, in George Skipper's pocket sketch-books.
RIBA Collections.

Frontispiece illustration
George Skipper, Architect, March 1901. Ink on Linen paper.
(detail) Front Elevation Drawing, Surrey House, Norwich.
Head Office of Norwich Union Life Insurance.

Contents page illustration
George Skipper, Architect, 1905–1909,
Photo: Stonemasonry around window, Sennowe Hall, Norfolk.

Chapter one

1856—1869

'... once more at Dereham, the place of my birth, whither my father had been dispatched on the recruiting service. I have already said that it was a beautiful little town – at least it was at the time of which I am speaking; what it is at present I know not, for thirty years and more have elapsed since I last trod it streets. It will scarcely have improved, for how could it be better than it then was. I love to think on thee, pretty quiet D—, thou pattern of an English country town, with thy clean but narrow streets branching out from thy modest market place, with thine old-fashioned houses, with here and there a roof of venerable thatch, with thy one half-aristocratic mansion . . . . . . Yes pretty Dereham, I could always love thee . . .'

George Borrow (1803–1881) *Lavengro*, (written in 1842 and published 1851. Borrow is remembering his childhood in Dereham in about 1810).

George John Skipper was born on 6 August 1856 in Back Lane, Dereham, Norfolk, the second son of Robert Skipper (1824–1904) and his wife, Elizabeth, both of whom were thirty-one years old. A sturdy, fair-haired little chap, George was mostly in the company of his brother, also named Robert, who was a year older. Other brothers were to follow.

His father, Robert Skipper, was an entrepreneurial builder and brick and tile manufacturer, who would buy plots of land, build houses and then sell them. He employed fifty men at a time and was capable of completing public commissions, for instance building King's Lynn Railway Station. He was also a lender and an underwriter to various property deals in Dereham and the vicinity.

George's mother, Elizabeth, born on New Year's day in 1825, was the second of four daughters of a former farmer and later tailor, Richard Wilemer, and his wife Ann, of Great Ellingham, twelve miles south of Dereham. The parish records of Great Ellingham, as well as those in Norwich, Aylsham, Dereham and Fakenham, show that there were legions of Skippers. It is a very common name in the county, and it is not easy to distinguish one Skipper family from another. There were at least three large Skipper families in Shipdham, five miles south of Dereham where Robert Skipper came from.

There were more Skipper families in Costessey, who were also brickmakers and terracotta mould-makers.

Dereham, or East Dereham as it was always known, is one of England's ancient market towns. If you do not know Norfolk, it is the upper part of the projecting bump on England's East coast, rich farming country, with good arable soils on a flat landscape. In the lower middle of this county is the city of Norwich, from which roads radiate in all directions. Dereham is seventeen miles to the West of the City, on the road to Kings Lynn, the Midlands, and the North of Britain.

It was a fine place for a boy to grow up in. There was an abbey church with a tower, a market place, corn exchange, assembly rooms, three banks, a post office, a mechanics institute, schools, a court of petty sessions, and six dissenting chapels. There were factories, maltings and a tannery, a steam driven saw-mill, and at least four foundries. Dereham had two coaching inns and was on the route of the cattle drovers and their herds heading to Great Yarmouth and Smithfield.

George's birthplace in the town is listed as Back Lane in the *Oxford Dictionary of National Biographies*. Back Lane cannot be located – there is no such street in Dereham these days. It was located in the area later occupied by Commercial Road. It was the new house, which Robert Skipper built, in Russell Place, in Commercial Road, which became the Skipper's family home for decades to come. Skipper senior had mastered the development of Commercial Road, not only buying plots, but by underwriting the purchase of the entire site by Thomas Studd from the trustees of Jane and George Hart in 1853. Moreover Skipper designed and built some of the houses there, starting with seven dwellings in Providence Terrace, being numbers 81–93 in Commercial Road.

So even at this stage, Mr Skipper of Commercial Road in Dereham, not yet thirty years old, was an able businessman. He could buy land, draw up his own plans, and use his own workforce to build handsome villas constructed of bricks from his own brickyard.

To follow George's life in art and architecture, it is very interesting, if speculative, to try to get a sense of his character. It cannot be done of course, but let us see the little boy as a blank canvas. The early circumstances of his family cast a shadow throughout his life.

For a start he was a second son, viewed as competition from older and younger brothers. As a second-born child he would for a while be playing catch-up with the older brother, though brother Robert Skipper junior (1855–1945) was only one year older. When George was two years old his mother gave birth to a third son, Arthur, who was born and died in June 1858. A fourth was Frederick Skipper (1860–1955). A year later, in December 1861, Elizabeth Skipper gave birth to Richard Wilemer Skipper (1861–1957). Finally, in 1863, she had another son, John Henry Skipper (1863–1901).

Five years later, Elizabeth Skipper died in March 1868. Everything changed. For George, only eleven years old, there can only have been grief. The one love, the mother love, the tenderness of the person who brought him to life was over. Death was something George Skipper learned about from early on. And, for all we know, this primal loss was compounded, because after a few months, the boys' father married again.

To begin with Robert Skipper had depended on the boys' aunts and his housekeeper and maidservants to look after the five youngsters. However, either through his work, or through an introduction, he became connected with Caroline Withers, the eldest daughter of John Showell Withers of Kelling. Withers was a maltster, brewer, auctioneer and surveyor, a socially elevated and educated man, at one time Surveyor for Highways in the Cromer district.

The couple were briefly engaged and married and Caroline Skipper (1830–1919) moved into the family home in Commercial Road. For the boys, here was their stepmother. There is no knowledge of whether the relationship was good, but we do know that the five Skipper boys were happy to live in their father and stepmother's home for many years to come, so it must have been a comfortable situation.

In the short term, however, the two eldest boys, eventually all of them, were sent away to the city of Norwich, to a handsome building in Bracondale, which overlooked Norwich's riverside and railways station. Run by a loose association of tutors and their assistants, it had gradually become known as Bracondale School, housing about fifty boys aged from eight to sixteen.

Maybe the two elder boys, George and his brother, Robert, aged twelve and thirteen respectively, would never have left home to become boarders in Bracondale if their mother had not died. Having the boys out of home for a while was inevitably easier for their newly wed father. It required a big outlay of money in school fees, one that he could afford.

The school in Bracondale had begun about forty years earlier, in 1821, when a Latin scholar and tutor, Daniel Bamfield Hickie, started teaching young gentlemen. Initially, languages were the tutors' forté, with coaching in Latin, Greek, French and Italian, and even Turkish. By the mid-1850s, the syllabus

Pl. 2
George's father, Robert Skipper (1824–1904).

Pl. 3
Bracondale School, Norwich.
Tinted print c.1835

had been extended. There were still only two teaching rooms downstairs, and only about fifty boys, who were all boarders to be accommodated in small dormitories, with boys of their own age. In years to come, notably from the 1890s, when another school combined with Bracondale, it would acquire better facilities and high standards, and survived until 1993.

By the time the Skipper boys were there, the range of tuition available included Art classes twice a week, conducted by a Drawing Master. The works of the artist, Henry Ninham (1796–1874), the painterly draftsman of Norwich, were a constant influence, and there was certainly a tradition in drawing and painting the buildings of Norwich. And here George would excel, because he had been conscious of buildings from a very early age. He could see elevations and styles of brickwork where other children would only see a front door and a smoking chimney. For young George Skipper to review his father's occupations was another part of his formative education, because Robert Skipper was an enterprising, ambitious and successful man. A tangible cornerstone of his success in surveying, designing, building and selling houses, maltings and factories was his business as a brickmaker.

While very many farms and villages had their own brickfields, Robert Skipper expanded his production to the level of a small industry. His first brickyards were down in Shipdham, five miles south of Dereham, where there were many other Skipper families, very probably interrelated. There was, for instance, Isaac Skipper, born in Shipdham in 1815, innkeeper of the Kings Head, with six children, and Henry Skipper, born in Shipdham in 1825, harness maker with seven children.

George's father had acquired another brickyard, which was much closer, in Dereham. *Kelly's Directory* of 1883 stated that the claypit and brickyard was next to the railway station, which was almost on the doorstep of the Skipper family's home. How many times George and Robert must have been up at the brickfield, or waited by the kiln while their father gave instructions to his brickmakers. Maybe he never went to his father's brickyards, and this is an imagined picture, but I doubt it. It was an exciting place to visit.

As he looked around, the men, and even a woman, continued with the heavy tasks. Everyone had different duties. At the clay pit a man known as the temperer moved the clay to the pug-mill, and oversaw the mixing and squashing of the material. As it was extruded, the tube of wet clay was cut off by the Pug-boy in chunks big enough to make three or four bricks, and this was carried to the moulding table. Sand was put on the table and kneaded into the clay, making the size and shape of the clay suitable for the mould. The brick-moulder, or brickmaker sanded the insides of the mould, and then threw the clot of clay into the mould, making sure to fill all the corners. After trimming off surplus clay from the mould, the brickmaker turned out the raw bricks onto a pallet. Then the 'Take-off boy' passed these raw bricks to the off-bearer, who wheeled the wet bricks on barrows to the stacks, where 'hackers' would pile the bricks in stacks to dry.

The firings were more or less constant throughout spring and summer, using up all the stacks of raw bricks. George must have felt the immense heat of the large kiln, and noted the careful attention paid to it. Actually loading the kiln took 'the setter' more than a day's work. The raw bricks still contained 10–15% moisture and so, to avoid these bricks exploding, the kiln could not be taken up to high temperatures straight away. During these hours steam would emerge. Then the kiln was allowed to get hotter. More coal was needed every couple of hours as the temperature rose to over 2,000 degrees Fahrenheit, going through a transformation, a hardening which meant that a brick could never dissolve in wet conditions. The kiln was kept at this temperature for four days, before the fire died down and the kiln gradually cooled for another three days. Only then could it could be emptied and the fired bricks separated into stacks of varying quality and colour.

The most significant aspect of his father's brickworks in Dereham was the proximity of the railway. Before locomotion the brickmakers did everything on a local level for the simple reason that moving bricks weighing five pounds or more was heavy work. A cart or wagon could only carry so many, let us say a ton, or four hundred and forty bricks. Once the railway arrived, the train could shift 100,000 bricks at a time. So Mr Skipper's bricks found a much larger market in Norwich, Kings Lynn, and even beyond. Authors John Thomas and David Turnock, writing in *The Regional History of the Railways of Great Britain* identify Dereham as one of the places that illustrated the power of nineteenth century railways to develop a small town:

> With an 1841 population of 3,837, Dereham already had several brewers and malsters, two iron foundries and various small industries geared to the needs and produce of what was described as the 'Garden of Norfolk'. But by 1855 (eight years after the railway arrived) it had grown to nearly 4,500 and had added a steam saw-mill, two further foundries, and a greatly expanded interest in the making of agricultural implements. *White's Directory* of that year recorded how the town trade had 'considerably increased' since the opening of the railways, and described the extensive

granaries which had been built near the station and through which extremely large quantities of corn were dispatched by rail. East Dereham in fact well illustrated the power of the nineteenth century railways to develop a small town when not too near a major centre and when conditions, in this instance the high fertility of the local soil, were right.

It had begun in 1845 when the Lynn and Dereham Railway Company and the Norfolk Railway Company were both licensed to build railway lines to Dereham. The Norfolk Railway, coming from Wymondham (via Kimberley, Hardingham, Thuxton, Yaxham) to the South reached Dereham in 1847. The Dereham and Lynn line, coming from Kings Lynn (via Middleton, East Winch, Narborough, Swaffham, Dunham, Fransham and Wendling) was ready a year later. Both lines were operated after 1862 by the Great Eastern Railway Company.

Not only, as mentioned, did the railways bring greatly increased trade and manufacturing opportunities to the town and surrounding farmlands, but they helped Robert Skipper in his business. He could take on bigger jobs further away from Dereham, for example shifting hundreds of thousands of bricks to the County School. This was an immense building, the Watts Academy, an inland naval training school for sons of farmers, since demolished. But it had its own nearby station on another line opened in 1849, going North via Fakenham to Wells-next-the-Sea.

Back in Norwich, George had been sent to an optician and now wore spectacles: they were a welcome improvement. He was also growing fast and needed measuring for a suit.

Pl. 3A
George Skipper, watercolour. Unidentified, undated, signed 'GJS'.

CHAPTER TWO

1870—1879

Young Skipper, still at Bracondale School, found that he enjoyed the Drawing lessons and was getting satisfying results, commendations and even a school prize for Art. He saw a glimpse of himself as a grown man and an artist. And why not? Norwich was a very painterly place, a traditional home for landscape and architectural artists, notably John Sell Cotman and Henry Ninham, to name two among about thirty disparate draftsmen and painters known to art historians as the 'Norwich School of Artists'. Some of these men were still alive in 1870 and gave lessons.

Whether Bracondale's visiting Drawing Master suggested it, or not, George decided that he wanted to attend Norwich Art School. And when he discussed this with his father the idea was approved, but with conditions. How many times have parents of artists influenced the course of art history? In George's case, the aspiring painter heading towards Norwich's Art School was encouraged to apply for two classes: one in Fine Art, and the other an Artisans' course specialising in Architecture. As a comment on George's father, who was paying his fees, Robert Skipper steered his artistic son towards buildings, and in this way it could be said that he 'made' his son into an architect. There is no suggestion that George was in any way unwilling.

The Art School in Norwich was by then operating as one of the new 'Government Schools of Art'. The origins of the Government Schools of Art were many years earlier in the Napoleonic Wars. The British had found new markets while the French were otherwise occupied. But by the 1830s the trade relationship was competitive, and the government was concerned because British goods suffered in terms of design. British manufactures were known for technical excellence, but their designs were unattractive compared with those in rival France, where pattern makers and industrial designers gave French manufacturers the leading edge. It meant that Britain was spending money importing those goods and hiring foreign artisans. Lack of design and artistry was impoverishing the country.

With this in view, the Government Select Committee on Arts and Manufactures sat for nine months until summer 1836. They heard evidence and listened to ideas from leading artists and theorists on how the situation might be improved. One idea to work in the long run was the establishment of Schools of Art and Design, the beginning of Britain's Art Schools.

The civil servant most active in later Select Committees was Henry Cole (1808–82). Cole's other ideas included introducing artists to manufacturers, for instance taking Herbert Minton, the great Staffordshire Pottery owner, to the studio of Norfolk-born sculptor, John Bell (1811–95) in London. Using the Society of Arts (soon to be Royal Society of Arts) to offer prizes, Henry Cole initiated a series of design exhibitions and won the support of Albert, Prince Consort. One of the earliest of these design exhibitions was in Norwich in 1840, the Polytechnic Exhibition, which was held in a bazaar in St Andrews Hall and organized by John Barwell, President of the Mechanics Institute, and his wife Louisa.

The Barwells campaigned for a Norwich School of Design, and in fact Louisa's sister married the painter Richard Redgrave (1804–1888) who was teaching at the South Kensington School. And so it was that for a period of five years, John Barwell, in conjunction with benefactors and subscribing supporters, discussed the prospect of an Art School that was to receive a government subsidy.

In the meantime, Henry Cole had been busy. The manufacturing exhibitions he had organized around the country had been successful, and with the help of Prince Albert he prepared what was to be the greatest show on earth, The Great Exhibition of 1851. And it was from the overall success of The Great Exhibition that Cole had enough money to build museums and promote the principles of design in industry through The Department of Practical Art of the Board of Trade. Beginning in the first Government Art School in the nascent South Kensington Museum (now the V&A Museum), Cole immediately expanded to link the system to more Art Schools throughout the country.

The system that Cole and his advisers set up was known as the South Kensington System. It provided certification to teachers and approved subsidies to the provincial art schools. It also organized visiting lectures and produced booklets on technique, such as *Rudimentary Art Instruction: Freehand, Outline from Outline*, by John Bell. The sculptor had studied at The Royal Academy Schools and previously at Sass's private school, and the methods of training were familiar, involving students copying from classical figures, and repeating techniques until they were proficient. By the time Cole retired Britain had ninety Art Schools, and trained Art Teachers throughout secondary schools

When George Skipper went to Norwich Art School for two half-year sessions in 1872–73 it was under Robert Cochrane. Headmaster for twenty-five years from 1859, Cochrane was the first to entirely adhere to the

London-led rules, hiring certificated teachers. He also had to balance a school of artistic young ladies and a smaller amount of artisanal students. The fees for the artisan classes were cheaper than those for the Private, or Public Ladies, or Gentleman's classes, because they attracted the government subsidy. The school operated morning and evening classes. Notices reminded students that all course fees should be paid in advance.

George attended the day classes at the Art School. Still only sixteen he stood somewhere above and between the fine artists and the artisans, because he was doing two courses, one in Fine Art and the other in first Elementary and then Advanced Artizan (sic) Classes specializing in Architecture.

In the Elementary class George learnt about 'Practical plans and Solid Geometry, Machine Construction and Drawing, Building Construction,

Pl. 4
Norwich School of Art in the 1870s, situated on the top floor of the Free Library at the corner of Duke Street.

Pl. 5
George Skipper, charcoal pencil on paper. Figures in the street, Belgium, 1873.
RIBA Collections.

Linear Perspectives, Free-hand Drawing, and Shading from the flat and round, Model Drawing and Elementary Colour'.

Proceeding to Advanced class his tuition included 'Drawing the figure from Casts, Painting Ornament, Flowers, Still-Life, Landscapes, etc'. Additional application, for male classes only, included Architectural, Mechanical and Engineering Drawing.

It is thought he lived at home in Dereham and commuted by train to the city, a journey of over twenty miles there and back each day. No doubt there were days when the train journeys were difficult, but for the young art and architecture student sitting in a railway carriage, there was so much to see. The details of arches, walls and iron pillars of the railway stops and small stations were of interest. At that moment his father was building the station at the other end of the same line, the terminus at King's Lynn. Skipper senior had managed the whole business. (Despite alterations, the station still operates with a train to London every hour).

Norwich citizens of today should not imagine Skipper, the young art student, inside the splendid buildings of present-day Norwich Art School. The five-floored brick building in St George's Street, overlooking the river, was not built for another twenty years.

Instead, the college was, in the days of headmaster Cochrane, on the top floor of the Free Library Building, at the corner of St Andrew's (Broad) Street and Duke Street. The building does not exist now, but it had a triangular floor plan and provided only about ten rooms. Nevertheless, there were shared studios, teaching rooms, a few plaster casts from classical items in Rome, and a small art library. With hindsight this period in the history of Norwich Art School might be seen as a difficult time, hindered by the government SKS (South Kensington System) regulations, which were old fashioned and artistically inhibiting from the beginning. Within a few years the SKS tests were dropped.

But George enjoyed his year at Art School and passed the South Kensington System tests. Marjorie Althorpe-Guyton, author of *A Happy Eye – A School of Art in Norwich 1845–1982* records that George Skipper also won prizes for excellence 'in freehand, geometry and model'.

His father had plans for George's next step. Either through his own contacts, or through his clients, Robert Skipper had arranged an apprenticeship with a London architect who was just starting a new practice.

Moreover, in the fashion of the newly founded Architectural Association, George was to go in search of inspiration to Belgium. A ferry service operated from Dover to Ostend in Flanders. Just as viable, he might have had a passage out of Great Yarmouth. The duration of the excursion, it would seem, was only one week, from Wednesday 20 August until 27 August 1873. Who accompanied him? There is no indication in George's little sketchbook, but it is extremely unlikely that he travelled alone. He was too young: George celebrated his 17th birthday just before his visit to the nearby continent. Could he have gone with an architect, paid for by his father?

George probably had other drawing materials, but the only information to be found is in his little sketchbook (the first in the RIBA collection). He

Pl. 6
George Skipper, pencil on paper, 26 August 1873.
'Gate at Malines'.
RIBA Collections.

sketched a timber-framed tower between Bruges and Ghent on 22nd August, and ten windows by an outside staircase in Bruges itself. He drew three separate spires and a gatehouse in Malines (Mechelen), between Brussels and Antwerp on August 26th. In the square around St Rombould's Cathedral he observed ten variations of the Dutch gable. On the 27th, before returning, he made a sketch of a double-arched sluice, and a quick scribble of the port of Antwerp.

Returning to England, George went home, and then set off for London. He was greeted by his new 'master', Mr John Thomas Lee FRIBA (c.1845–1920) of Regent Street, and later of 16 Great James Street, Bedford Row. As mentioned, this was Lee's inaugural year as an architect with his own practice, and without being too cynical, it could be that Lee took on George as an Articled Assistant because not only could George make a contribution, but he (his father) might even pay for the privilege.

The circumstances of an architect's training were in flux. If a few years earlier George would have worked in a different system. Any later and he would have had to undertake the RIBA's compulsory exam, instituted in 1882.

The Architectural Association's notes on its own foundation state that the Association began in response to malpractice in articled pupilage:

> The Architectural Association was founded in London in 1847 by a group of young articled pupils as a reaction against the prevailing conditions under which architectural training could be obtained. Unlike continental models such as the French L'École des Beaux Arts, which imparted a degree of state-direction and control on architectural education, Britain with its liberal democracy and traditional fear of powerful centralised government had adopted a system of articled pupilage, whereby large premiums were advanced to private architects in return for imparting an education and training. This practise was rife with vested interests and open to abuse, dishonesty and incompetence.

Pl. 7
George Skipper, pencil on paper, 27 August 1873. 'View of Antwerp'. RIBA Collections.

Naturally, under articles to Lee, George had to do his master's bidding, attending site meetings, functioning as a clerk of works, talking to clients and contractors, as well as drawing up plans. The pupil also had to prove he had the required knowledge of geometry, measurements and mechanics. He had to demonstrate 'a reasonable knowledge' of classical architecture, as well as that of the middle ages. He had to show that he could handle the responsibilities of a clerk of works on a sufficiently important public building.

John Lee was affiliated with two other architects, whose influences were far reaching. One of these was Alfred Waterhouse (1830–1905) who, in the year that young Skipper arrived, started building the Natural History Museum in South Kensington. It was Waterhouse's best-known work, displaying large quantities of terracotta details, inside and out.

The intended architect (and military engineer) had been Francis Fowke, (1823–1865) who had already designed parts of the adjacent Victoria and Albert Museum, the Albert Hall and other museums and national galleries. Working from and extending Fowke's ideas, Alfred Waterhouse added a large amount of terracotta embellishment, described as 'details of enrichment of the new museum'. Many of these details had been made by Mr Dujardin, the French foreman at Farmer and Brindley, the well-known firm of Architectural Sculptors. They included bas-reliefs, medallions and sculpture in the round, depicting flora and living and extinct fauna, as well as columns and window surrounds.

Seeing these terracotta architectural enrichments, it would be a fair assumption that young Skipper thought about his own father's brick kilns, and those of his father's contact outside Norwich, George Gunton of Costessey brickworks.

The second architect with whom George Skipper's master worked was William Eden Nesfield (1835–1888), whose father, the better-known landscape architect and artist, William Andrews Nesfield, was still alive. Known for a number of buildings designed in a style described as Queen Anne Revival, the younger Nesfield also wrote and painted. Almost all architecture of the Victorian era can be seen as a series of revivals – of Gothic, of Classical, of Baroque, of Jacobean and many others, and Nesfield was a successful exponent, designing mansions with turreted roofs, associated estate cottages and ornamental gatehouses. His partner in design was the eminent architect Richard Norman Shaw (1831–1912), whose interests were similar, though perhaps on a grander scale. Shaw's works included Cragside in Northumberland and the Royal Geographical Society's HQ in Kensington Gore. His designs also showed an admirable tendency to combine with sculptors, especially on the grand fountain at Witley, for the Earl of Dudley, or the Flora Fountain, shipped to Bombay.

We can get an impression of George Skipper's growing view of architecture. He was working beneath and among the greatest architectural figures of that time, in the biggest and busiest and richest city in the world, where great patrons and institutions commissioned. We cannot be sure of the extent of personal contact between these great men and the young pupil from Norfolk, not yet twenty years old. As well as studying, George probably carried drawings and ran errands. With his background in Dereham, the young man knew how to make himself understood by builders and suppliers – he had his uses. Most importantly, he could draw, and this will have been noticed.

And what young person, whether of architectural inclination or not, could not be in awe of the metropolis, now or then? There was building in progress on a massive scale. Much of 'Albertopolis' – Exhibition Road in Kensington, where all the museums are – was still being built. The Thames Riverside, with Bazalgette's extensive drainage schemes, was being established with a mighty embankment and two new bridges. Teams of navvies were digging out the first Underground railways, street lighting was being introduced and steel tramways were laid into roads. The city roared with construction work.

Where George lodged, probably arranged by John Lee, is not known. However, a significant event happened before he left London whereby he joined the Plymouth Brethren. Steven Thomas's conversation in 2004 with Mrs Betty Skipper, (George's daughter-in-law), records that George had been approached by one of the Brethren at his place of lodging, and that was where a conversion took place.

Before anything it should be noted that a career in the architectural profession was reasonably normal for non-conformists. Alfred Waterhouse and Richard Lane were Quakers, William Hill and F.J Jobson were Methodists, Henry Sulley was a Christadelphian, Thomas Worthington was a Unitarian. Furthermore George came from a town and county known for all varieties of nonconformism. In fact several of the neighbouring houses in Commercial Road, Dereham, belonged to nonconformist ministers.

Nevertheless, this conversion was a profound move, one that could not be taken lightly, or ignored, then or now. The Brethren are special among nonconformists. They are an Evangelical Protestant Christian group that has, to an extent, isolated itself from the church by doing without priests, vicars and bishops. Men and women meet in a fellowship and all beliefs are centred upon the bible; there are some Six-day Creationists in the following. Without doubt they are sincere, family-oriented people who conduct their lives in a moral way and meet regularly with others of their faith. They are conservative and low church, meaning that they are not interested in the pomp and ritual, or ornament, of some Anglican or Catholic congregations.

The fact that Brethren mostly confine their social activity to their own kind was bound to isolate them. Some leeway was allowed, for example, regarding the rule against 'breaking bread' (having a meal) with any non-Brethren, whereby lenience was permitted if any other Brethren were present.

But questions spring to mind: how would conversion to the Brethren affect this young architect at the outset of his career? In particular, would a puritan anti-ornament style constrain his designs for buildings?

Pl. 7A *(facing page)* George Skipper, pencil on paper, 1877. 'A Chimney'. RIBA Collections.

At this point George left London. There has been some confusion over the dates of George's apprenticeship, and other writers have supposed that George Skipper spent the years of a long apprenticeship in London. Some apprenticeships lasted six years, but at that time articled clerkship to an architect would last only three years. George Skipper signed his indenture to John Lee in late 1873; they were completed by end of 1876. Instead of seeking his fortune in London, George went back to Dereham to work in his father's office, starting in early 1877. (These dates are verified by Skipper in his own handwriting on the Candidates Statement of his application to RIBA dated 2 March 1889). In the same document he wrote that after articles in London with Lee, '(I) entered builder and contractor's employ to gain practical experience of building operations, taking part in management of same'. He did not add that the builder/contractor was Robert Skipper of Dereham. He added, however, that he began his architectural practice in 1879, and relocated to Norwich on 25 June 1880.

The reason for leaving was probably by pre-arrangement with his father, who had paid for his training. It would have been possible, if necessary, for John Lee to be able to transfer George's indenture to his father, because Robert Skipper, as stated, was a great deal more than 'just' a builder. He came from a generation of master masons, rather than architects, and a time before the Architectural Association or RIBA testing. In fact other would-be architects were articled to him in Dereham, for example, the architect Augustus Frederic Scott (1854–1934). (Scott was not related to the illustrious family of architects. His father was a Primitive Methodist minister and Augustus was a teetotal vegetarian cyclist. Later he would be George Skipper's rival in gaining commissions in Norwich and Cromer. Scott made many Methodist and Baptist chapels, a decorative example being Potters House Chapel in Norwich).

Twenty-year-old George Skipper was back in his home. His working hours were spent in the Skipper senior's office, and out on sites, engaged in very practical schemes. He walked daily in the town, greeting old acquaintances and answering their enquiries. He lived in his father's house. Younger brother Fred was still at Bracondale, but older brother, Robert Skipper junior, was in Dereham too. He now worked in Dereham's shoe and boot factories, in conjunction with a new tannery, all of which had been raised two years earlier by Mr Uriah Skipper, one of his father's family. Pevsner notes that Skipper's leather-works employed a hundred people. It was a large building of three-storeys, with two wings and associated cottages. All in redbrick, this was another of Robert Skipper senior's many projects in Dereham.

George's work as an architect and draftsman in his father's building and contracting offices involved a constant flow of residential and utility building work. There are so many buildings in and around Dereham built by Robert Skipper and his team that they have not all been counted. One that George Skipper dates as

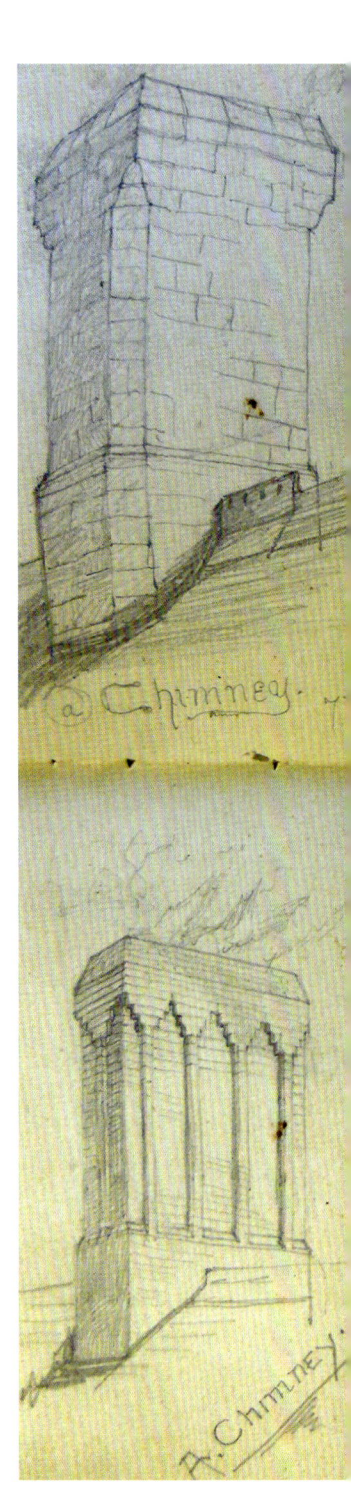

21 August 1878 in his notebook was a pair of cottages for Mr Sparkes in Mattishall. It was traditional in appearance, with brick fronts and gables, and a high-pitched thatched roof with twin dormers.

After two years working for his father, George altered the arrangement so that he was then an architect in his own right. The work remained the same. He designed houses for Mr Thurston in Dereham, he surveyed a drainage plan for a housing development in Crown Road, Dereham. In Lowestoft, Suffolk, where his father had bought certain plots of land, George designed terraced housing in Lorne Road for Mr Crisp, and in New Road for Mrs Seago.

Another small commission in 1879 was connected to the various nonconformist congregations in Dereham. George was asked to design an inexpensive chapel for immediate construction on a small plot in Whinburgh, just south of Dereham, for a congregation of Primitive Methodists. He drew up a low-pitched, three bay, brick and tile structure with classical proportions. At each elevation a pair of tall windows let in as much light as possible. Those at the gable front were arched and placed either side of the doorway. The entrance was surrounded by cream-coloured bricks and mantled by a small pediment, an echo of the real pediment above, enclosing a circle and horizontal band of pale brickwork. It was a modest but elegant treatment. (The chapel was in use for eighty years until the 1960s, when it fell into disuse. More recently it was converted into a three bedroomed house).

Pl. 8
George Skipper, Architect, 1879, Primitive Methodist Chapel, Whinburgh, Dereham, Norfolk.

The Hospital, Shepton Mallet.

However, the relative mundanity of these small local commissions paled in comparison to winning his first architectural competition. George had entered a design for a hospital and associated cottages in Shepton Mallet in Somerset, and this was chosen above sixteen other entries from architects throughout England.

The hospital building in Princes Road in Shepton Mallet was taken out of service in 1992, but still exists as a series of eight apartments known as Carlton Court. A new wing was built in the 1920s, and another, with a third gable, was added at a much later date. Otherwise the exterior is much as it was originally built, with two-storeys, a steeply-pitched tiled roof, and three chimneystacks. The exterior walls were built of the local Doulting quarry stone, roughly finished, but cut with two continuous bands of a lighter-coloured dressed stone. The building was lit with sash windows and a canted bay window on one of the two gabled bays. A verandah at the front added character with carved supports and ornamental ironwork. The entire appearance was that of a handsome country retreat.

On Saturday, 25 October 1879, George took the train to Shepton Mallet to witness the laying out of the hospital's foundations. He must have appeared very young as he met the man who would be his first patron. This was Richard Horner Paget (1832–1908), later baronet of Cranmore, MP, Deputy Lieutenant of Somerset, and a man with considerable influence. Paget's daughter married the son of four-times-Prime Minister, William Gladstone.

Prestige, a degree of notoriety, money, and more work to come – all this would result from entering the competition.

Pl. 9
George Skipper, Architect, 1879, The Hospital, Shepton Mallet, Somerset.

The Builder

AN

ILLUSTRATED WEEKLY MAGAZINE,

FOR THE

ARCHITECT, ENGINEER, ARCHÆOLOGIST, CONSTRUCTOR, SANITARY REFORMER, AND ART-LOVER.

CONDUCTED BY

GEORGE GODWIN, F.R.S., F.S.A.

LATE VICE PRESIDENT OF THE ROYAL INSTITUTE OF BRITISH ARCHITECTS;

Honorary Member of various Societies; Author of "History in Ruins," "Town Swamps and Social Bridges," "Another Blow for Life," &c.

"Every man's proper mansion-house, and home, being the theater of his hospitality, the seate of selfe-fruition, the comfortablest part of his own life, the noblest of his sonne's inheritance, a kinde of private princedome, nay, to the possessors thereof, an epitome of the whole world, may well deserve, by these attributes, according to the degree of the master, to be decently and delightfully adorned."

"Architecture can want no commendation, where there are noble men, or noble mindes."——SIR HENRY WOTTON.

"Our English word TO BUILD is the Anglo-Saxon Bylban, to confirm, to establish, to make firm and sure and fast, to consolidate, to strengthen; and is applicable to all other things as well as to dwelling-places."——DIVERSIONS OF PURLEY.

"Art shows us man as he can by no other means be made known. Art gives us 'nobler loves and nobler cares,'—furnishing objects by the contemplation of which we are taught and exalted,—and so are ultimately led to seek beauty in its highest form, which is GOODNESS."

VOLUME FOR 1870.

LONDON:

PUBLISHING OFFICE, No. 1, YORK STREET, COVENT GARDEN, W.C.

Chapter Three

1880—1889

Living and working in Norfolk, Skipper's next ten years of work were shaped by the prize he had won. There were associated commissions to design small hospitals, schools, as well as additions to a model factory and a new 'old village' on the other side of England.

The open competition and the prize of the Shepton Mallet hospital commission, and indeed, all the architectural prizes of the mid-19th century, derived from the lifelong efforts of another architect.

This was George Godwin (1813–1888) whose supreme achievement was in editing *The Builder* for very nearly forty years from 1844 onwards. Published weekly, it was a Victorian phenomenon, providing announcements and descriptions of architectural and urban planning, new machinery and art, especially sculpture.

Godwin elevated the status of *The Builder* from a trade journal into an indispensable resource, still very much valued by architectural historians. Illustrations were reproduced in engravings, lithographs and eventually photo-lithographs, and although Godwin employed a staff of five, he wrote most of the articles himself. He also issued collections of his own magazine articles in book form, for instance *History in Ruins*. Such interests led to his election to the Society of Antiquaries and The Royal Society.

Illuminating all, the journal's emblem was the lamp of knowledge. Up in Norfolk George Skipper read every page of *The Builder*. It featured pages of announcements about building projects, and architectural commissions and competitions. George Skipper entered other competitions announced in the journal and won prizes. His drawings of his own buildings were printed in *The Builder*. Within the profession there could be no better advertisement.

To begin with in 1880 he moved his own new architectural practice to Norwich. The new office in Bank Plain was where he would keep his wooden draftsman's table and T–square, his box of technical drawing instruments, his large drawings and floor plans. There was probably a survey level scope theodolite and folding tripod in the corner.

Pl. 10 (*facing page*) Title page: *The Builder,* Illustrated Weekly Magazine, 1870 Vol.

He travelled every day by train from Dereham and was still living in the house in Commercial Road at the 1881 census. Residents were listed as follows:

— Robert Skipper - Head - age 56 - Builder & Brick Manufr - Shipdham, Norfolk.
— Caroline Skipper - Wife - age 50 - Kelling, Norfolk.
— Robert W Skipper - Son - single - age 25 - Boot & Shoe Manufr - Et Dereham.
— George J Skipper - Son - single - age 24 - Architect & Surveyor - Et Dereham.
— Fred W Skipper - Son - single - age 21 - Et Dereham.
— Mary M Lincoln - Serv - age 19 - Domestic Servt - Yaxham, Norfolk.
— Susanna Pease - Serv - age 18 - Domestic Servt - Shipdham, Norfolk.
— Sarah Ann Tolman - Serv - age 17 - Domestic Servt - Carbrooke, Norfolk.

Pl. 11
George Skipper, Architect, 1881, Butleigh Hospital, near Glastonbury, Somerset.
photo:
S. Thomas 2005

Soon after the census George had left for Norwich. His elder brother, Robert, also went to the city where, in addition to being a leather merchant, he took up a new career as a mustard manufacturer in a joint-owned company, Skipper & Withers, based in Number 5, St Faith's Lane. In later life Robert also worked as a house agent. Both brothers had reasons to leave home, with thoughts of marriages to come.

It was from George Skipper's first Norwich office in Bank Plain that the young architect generated a large amount of designs for houses, shops, hospitals and schools in Somerset. All of these were to be built in stone. Some of the intended buildings were only one mile distant from the quarry, which was owned by his patron.

Paget had evidently taken a shine to Skipper. Following on from the hospital in Shepton Mallet there was to be a smaller hospital for Butleigh, just south of Glastonbury. George notes in his 1881 sketch book that its construction, discounting materials, would cost £2,200, with a further £1,800 for the adjacent Medical Officer's house. It was to be a twenty-five bed 'cottage hospital', later known as the Sir George Bowles hospital. It closed in 2005, suffered arson in 2013, was demolished in the same year, and replaced by fifteen houses.

A photograph in Steven Thomas's dissertation 'The Architecture of George John Skipper' shows the little hospital in 2005, a few months before its destruction. A few cars are parked at the south front. Built of rough and smooth stone, the building had two projecting gabled façades with stone mullioned windows, a steep tiled roof, and four tall brick and stone chimneystacks. A timber-framed verandah around the entrance lent an air of a small hotel by the sea.

These cottage hospitals, some of which were convalescent homes, or isolated quarantine hospitals, existed in large numbers all over Britain. Built in the second half of the 19th century and the object of local charity, or patronage, they are fondly remembered. Nearly, but not quite all, have been taken out of action as the National Health Service seeks to centralise all health care.

As early as February 1880 George Skipper had already attended a site meeting and issued quotes for a plan for Patrick Stead Hospital in Halesworth, Suffolk. He drew up plans for a surgeon's room, matron's room, isolation rooms, WC, baths, and all drainage. Still aged only twenty-three, George did not win the commission, which went instead to an older architect, Henry Hall (1826–1909).

Nevertheless, in preparing his plans and applications, Skipper's research into the technicalities of ventilation was professional, almost medically so. This was in an age when tuberculosis was at last understood to be a bacterial infection

Pl. 12
George Skipper, Architect, 1882–83, St William's Hospital, Rochester, Kent

taken into the lungs. In his notebook GS made notes (26/2/1880) on the ideal axis of hospital wards:

> 'The most simple form of structure for insuring ventilation and light is to build hospital wards in straight lines with windows on both sides, back and front, the length way of the ward being the length of the building, and the administration in the centre by such an arrangement as above. However no more than 4 wards could be obtained if the building were two storeys high. For small hospitals intended to receive only the sick, this plan will prove efficient and economical. The direction of the axis of such building should be N–S, a little inclined to the East so as it secures the sunshine, and to protect it from the winds'.

Almost immediately after Shepton Mallet and Butleigh, another design for a small hospital was commissioned, probably through the auspices of *The Builder*. This was the Chatham and Rochester Infectious Diseases Hospital, known as St William's, in William's Way on the outskirts of Rochester. It was not the same as the Somerset hospitals, because it was built in cream brickwork with a shallow-pitched slate roof. Set on a slope and surrounded by a stone wall, it consisted of two separate two-storey buildings. One had banded

Pl. 13
George Skipper, 1881,
Watercolour on paper: first design for Sexey's School in Bruton.

coursework and 'eyebrow' mouldings over first-floor arched windows. The other, housing the wards, was well lit by extremely tall windows. Building work was completed by 1883. The hospital was closed in 1996.

Cottage hospital buildings were not dissimilar to schools. George drew a perspective sketch for a Somerset County School in Paget's ancestral village of Doulting, with shaped gables in a French or Belgian manner. His plan for Sexey's School in Cole Road in nearby Bruton, was the prizewinner in open competition. The school was named after Hugh Sexey, auditor to Queen Elizabeth I, a perpetual benefactor in his will.

George Skipper's original design, a watercolour depicting a much larger structure, was at variance with the actual building, begun in 1882, but not completed until 1891. Sexey's School was built of rough-cut limestone with mullion and quoin details in dressed stone of a paler hue. Facing South-East, it had projecting gables, two of which had oculi or porthole windows close to the apex, and a slate roof with a lead-roofed miniature bell-tower. Further details included buttressing, stone chimneystacks, and a prominent main entrance protected by a porch with a moulded pediment. The school opened in 1892 with only fifteen boys. Today it is a state Boarding and Day school with six hundred boys and girls.

Pl. 14
George Skipper, Architect, 1882–91, Sexey's School, Bruton, Somerset.

Pl. 15
The Builder,
24 August 1889.
'Cottages at Doulting, Somerset.— Mr George Skipper, F.R.I.B.A, Architect'.

Pl. 16 *(facing page)*
George Skipper, Architect, 1882–91, Arch Cottage, North side of Doulting, Shepton Mallet, Somerset.
(Photo 2019)

At the heart of Skipper's work near Shepton Mallet were the Paget Terraces of estate cottages in Doulting. They present the appearance of a 17th century traditional village street, or even earlier, and this is the success of Skipper's neo-vernacular style, which Historic England, giving them Listed status, describe as 'a Tudor style'.

In pages to come there will be much mention of Listed buildings in connection with George Skipper. For anyone unfamiliar it should be explained that Listing is conducted by the authorities at Historic England. This is the executive non-departmental public body of the British Government, sponsored by the Department for Culture, Media and Sport. When a building is Listed, it is protected by enforceable legislation.

Behind all the alterations to Paget's Doulting estate was the construction, ten years earlier in 1871, of a new section of the Frome to Shepton-Mallet road, running through his land. The new layout created a new centre of the village.

This is where Paget wanted the almost theatrical effect of faux-historical housing in stone from his nearby quarry. The terraces are more than effective, and any first-time viewer could be excused for being far off the mark when

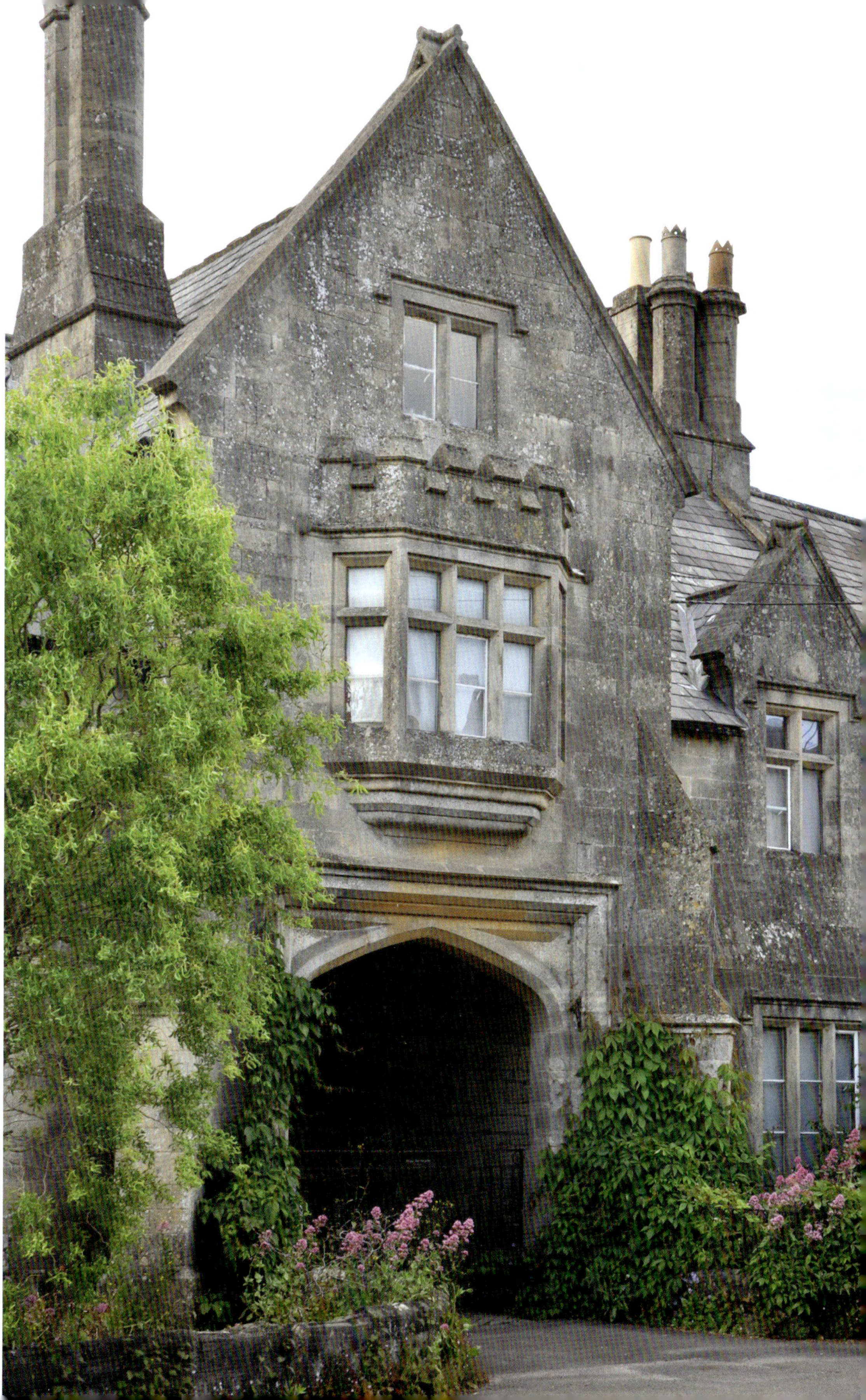

Pl. 17
George Skipper, Architect, 1882–91, 24–29 Doulting, Somerset.

guessing their age and origins. They were all part of Skipper's 1880–82 plans, and were not all completed until later. One cottage was marked 1882, while the shop doorway carried the date 1900.

The buildings formed part of a continuous stone street on either side of the road, known as Numbers 24–29 Doulting, (southern terrace) and Numbers 47–51 Doulting, (northern terrace) all of which are now Listed Grade II. Both were illustrated, after their construction, in lithographic prints in *The Builder* (10/9/1887 and 24/8/1889).

They were not identical. The north-facing six dwellings, 'Numbers 24–29 Doulting' were built in two stages with 24, 25, 26 in place by 1882 and 27, 28, 29 finished in about 1900. Beneath steeply-pitched slate roofs and five large chimneystacks with diamond-section shafts, the street-facing elevation presented two projecting gable fronts. They were of different sizes, one with a canted oriel, and three half-dormers, all lit with a generous quantity of windows with stone mullions and hood-moulds and small panes. They were mostly one-and-a-half storey, and their exterior doors cannot all be seen from the front. A plaque showed Paget's initials 'RHP' and beside it, '1882'. How people must have wondered when noticing that date.

Adjacent to Numbers 24–29 Doulting, is the former public house, The Abbey Barn Inn, and the next-door house, known as Number 30 Farm Road East. They constitute an additional commission from Paget, and are also Listed Buildings, all of a piece with the rest of Skipper's village plan.

The old pub was five bays deep, with two-storeys and an attic beneath a tiled roof. Like the other Doulting buildings, Skipper designed the inn with two and three-light stone mullioned windows and gabled dormers above. Close to the centre was a five-light canted bay window, with a lead covering. A hooded arch surrounded the main doorway to the bar. As is well known, England's village pubs disappeared in the late 20th and early 21st century at a rate of four or five a week. The Abbey Barn Inn closed in 2006, and the building's use was changed to residential.

Pl. 18
George Skipper, Architect, 1882–91, Entrance to Abbey Barn Inn, Doulting, Somerset.

The other buildings, across the road, were the northern (south-facing) terrace. They were of the same high architectural quality and are also designated Listed buildings. The terrace comprised seven houses in Church Lane, referred to as 'Numbers 47–51 plus Numbers 53–54 Doulting'. Described as cottages, they were quite grand, all of two-storeys, or more. The large slate roof was steeply pitched with a number of substantial chimneystacks rising from the ridge.

The northern side centred on Number 50, previously known as Arch Cottage, because it had a formal arched carriageway at ground level, and above it a castellated oriel window. The stonework was of the best quality, with carved mullions, hood-moulds and label-stops around the arch, oriel and numerous smaller windows and doorways. The far end of the row, Numbers 53 and 54 were of two bays only and had a different conformation of windows, including arched ones. Again the components of this continuous stone street were built at different times, from the early to the late 1880s.

With its archway and oriel, Skipper's design could appear like an Oxford quadrangle, or a fortified castle in Camelot. And there are those who claim to despise contrivance and replication of architecture. Their modernist hearts would relent to see the apparently aged stone beauty of Skipper's Doulting. Seen close-up, the freestone blocks of Doulting stone are cleanly cut and dressed. It is an Oolitic limestone, a near-perfect building material of uniform texture, its colour varying from cream to brownish-yellow.

One lingering impression of Doulting is that Sir Richard Paget did not know that his Neo-Tudor village centre, passed slowly by carters, drovers and packmen, would, within ten years, be roared through by the first motor-cars. The place is nowadays an inconvenient 'S' bend on the A361, driven through at 50 mph. Car passengers barely have a chance to see a remarkable instance of historicized architecture, appearing to be five hundred years old, though actually less than one hundred-and-fifty.

Another building in the village, also conceived by Skipper, is now known as the The Old Bell House. It was formerly the Somerset County School in Doulting, first appearing as a sketch in George's notebook as early as 1881. The old school building was a five bay terrace of two-storeys, with a slate roof and two relatively plain chimneystacks. The stone mullioned windows had the same distinctive hood-moulds with label-stops as the Paget terraces. The central bay of the front elevation had an entrance porch, and to the left of this was a projecting wall supporting a slender roofed tower that housed the old school bell. The Old Bell House ceased to function as a school, and was replaced many years ago by another Primary school. It is now a private residence.

Additional work for Sir Richard Paget was for a pair of cottages in Chelynch, one mile North of Doulting. Completed in 1885, they had a simple layout with a living room, pantry and scullery downstairs, and three bedrooms with dormers upstairs. The windows were mullioned with hood-moulds and label-stops, practically a signature for Skipper in his Somerset work. The Chelynch cottages are not Listed .

Sir Richard Paget also encouraged his young Norfolk architect to enter other competitions in which he was one of the judges, introducing him to the Marquis of Bath and Sir Neville Grenville, who was Paget's predecessor as MP for Mid-Somerset and High Sheriff of the county. The most fruitful introduction, in terms of architecture, was to William Clark of Clarks Shoes in Street, a small town on the road to Taunton, and some twelve miles West of Doulting.

In the meantime, back in the East of England, a major event was taking place. George had met and proposed marriage to someone in Norwich. Previously in service, and then a dressmaker, she was sixteen years older than George, and one of a pair of sisters attending the same meeting-house as him.

George married Elizabeth Tills Baines in the summer of 1883, and this was why he moved out of the family home in Dereham. The young architect with his bride had bright prospects, with their first home and a recently established business.

Where the newlyweds first lived in Norwich is not known. George Skipper's name appears on the 27 September 1881 purchase of a land plot for development in Hellesdon, to the West of the city. In the same year he created plans for work in King Street, for a property that may have been owned by his father. Even closer to the city centre, George drew plans for a building in St Andrew's Hill, the narrow old street leading up from St Andrews Street, dated 30 May 1883.

As well as working as first draftsman and designer, drawing up architectural plans and artistic impressions of the work for Clarks in Somerset, Skipper had a string of Norfolk projects. Owners and patrons were beginning to seek him out. One of his Norfolk jobs in 1882 was to plan an extension for The Woodhall, in Hethersett. The task was to build a cross-wing to the left front of the house, its roof reaching to a crow-stepped gable. The house was owned by Rev William Waite Andrews, whose disagreements with the squire, Sir John Boileau, are well recorded in Owen Chadwick's 1960 book, *Victorian Miniature*. The clergyman believed that, by employing Skipper, he might, 'conserve, or even emphasise the rustic pedigree of the building'.

Pl. 19
George Skipper, pencil on paper, 3 June 1880.
'Cap & octagon shaft brought to circular in nave of Hunstanton church. West pillar'.
RIBA Collections.

Pl. 20
One of George Skipper's forty-seven pocket sketch books. RIBA Collections.

Pl. 21 (*facing page*)
George Skipper, Pencil on paper, 21 July 1884. 'South Porch arcade, Sherborne Minster'. RIBA Collections.

George Skipper was without doubt employing assistants and other draftsmen in his office. For all the buildings so far mentioned, we have only looked at the front elevations, the faces that houses show to the street. Skipper was extremely good at depicting these because, as he often reminded others, 'an architect needs to be an artist', which he was. But for all the other elevations, floor plans, surveys, and the 'nuts and bolts' of architectural practice, Skipper needed a staff of at least four or five people, even at this early stage.

It is important, in order to understand Skipper and how he managed to undertake work throughout his career, to know that the architect did a great deal of preparation and study. For example, when drawing up the first hospital for Somerset, Skipper had already made drawings and plans of Maidenhead Cottage Hospital. The same was true regarding schools: he had studied schools designed by other architects, and he had drawn up his own plans for other schools, for instance Cheltenham Girls School in 1885, though these were not followed through.

These preparatory studies, which were eventually supported by his own books, lovingly collected and often used, also included his own sketches of buildings in Norfolk, London and in Belgium. The drawings showed a clear preference for Classical and vernacular architecture, but also demonstrate his observation of details, some of them very similar to those that stonemasons were adding to his Somerset projects – stone hoods, copings, arches – that might be seen in English churches.

George Skipper's sketch/note books covering more than sixty years (the RIBA collection in the National Art Library) contain (especially in the 1880s) his quick but competent drawings of – for example, an arched door, an urn, a corner turret, a porch, a self-closing iron door catch, a newell post, a keystone, a cupola and finial, a buttress – and even an impressive gothic dog kennel.

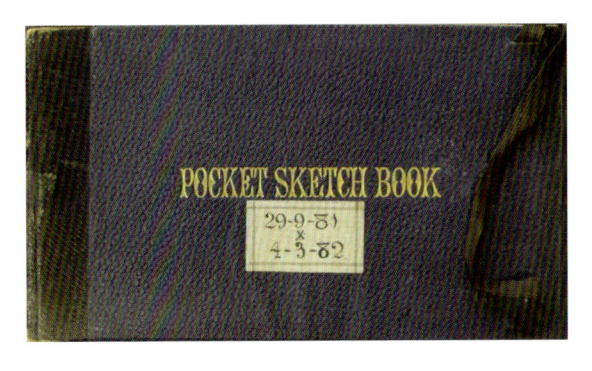

Although confined to a small pocket-book format, (approximately seven inches by four inches) some of the sketches from the 1880s are of a better quality than others. He went, for example, to Hunstanton to sketch the interior of the church on 3 June 1880; he made a visit to Castle Rising in Norfolk on 4 June 1880; he stood in the street to sketch the exterior of a house in Bristol on 13 August 1881; he entered Glastonbury Abbey in Somerset on 11 April 1882; he made an excursion to Haddon Hall in Derbyshire, renowned for its stonework, on 29 July 1883; and another to Sherborne Minster on 21 July 1884. When he entered a church to examine some architectural detail, he would take out his measuring tape and dividers, and assess every curl and return down to the last quarter of an inch.

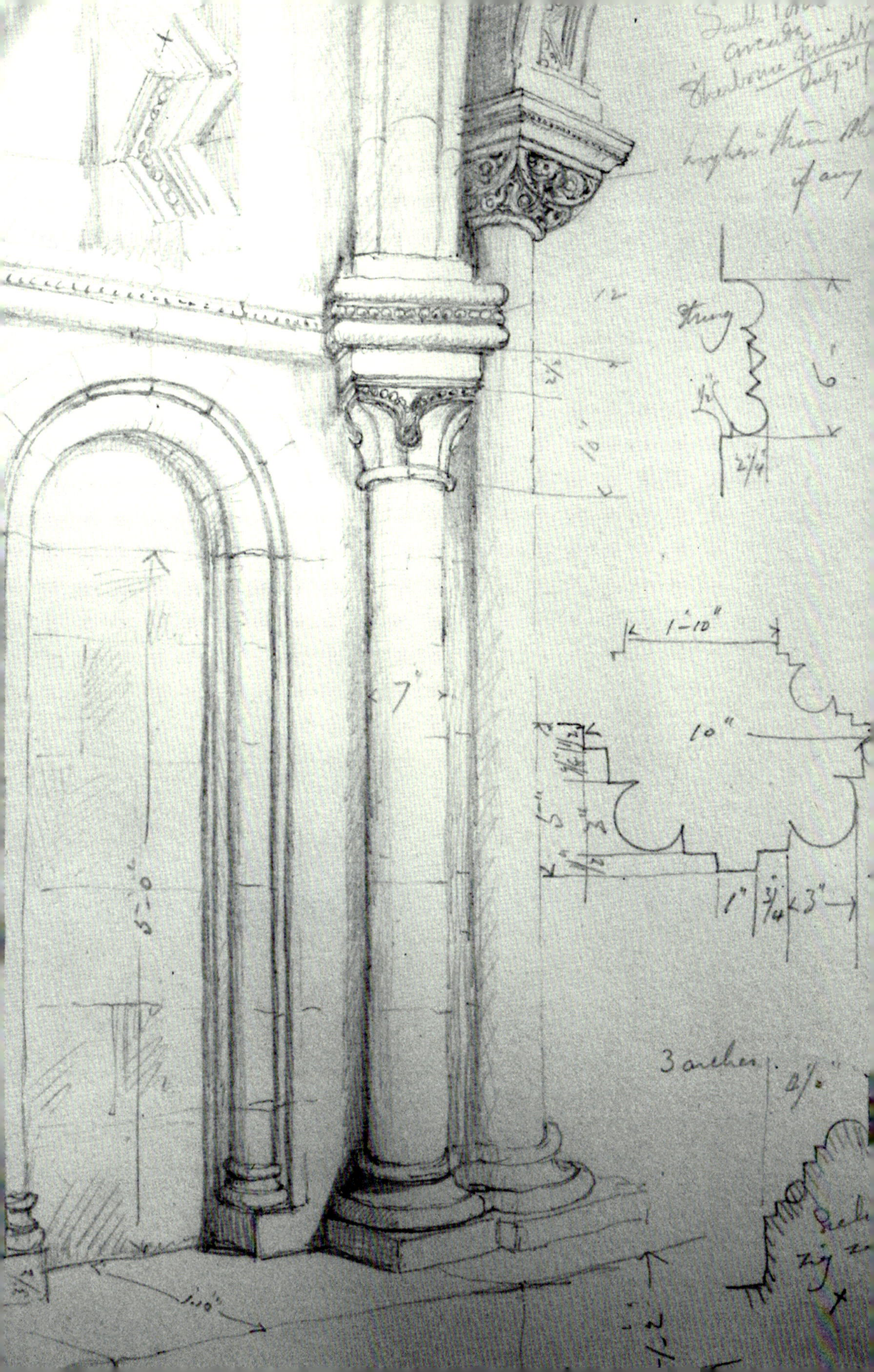

George Skipper took on an apprentice, or articled assistant in 1883. This was George Ratcliffe, aged sixteen, from North Norfolk. Ratcliffe stayed under Skipper for ten years, before leaving for London to work in the architect's office of the M&GN Railway. Even before Ratcliffe, Skipper had taken on a pupil, Ivan Kent, when he started in Norwich in 1880,

For historians curious about the arrangement, or contract, under which apprentices worked, the actual conditions were handwritten in copy by George Skipper in one of his sketchbooks:

Pl. 22
George Skipper, Architect, 1883, Crispin Hall, Street, Somerset.

(View from Leigh road).

<u>Mr Skipper's proposals as to George Ratcliffe's apprenticeship</u>

— *under will* —

1. Board, Lodging and washing etc — instruction in profession
£50 per year for five years   = £250
Half, or £125 payable at commencement of term,
and half, or £125 payable at two-and-a-half years.

2. Supplementary Grant
from the ward, payable at his coming of age:
£25 per year for five years: = £125

Skipper's work for William Stephens Clark of C. & J. Clark Ltd, shoe manufacturers in the town of Street, in Somerset, began with Crispin Hall. Its date, marked on a plaque, was given as 'Club and Library 1883', which indicates that it was begun at the very least fifteen months earlier, and that Skipper designed it in 1880 or 1881. Moreover, the date showed that Skipper's work for Paget in Doulting, and Clark in Street, were both done at near enough the same time.

Crispin Hall was not built of dressed stone, but of squared rough blocks of local Lias limestone in irregular courses, all of which were cleaned in a recent 2018 restoration. It stood on the South side of the High Street and was actually two buildings, an overall ' L'–shape plan, with more road-frontage around the corner in Leigh Road. It was mostly two-storeyed with an attic, and roofed with red clay tiles.

At Crispin Hall's corner (of High Street and Leigh Road) Skipper planned a turret with an eight-section conical roof. The roofline was also broken by a wooden bellcote and an ornamental weathervane. At either end of the right-angled plan were projecting gable-fronted extensions, and the one in the High Street had an entrance with an extending porch. The windows were the strongest feature, a combination of 2,3,4, 6 and 9-light stone-mullioned windows, all with dressed stone hood-moulds and label-stops. The ones on the central hall were very large, five of them occupying the entire wall. The double doors in the carriage entrance, also at the corner, were of ribbed timber with black iron brackets.

It was a serviceable public building, a *tour de force* in the twenty-seven year old architect's newly acquired Neo-vernacular style. Again, if seen from certain

Pl. 23
George Skipper, Architect, 1883, Crispin Hall, Street, Somerset.

(View from High Street).

angles, Skipper's hall appeared four hundred years old on the day it was built. William Stephens Clark was impressed.

Some years later in 1922, the famous composer, Gustav Holst, conducted an orchestra in Crispin Hall to accompany a piece of music by the polymath and mystic, Alice Buckton. These days the hall is managed by the Crispin Hall Trust Charity, and still offers a large public room, a dance floor, community centre, café and emporium selling local crafts. Street's library has been moved to a new building on the other side of the road, and green-painted tubular steel bus shelters stand outside the main hall.

Following the success of Crispin Hall, William Clark turned to the rest of his philanthropic scheme. Following in a tradition of Liberal or Socialist factory owners, he wanted to provide workers with better housing and communal facilities. From Public Hall and Library, the plan would extend to town housing, recreational facilities, a clock tower out of a history book for the factory, workers' housing, a vestry and fire engine house. Finally, Skipper had designed a large home for Mr Clark at Millfield House, later to be an independent school.

For all his work for Clark, Skipper received £9,000, an enormous amount, equivalent to more than a million in 2020. (This figure was noted in Steven Thomas's study and taken from Skipper's notebooks in the RIBA Collection: Thomas expressed a degree of shock at the size of the prize).

Aided by prominent date plaques on the buildings themselves, we see the next in sequence to have been a terrace of twelve cottages, quite close to the factory, in Wilfrid Terrace, (odd numbers 1–23) on Wilfrid Road, Street. Made for workers, and dated as built in 1885, the quality of the architecture is such that now they are Listed buildings. The Listing authority makes note that 'the great attention to detail and the spacious planning give this part of the town the atmosphere of a garden suburb'. As mentioned before, in relation to the appearance of Wilfrid Terrace, indeed most of Skipper's buildings, they seemed to be part of history the moment they were built. One might have expected their creator to have been a Wessex man, familiar with stonework, instead of an East Anglian.

Redbrick chimneystacks loom over the terrace's red tiled roofs. Below this the stonework consists of irregular courses of squared rubble, with dressed limestone details around doors, windows, and arches. There are alternate projecting gable fronts, dormers between them, a central carriageway entrance with chamfered edges, arched doorways and the now familiar mullioned windows, in irregular three and four-light sizes.

PL. 24
George Skipper, Architect, 1883, (detail)
Connecting turret, Crispin Hall, Street, Somerset.

At more-or-less the same time Clark's builders followed Skipper's plans for a group of four almost identical cottages known as Strode Cottages, dated 1886. They were actually Numbers 63–69 High Street (south side) in Street, and named after William Strode, a local hero of the English Civil War. These too are now Listed buildings, and shared many of the features of Wilfrid Terrace, but they were smaller, with one-and-a-half storeys, with two projecting gabled bays to the front, and two dormers on the roof in between. The stonework was the same irregular coursed squared rubble, complemented by dressed stone details above the mullioned windows. The redbrick chimneystacks of Strode Cottages were more imposing than those of Wilfrid Terrace.

When we see the information about these works by Skipper, it is often stated that a particular building was 'built by George Skipper'. This is of course not strictly true and a number of builders and masons in Somerset would say that it was they who did the building work. Their hands were calloused, their eyes stung with grit, they had got soaked on the roof. Although the Skippers, or at least George's father, had teams of men, wagons and bricks in Norfolk, George's role in Somerset was as the clever young architect who made Clark's ideas real on paper and plan. Skipper's cottages for Clark were meat and drink to local builders. In their view the cottages were traditional and blended with other old dwellings. One imagines they took some pride in the work. The next part of the plan was not so utilitarian, and may not have been built by the same group of workmen.

Pl. 25
George Skipper, Architect, 1885, Wilfrid Terrace, Street, Somerset

The clock tower at the factory was a thing of beauty. It was to be the town's Queen Victoria Golden Jubilee Clock Tower. It would stand among factory buildings that dated from 1825, and an adjacent water tower by the architect William Reynolds. Skipper's design for the sixty foot tall tower was reputedly based on the clock tower at Thun in Switzerland, but a quick glance at a photograph of the clock-bearing *Stadtkirche* Bell Tower in Thun indicates that there is no resemblance at all. Clark's Clock Tower of 1887 was far more attractive.

As with Skipper's other works in the town, the Clock Tower's building material was squared rubble, raised in irregular courses with details in dressed limestone. These details comprised carved stone framing around the four-centred, arched doorway at the base, frames around the arrow-slot windows that lit the internal staircase, and a concoction of plinth band and corbels. Clocks with Roman numerals were inset between quatrefoil piercing on each face. Above the clock(s) were three arched vents and a graceful pyramidal roof, clad with peg tiles, and a gablet, topped by a conical lead cap supporting an ornate weathervane.

Pl. 26 *(facing page)* George Skipper, Architect, 1887, Queen Victoria Golden Jubilee Clock Tower, C.& J. Clark Ltd, Street, Somerset.

Unsurprisingly the Clock Tower is a Listed building. The ground floor doorway is perpetually open, because it was altered, thirty years after construction, to accommodate Clark's First World War Memorial. The appearance of the tower does evoke a view in an old town in northern Switzerland, Slovenia, or Austria – and yet seems not an inch out of place in a Somerset town. Clark's Jubilee Clock tower was Skipper's first bit of fun and, although the description may seem unsuitable, it was a folly of sorts. My impression is that Mr Clark did not want too much embellishment for the tower, and that Skipper got it just about right.

All the stone for all the projects in Street came from the town quarries, initially on Ivythorn Hill at the western edge of Street, dug from the 1300s. The stone was Lias, a blue-grey limestone derived from compressed marl from the first Jurassic era, more than a hundred million years ago. By the 19th century there was an established corps of stonemasons, stonecutters and quarrymen in several quarries on the western side of town. Stone merchants bought leases and traded the stone to other areas. At the time of Skipper's works there were as many as ninety-nine stoneworkers in the quarries and several more involved in building.

The stonemasons and labourers moved to other sites in the town, where the foreman would again peruse Skipper's plans and drawings. First of these was the Vestry in Leigh Road, completed in the same year, and possibly also in connection with the Queen's Golden Jubilee. Clark had bought the land and donated it to the parish, and it may have been the parish that supported its upkeep. It was intended to provide an office space for parish church business, and, for a while, a place downstairs to park both the voluntary brigade's fire engine and a hearse. Another portion of the vestry included a three-bedroomed house with an outside well for water. It is not a Listed building, though it has

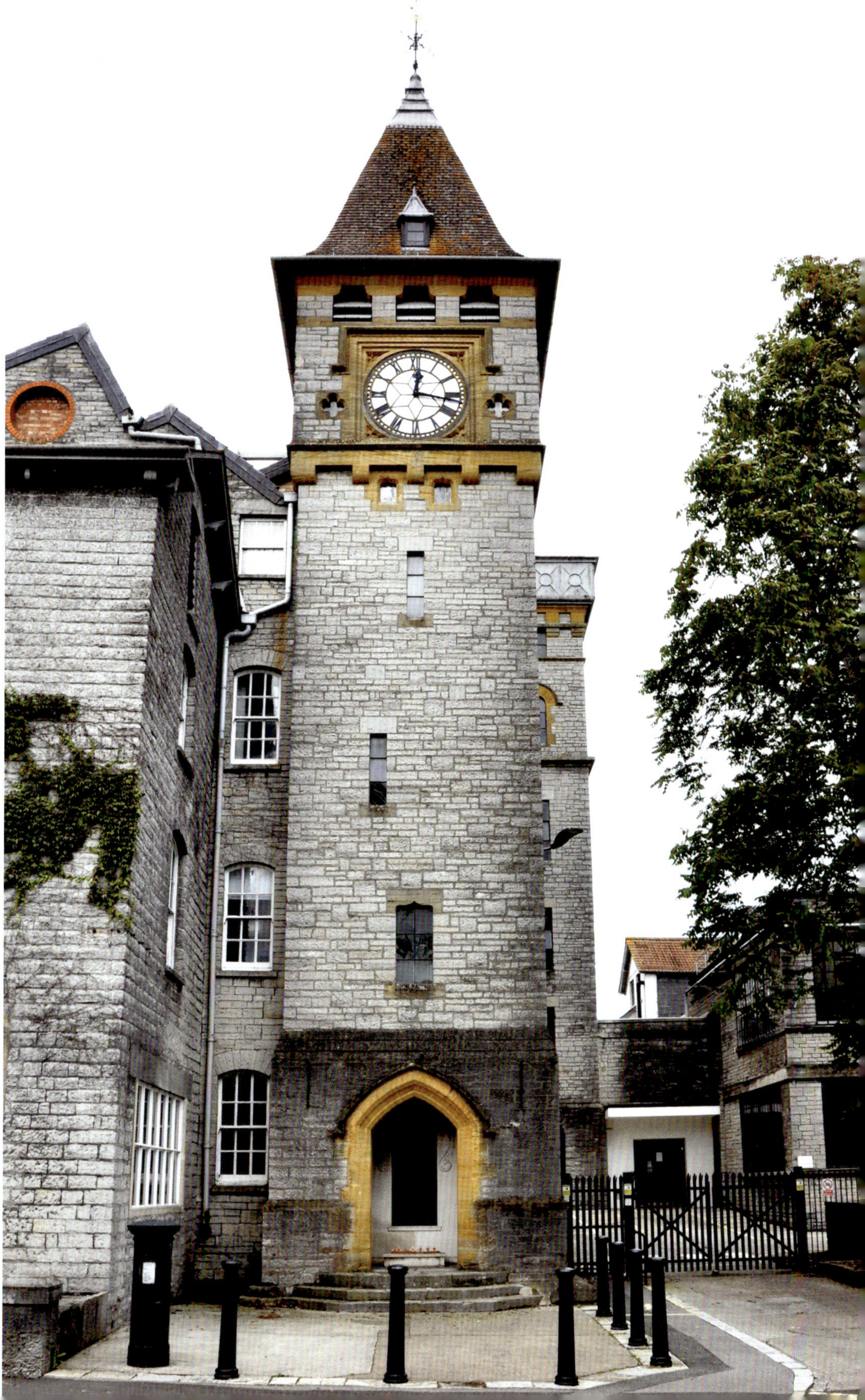

much in common with Skipper's other work in town. It had the same stonework and red tiled roofing; at either end were gabled cross-wings with irregular mullioned and casement windows. The chimneystacks in redbrick with oversailing courses were noticeably tall, an unnecessary feature these days. After it was no longer of use to the parish, the Vestry building was used by the Street Urban District Council. Still later it became extra office space for Clarks, and finally it was sold for residential use.

Incidentally, up in Norfolk, the architect was making another Golden Jubilee Memorial in brick, oak and iron, to go on the green of another model village. We shall return to Skipper's homeland soon enough, though the list of his works in Somerset is not complete.

The building team in Street, this time led by Mr J. Pursey, turned back to housing to make another Skipper terrace of nineteen houses to form Numbers 20–58 Wilfrid Road. It was named after Richard Cobden, a 19th century liberal manufacturer turned politician who co-founded the Anti-Corn Law League. The housing was ostensibly for workers, and had been commissioned as such. Today they are Listed buildings.

Pl. 27
George Skipper, Architect, 1889, Cobden Terrace, Street, Somerset.

Cobden Terrace employed all Skipper's characteristic features, with projecting gable-fronted bays, small gablets, and mullion and casement windows with hood-moulds. Grouped redbrick chimneystacks rose from the red tiled roof, as did an arcaded cupola with an ogee-shaped roof. This was at the centre of the terrace, and beneath, at ground level, were two doorways on either side of a passage way to the rear. These were all surrounded by smooth, chamfered stone with an upper panel inscribed COBDEN TERRACE ANNO 1889 DOMINI. The entire effect was handsome and broadly undateable, if you could not see the inscription. The Listing authority describes the style as elaborate Jacobean, but it was Skipper's by now familiar version of Neo-vernacular, a successful blend of traditional features from different centuries. Mrs Clark, wife of his patron, referred to some aspects of Cobden Terrace as 'folksy'. Her own home, designed by George Skipper, was being built at the same time.

The last of Skipper's Somerset work was Millfield House, built concurrently with Cobden Terrace in 1889. Although this was to be W.S. Clark's own home, and has since become a prestigious school, it is not a Listed building. In fact, and I take this to be a telling observation, it has been directly compared in appearance to his worker's cottages in Wilfrid Road.

Pl. 28
George Skipper, Architect, 1889, Millfield House, Street, Somerset

There have been a variety of further buildings at the school, but Millfield House is much as it was in appearance. From the front we see the squared Lias blocks in irregular courses. The redbrick stacks and red tiled roofs are familiar, as are the dormers and gabled cross-wings at each end. Dressed stone hood-moulds and label-stops surround the mullion windows. There are also features that Skipper used less often, in this case a canted bay window, and a pitch-roofed porch entered by a chamfered archway, reminiscent of a church porch. These days the school possesses eighteen other boarding houses, while William Clark's original home is surrounded by neat hedges and lawn, and its walls are festooned with climbing greenery. The philanthropic Quaker shoemaker and his family lived there until 1935.

As a last word on Skipper's numerous buildings in Street, it is interesting to note, that when visiting the town, one sees a number of buildings of a later vintage than Crispin Hall or Cobden Terrace. These are not by George Skipper, though they display techniques and details copied from his 1880s repertoire.

By travelling on the train on the Great Western to Paddington, then on to the Great Eastern out of Liverpool Street, the architect could reach Norwich in six or seven hours. Skipper must have made this journey many times during the 1880s. With his two extensive Somerset projects complete, practically a decade's work, George could concentrate on Norfolk and Suffolk commissions. He had acquired some valuable experience, firstly in relation to patrons, and secondly with regard to building with stone, a soon-to-be useful expertise that he could not have found in East Anglia.

In 1886 George moved his office from Bank Plain to Castle Chambers in Opie Street, still close to the centre of Norwich. The chambers were actually leased to the Norfolk and Norwich Traders' Association, and Skipper sub-leased. Other sub-lessors included Mr Partridge, a land agent, and Mr Hill, a solicitor. Three years later in 1889, George was elected a Fellow of the Royal Institute of British Architects. It was the stamp of approval, and this came from his peers: he had been proposed for RIBA Fellowship by architects E. Boardman, H.H Statham and J.B Pearce.

Furthermore, at the behest of his father, George entered a working partnership with his brother, Frederick Skipper, who would function as a surveyor within the partnership, although he was not qualified or professionally trained. Brothers can be so irksome – there are suggestions that the partnership was not an ideal arrangement for George. Many years later, George's son would comment that his father and his uncle had 'incompatible temperaments'. Frederick had moved into Norwich and married a Miss Harriet Amy Hayward from Birmingham.

George Skipper's Queen Victoria Golden Jubilee Memorial in Norfolk was in Heydon, concurrent with additions to Heydon Rectory and minor alterations to Heydon Hall, (work to the Hall had been originally suggested by Sir Henry Bulwer, though he had died some years earlier). The hall is an Elizabethan mansion and rightfully a Grade I Listed building; the alterations did not amount to much and are not mentioned by the Listing authorities. It was Wiliam Earle Gascoyne Lytton Bulwer, then about sixty-five years of age and living at the hall, who commissioned the Jubilee Memorial. He was nominally head of the much-branched family that has included politicians and writers.

The Jubilee Memorial took the form of a hexagonal brick-built Well-house, surrounded by four arched openings with stepped buttresses. The brickwork was of the best quality and included moulded brickwork from the Costessey brickworks, to be known as 'Cosseyware'. The roof was a substantial oak-framed hexagonal structure clad with machine-made peg tiles and lead flashing. At its peak stood a lead finial and an iron weathervane, surmounted by a wrought-iron outline of a two-masted ship, nowadays painted in gold. Inside

Pl. 29
George Skipper, Architect, 1887, Queen Victoria Golden Jubilee Well-house, Heydon, Norfolk.

the well-house was the well-head, covered with a lid and a cage of iron railing. The specially moulded brick eaves were shaped with fleurons, and a stone plaque was carved with a crown and the inscription: ERECTED BY COLONEL W. E. G. LYTTON BULWER TO COMMEMORATE THE JUBILEE YEAR OF THE REIGN OF HER GRACIOUS MAJESTY QUEEN VICTORIA 21 JUNE 1887.

Pl. 30
George Skipper, pencil on paper, 1884
Self-portrait, (untitled).
RIBA Collections.

The quality of workmanship in brick, oak and iron was superior. The Well-house too is a Listed building, and there are a further five Listed buildings within a few yards of the village green. The Listing authorities stated that the reason for the inclusion of the Jubilee Well-house is architectural interest. 'It demonstrates a high quality of design in a Tudor Revival manner and is associated with an eminent architect with nineteen Listed buildings to his name'. But the comment is premature for this text, for we have yet to see Skipper's rise to eminence. The steepest part of this would be in the next twenty years.

George Skipper and his brother, both qualified and ensconced in the new offices, began to take in more work in Norwich. Small orders and requests came in, and sometimes a larger undertaking. In the former category was a small adjustment in 1889 to houses in Earlham terrace in Norwich, whereby a series of bay windows were added to the terrace that had been built in 1858. Of more consequence were plans supplied to Mr H.H Cole Esq, in regard of a residence in Brundall, Norfolk. For George, these were little more than plans and drawings; for Frederick there was the task of costing the job and reporting to the client. More lucrative were jobs for James Young's builders of Chapelfield (whom Skipper would co-operate with for many years, and who still trade in Norwich in 2020). One of these was an 1887 order for plans for a shop and two houses in Grove Road North, Norwich. This was followed by another order in 1889 to design twelve houses in Ella Road, Norwich, for another builder, Messrs E. and J. Duncan. Outside the city, twenty-five miles distant in Lowestoft, the Skippers drew up plans for seven houses for a property owner, William Bell.

In years to come Skipper was to do more work in Lowestoft, to include a country mansion, terraces of houses, several large maltings and malt-houses, and finally a supremely innovative Arts and Crafts building by the harbour.

CHAPTER FOUR

1890—1899

The *fin de siècle*, the time of promise, of artists and thinkers, of art nouveau and magical displays — the decade began terribly for George Skipper.

His wife, Elizabeth Skipper, died on 17 June 1890. They had only been married for six or seven years. We know next to nothing of George's first wife, other than knowing she and her sister were members of the Brethren congregation. Readers and writers who wonder about George Skipper's character will note that he contained his grief. Perhaps it kindled the childhood ache at the loss of his parent, also named Elizabeth.

He received succour from the Norwich congregation of Brethren and it was his co-religionists who introduced him to Miss Rachel Marion Bareham, thirty-eight years old, and the daughter of Robert George Bareham, a farmer, blacksmith, and self-styled veterinary surgeon in the area around Aylsham, half-way between Norwich and Cromer.

In the following year, George and Rachel were married on 1 September 1891. A pertinent commission arrived at the same time. This was for a meeting house in Aylsham to be known as the Gospel Hall or, more commonly, the Cawston Road Brethren Chapel. The commission was doubtless connected with his marriage to Miss Bareham, who was also one of the Brethren congregation in the Aylsham area. Skipper's initial design drawing, actually a watercolour, can be seen inside the hall. The caption stated that the order was placed and paid for by a wealthy member of the Brethren congregation, George Pretty, a shopkeeper in the town.

The Gospel Hall was more substantial than the Nonconformist chapel at Whinburgh that he had designed twelve years earlier in 1879. With internal measurements of 55 ft x 25 ft, the Gospel Hall had a small lobby, a main hall, a baptistry with facilities for full immersion, and a small room with a stove at the far end, suitable for Sunday school. Built of brick, it had five large casements on either side, a 45 degree pitched and tiled roof, with a modest chimneystack, and a small projecting air vent on the ridge.

Any architectural quality the hall possessed was confined to the street-facing gable-end. In between a pair of relatively plain windows was a porch with a

Pl. 31
George Skipper, Architect, 1891 Gospel Hall, Aylsham, Norfolk.

recessed doorway behind a three-centred arch. Above this was a pediment beneath an unusual broken arch with a second and smaller pediment, all set in custom-made bricks from Guntons of Costessey. Still further up was an arrangement of an oculus, framed by four keystones, and pilasters that rose above the ridge and terminated with a segmental pediment against the skyline. Beneath the oculus a stringcourse crossed the pilasters and met the diagonal profile of the roof with short pillars topped with globe finials.

All in all the use of historical features, some of them copied from the magnificent Jacobean hall three miles down the road at Blickling, was excessive in the context of a single-storeyed Brethren meeting house. It was not one of the architect's finest creations, although Mr Pretty and the congregation were undoubtedly pleased with the outcome. The Gospel Hall was internally modernised in 1974, at which time the congregation was combined with another, and the hall renamed as the Emmanuel Church Hall. It is no longer exclusive to the Brethren.

According to the 1891 census, George and Rachel Skipper's home was 'Kingsley Villa', 50 Mill Hill Road, Norwich. (As an aside, and thinking of the years to come, George would later vacate this address, and return some years afterwards. His family would stay in Mill Hill Road until 1975).

Apart from these important changes in Skipper's private life, his architectural practice had been preparing ideas, competition entries, and proposals. Commissions were now coming to the Skipper brothers from all directions – from Norwich, and Lowestoft (Oulton Broad), but mostly from Cromer, a North-facing cliff town on the Norfolk coast.

The Norwich works were an assortment of smaller commissions, many of which were in conjunction with Youngs builders. The Skippers drew plans for houses being built in College Road, firstly in 1891 for four houses (odd numbers 55–61) and again, two years later, for another four, to be built by Mr R. Wegg. Two of these were owned by George Skipper himself. All the houses in College Road were of red brick: Skipper's little two-storeyed terrace was noticeable in the long road as having tall chimneystacks over a slate roof, distinctive rusticated double arch doorways, and bay windows at ground floor level. There were terracotta details above the arches and window surrounds, and these are nowadays finished in white paint. Other small schemes in Norwich included small additions to a pair of houses in Chapelfield in 1892, drawn up for Youngs builders, whose builder's yard and office were at 99 Chapelfield Road. Skipper also planned for the construction of six houses in Marlborough Road to be built in 1893.

In the same year the architect was approached by custodians of Gildencroft Chapel in Quakers Lane, Norwich. The Society of Friends was long established and influential in the city. Their request was for drawings and ideas for additions to the 1820s chapel, described in *Buildings of England: Norfolk* as 'one of the largest and stateliest of the Quaker Meeting Houses'. Nobody is sure what these additions were; the building was destroyed by fire in Norwich's blitz of 1942.

It can be seen that an architect was expected to make alterations and extensions to existing houses designed by other architects. This was standard practice for the profession and in no way unusual in England, a country of historic buildings. In a few years' time some of Skipper's more prestigious commissions would be for amendments and additions to grand buildings.

Even in Dereham, a few doors down from his father's house in Commercial Road, the plan for Number 21, known in Skipper's day as 'The Pallant', was actually the 1891 'refronting' (surely architects have a word for this) of a house built in the 1840s, when it had been known as Lindfield House.

George Skipper's rearrangement to the front of Number 21 was so complete that it is these days a Listed Building. The brick front of the two-storey townhouse was raised with projecting bays on either side of the door, which had a lunette and wrought iron canopy. Both bays, extending to the eaves, had three sash windows, and the same upstairs. At the lower level was a band of dog-toothed gault bricks, and two more of these bands ran across the upper level. But it was at roof height that Skipper's playfulness was most noticeable – primarily in the 'tented' lead cones which covered the two bays. On the outside of either lead cone were double and triple chimneystacks in crenellated brickwork, detailed with thistle-heads and clover leafs. These were, of course, from Costessey brickworks.

Pl. 32
George Skipper, Architect, 1891, (detail)
Terrace in College Road, Norwich.

Pl. 33
George Skipper, Architect, 1891, 'The Pallant', Commercial Road, Dereham, Norfolk. (photo from estate agency).

The origins of 'Cosseyware' and Gunton's brickworks at Costessey connected with Costessey Hall, an ancient site just outside Norwich. In the 19th century, the owner, Sir George Jerningham, commissioned the architect, John Buckler (1793–1894), to extend it to a truly vast mansion-castle, with innumerable towers, battlements, and soaring chimneystacks. Construction work lasted from 1826 until 1855. The brickworks were established in 1836 and their initial purpose was to make bricks for the construction of Costessey Hall. As the Hall became closer to completion, the Gunton brothers turned to the public, offering a range of ready-made specialized bricks, as well as the capacity to produce ornamental terracotta, to be fired in the same kilns. They gave notice in the *Norwich Mercury* (5/4/1851), announcing:

> GEORGE GUNTON RETURNS HIS SINCERE THANKS FOR PAST FAVOURS, AND RESPECTFULLY BEGS TO ANNOUNCE THAT HE HAS ON HAND A LARGE ASSORTMENT OF ORNAMENTAL CHIMNEYS, NORMAN AND ELIZABETHAN WINDOW FRAMES, CORNICES AND COPINGS, AND EVERY DESCRIPTION OF MOULDED BRICKS AT REASONABLE PRICES.

By the 1890s Gunton's business was thriving, and other brickyards were opened at Barney, near Fakenham, Little Plumstead, and East Runton.

George Skipper was still entering competitions. In 1893 he submitted drawings for Mills Grammar School in Framlingham, Suffolk. On this occasion he was beaten to second place, and his plan did not go ahead. But in a high percentage of the competitions he entered, Skipper did win, and

Pl. 34
George Skipper, Architect, 1891, (detail)
'The Pallant', Commercial Road, Dereham, Norfolk.

a lot of the successes came down to the drawings themselves. Whatever else may be said, the architect demonstrated a certain flair as an artist-draftsman.

Elsewhere, in South Norfolk, Skipper drew plans for a residence in Pulham St. Mary for the District Medical Officer and Public Vaccinator, Dr Job Nathaniel Legge-Paulley. It was to be known as South House and has proved difficult to locate these days. All that could be found was a report of an unusual accident in the *Diss Express* of 10 November 1893:

> 'On Tuesday a serious accident befell a young man named Youell, in the employ of Mr. G. Hood, miller. Youell was standing on the cart near the mill, which was in motion, when one of the sails caught him on the head, causing scalp wound, from which blood flowed very freely. He was conveyed to Dr. Legge-Paulley's, who promptly attended to the unfortunate man's injuries. The patient is progressing favourably'.

Still more of Skipper's work was for Lowestoft, firstly in the drawing up of designs for cheap municipal houses, specified as 'second, or third-rate' housing, with costings to both. Some of these were intended for Gunton Cliff Esplanade. But the architect's other work in Lowestoft, actually slightly inland at Oulton Broad, was for a country mansion.

Pl. 34 *(facing page)* George Skipper, Architect, 1891, (detail) South-West front, Mancroft Towers, Oulton Broad, Suffolk.

This was Mancroft Towers, which Skipper had conceived on plan in 1889 and was actually built between 1891 and 1893. It was commissioned by Lt Colonel Philip Edward Back (1860–1930), chairman of Back's Wine Merchants in Norwich; he brought the name 'Mancroft' from the name of the Norwich parish and city-centre church. There was a sketch of a large Elizabethan-fronted house in one of Skipper's earlier notebooks, and this suggests that the architect had part of a plan to begin with. The final design, as agreed with the client, differed slightly. Skipper also came to Mancroft Towers some years later in 1898 to supervise additions requested by the client.

The words, 'An englishman's home is his castle', are used to make a legal point. At Mancroft Towers the phrase is literal. Spectacular in appearance, the battlemented house has the air (to my mind) of a location for a film of an Agatha Christie book. It was as Neo-historic as Skipper's houses in Doulting in Somerset, but those had been in a vernacular style; their stone walls gradually gathered lichen, and aged to merge with older buildings in the village.

At Mancroft Towers, the building was in isolation in its own land, with a drive to the door. Its central feature was a castellated tower (one of three) and the 1890s Neo-historic style was not unique in Oulton Broad. There are, of course, real 16th century houses throughout Suffolk. A strong and handsome building, it has received H.F. Grade II Listing.

Mancroft Towers was built in a soft-toned red bricks from nearby Somerleyton, and embellished with terracotta 'Cosseyware' details. These comprised a panel with the name 'Mancroft Towers', hood-moulds, label-stops and moulded pediments above main windows, which were brick mullioned casements. There were also red terracotta details in the spandrels around the

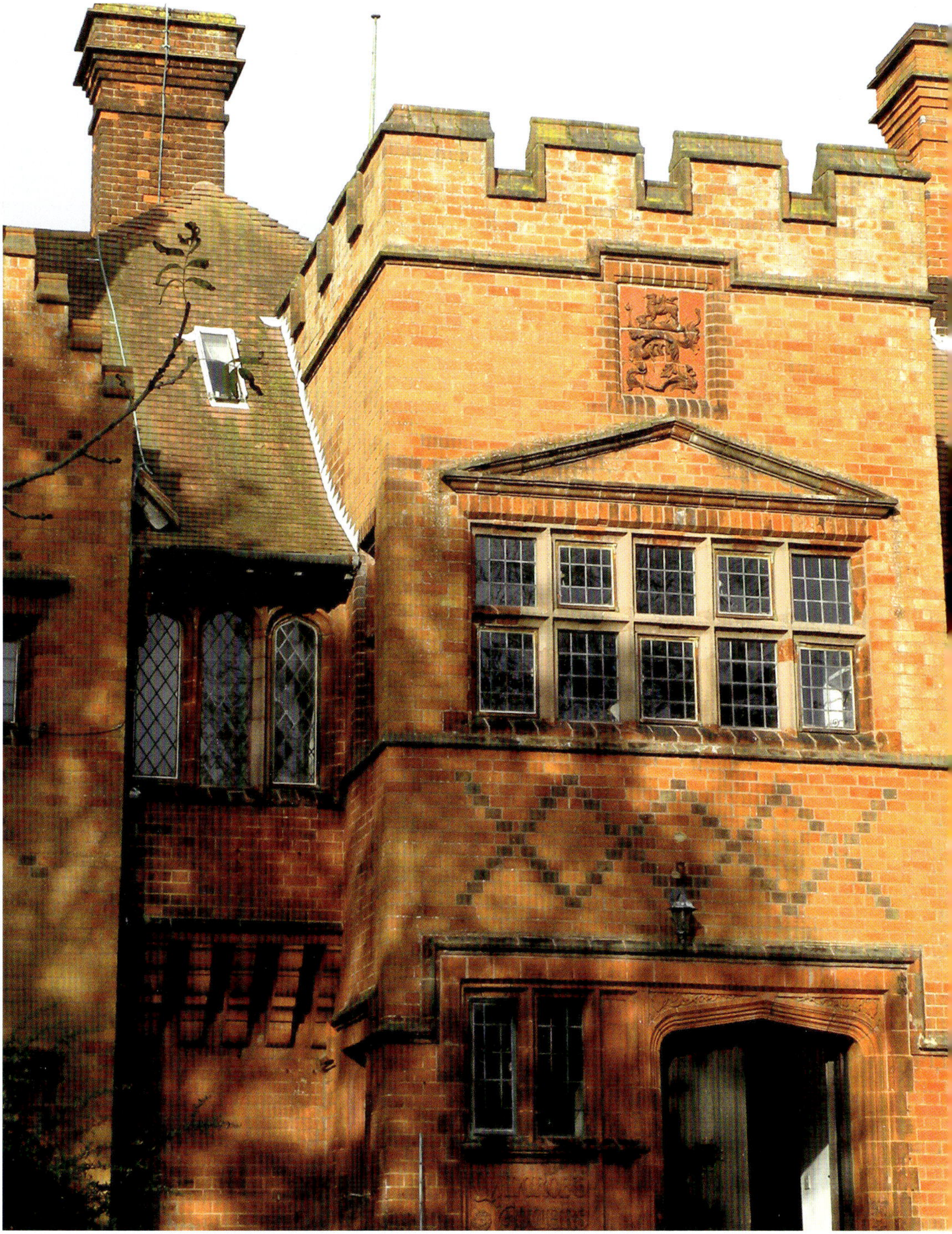

Pl. 35
George Skipper, Architect, 1891, South-West front, Mancroft Towers, Oulton Broad, Suffolk.

doorway, and a series of 10 inch square items in terracotta – a flower, a man's face, a fiendish crouching bat, a king's head and crown – on a stringcourse high up one of the towers. The main front, facing South-West, carried stepped gable wings at either end. These walls and the mid-section of the central tower were patterned with latticed courses of darker bricks. The north front, facing the garden, was centred on the second and larger tower, and had four-storeys and an internal stair turret. There were additional mullioned windows, and a single dormer in the roof that was clad with machine-made red tiles. Four tall brick chimneystacks stood high over the ridge. Mancroft Towers had the same features as some of Skipper's Cromer works, and were built by the same firm, Youngs of Norwich.

Lt Colonel and Mrs Back and their four sons and two daughters lived in the house for many years. The youngest son, who was about three years old when moving to Mancroft Towers, grew up to be a promising young artist who went on sketching expeditions with Alfred Munnings in the early 1900s.

The interior of the house was noted for its panelling, timber framing, and further 'Cosseyware' details. One of these was a rebus, or visual pun, consisting of small terracotta mouldings around the large fireplace in the hall. Some were tiny owls and others were small barrels, which denoted 'tuns', the largest wine casks used in England. Together the owl and tun made Oulton. One wonders whether this was Skipper's humour, or the idea of the terracotta artist at Gunton's, James Minns. Among other features were oak newell posts, surmounted by carved griffins, emblems of heraldry. Also in the curtilage of Mancroft Towers was a single-storeyed lodge of less consequence, with wooden casement windows and an attic room. A pattern of latticed coursework on the gable related to the brickwork of the main house.

    A few more commissions came from Lowestoft. At the junction of Suffolk Road and London Road Skipper made alterations and the addition of a tower, or tourelle, above the entrance to Mr Leach's shop in 1894 (since demolished). More profitable was the 1896 scheme for Miss Cator, in Pakefield Road. The plan, for a site opposite Lowestoft's Grand Hotel, was for seven large semi-detached houses. In the same year he planned a business premises in Oulton Broad, (Lowestoft) for Mr J.K Jones, and four cottages for Mr E.A Harrison, also in Oulton. Another plan, a year later, was for The Victoria Mansions Hotel on Kirkley Cliff in Lowestoft, with three associated double-villas nearby.

    Later renamed, the Victoria Hotel's two elevations, landward and seaward, were bold. Entirely of brick, it was about half the size of the big Cromer hotels. Facing inland the building was three and four-storeyed, with two projecting two-bay wings with Dutch gables at either end, and a single bay Dutch-gabled

Pl. 34
George Skipper, Architect, 1891, (detail)
Tower at North–East front, Mancroft Towers, Oulton Broad, Suffolk.

Pl. 35
George Skipper, Architect, 1897, Victoria Hotel, Lowestoft Suffolk.
photo: 1930s postcard.

centre. The casements were plain: those on the top floor were pedimented; some of those on the ground floor were arched, as were the doorways, beneath broken pediments. Four tall distinctive linear chimneystacks, stood across the ridge. The hotel is still operating in 2020, though modern additions have altered the appearance of the west face. The seaward elevation is much as it was, and shows three bays of four-storeys, topped by elaborate gables with fine coping and single pediments over double dormers. The construction of the Victoria was signed off by Frederick Skipper in 1897.

Very little work was found in Great Yarmouth, apart from The Cliff Hotel at Gorleston-on-Sea. It was enormous, with three storeys and a dormer attic, and two broad wings leaning at a shallow angle away from the sea. Between these wings was the gable front, and on either side, like gateposts, tall round towers reaching above the roofline. Another two turrets, slightly smaller, were at the extremities of the front; all four were topped with leaded conical roofs. The Cliff had one hundred-and-thirty-nine bedrooms, and a separate stabling block. A year after opening, the hotel was visited by Edward, Prince of Wales.

Just a few years later The Cliff was destroyed on Boxing Day 1915. A fierce fire fanned by a southerly gale razed the hotel to a burnt-out wreck. It has been rebuilt in stages and functions as a hotel to this day. For architectural purists the rebuild does not resemble the original building, and cannot be regarded as a Skipper work. In Great Yarmouth proper, Skipper also made minor additions to a factory owned by Jarrold of Norwich, (his neighbours in London Street) to include classical details around the manager's office.

Pl. 36
George Skipper, Architect, 1891, The Cliff Hotel, Gorleston-on-Sea, Great Yarmouth. photo: 1904, Donald Shields.

Skipper's order book for the turn of the century period was full. There were endless Norwich works: an unusual job in 1897 involved alterations in Magdalen Street to accommodate Norwich's Electric Tramways, with rebuilds to the fronts of Numbers 167–68 and 177-78. A year earlier he had designed five houses for Mr Parker in the same street.

Another task for the Skipper partnership, in what was to become a new architectural service, was in surveying and plotting out twenty-eight houses in the area between the Jenny Lind Infirmary and Mile End Road. This was prescient, a first instance of George's ability as a Town Planner. In the next century he would be showing what he could do in a variety of municipal housing schemes.

Ipswich also called for Skipper. In 1895 he designed a house and maltings (since destroyed) for Mr E. Webb, at a site adjoining Great Whip Street and New Cut West. In the following year he prepared alterations to a shop front in Westgate Street for a Mr Cade. Lastly, in 1899 he drew plans for maltings at New Cut West for Ipswich Malting Co. This was no common job, as East Anglian maltings are important places of economic significance. Skipper had seen three of them built by his father in Dereham, and had already planned some in Lowestoft.

But we are running ahead of our subject, and getting drowsy with the thought of so many achievements! Before heading to the North Norfolk coast to join the architect in Cromer, there is a moment to pause and wonder about George Skipper himself. Concurrent with the continuing list of works, his life was changing in many ways. Rachel Skipper gave birth to a baby boy on 11

February 1894. George was undoubtedly happy and proud of his wife and new son, George Theodore, or 'Theo' Skipper (1894–1958). To be a father is transformative.

Other Skipper babies were born. Fred's wife, Harriet Amy Skipper, (née Hayward), had had a son, Reginald Skipper (1891–1983), a daughter, Gladys Skipper, who emigrated later to the USA, and another son, Eric Hayward Skipper, (1897–1982) who would become another architect.

As for George Skipper's architectural practice, it was outgrowing the chambers in Opie Street. He secured a freehold a few hundred yards away in London Street, and drew up plans for a new office. Building work was contracted and very special orders made to Gunton's Costessey brickworks. We shall return to Skipper's office, still in construction, while his staff prepared for the move. Once in the new premises in 1896, the number of employees in the Skipper brothers' firm would rise to as many as fifty people.

Another radical alteration to George Skipper's circumstances was that he took on another Articled Clerk. The apprentice architect was John Owen Bond, the third son of Robert Bond, founder of the Department Store at Norwich's All Saints Green. Bond worked under Skipper for six interesting and very busy years. From Skipper's view, he had someone who could undertake tasks on his behalf, and share the high volume of work at that time. In due course Bond would qualify and work in Norfolk. The Bond Partnership continued its architectural practice in Norwich until very recently.

And now to the sea, because among Skipper's earlier 1890s works, the biggest in size, if not in importance, was the Grand Hotel in Cromer. It was actually completed and opened in summer 1891, so it must be assumed that Skipper had drawn up his plans for the project much earlier, probably in 1889. Even so, it was not the first Skipper work in Cromer because, before its completion, there was a request for another building, a town hall.

It might be confusing to review so many Skipper buildings, raised in the same period, and all of them in close proximity. Clarification comes from a local author. Glenys Hitchings has unravelled the entwined histories of all of them in her text, *George John Skipper: The Man Who Created Cromer's Skyline* (2015), illustrated by the photographs of Christopher Branford.

Some threads of the story of Skipper in Cromer went back many years. He lived through a period in British history during which time any number of fishing coves and small ports were made accessible by railway. In the case of Cromer, its rise as a respectable seaside destination had taken a steep turn.

In addition to the Victorian 'discovery' of the seaside and the concept of healthy leisure, there was a cultural angle. A mythic romance became linked to the North Norfolk coast, originating in the writings of Clement Scott (1841–1904), who visited Cromer in 1883. Described as a playwright, lyricist, translator and travel writer, he was also drama critic at the *Daily Telegraph*. Scott made his way two miles eastwards to Overstrand, and found lodgings there.

Enchanted by the sight of Louie Jermy, the miller's daughter, Scott dreamed up the notion of a peaceful English backwater that he referred to as 'Poppyland' in a poem titled 'Garden of Sleep'. The town later acknowledged his influence, which enticed other literary tourists, with a granite Drinking Fountain and Horse and Cattle Trough in Cromer. The inscription was: 'To Clement Scott, who by his pen immortalised 'Poppyland'. Erected by his many friends, November 1909'.

The development, eventually a series of hotels, had begun with a land sale some years earlier. Already fashionable among Norfolk gentry, the clifftop area of Cromer was previously owned by the Cromer Hall estate of Maria Windham, Countess of Listowel. On her death it was purchased by a London lawyer, Benjamin Bond Cabbell, who passed the land to a cousin, who then passed the deeds to his son, who had the same name as the original purchaser! BB Cabell II made plans to sell land and build hotels and promenades; when his plans did not materialise, he decided instead to auction plots. The London auctioneers invited hundreds of potential buyers for different sized plots; the

Pl. 37
George Skipper,
Pastel on paper,
c.1896.
(Assumed to be sunset on North Norfolk Coast).
RIBA Collections.

Pl. 38
George Skipper, Architect, 1890, The Town Hall, Cromer.

salty old town was seen as an investment opportunity. Numerous plots were sold and various house plans were drawn up for approval.

At the same time a meeting was held in Cromer's Lecture Hall in February 1889, at which the proposal to build a town hall was put in motion. Shares were issued and a committee with a chairman, Benjamin Bond Cabbell II, decided to offer an open competition for an architectural scheme for Cromer Town Hall.

Among twenty-seven entries the winning design was George Skipper's. His drawing for the Town Hall was made into a lithograph and printed in *The Builder*. And so it was that an inaugural foundation ceremony took place in January 1890, with Cabbell's wife using a symbolic gold trowel. Building work by Chapman & Son started immediately. It continued at a pace and the building bears a panel inscribed 'Town Hall 1890', though it must have taken longer to complete. Nevertheless, its construction preceded the Grand Hotel, and was Skipper's first completed work in the town.

Cromer Town Hall comprised a heavily detailed two-storey Queen Ann revival building, with a red tiled roof and brick chimneystacks at each end. The front, facing Prince of Wales Road, has five bays and gabled ends that are pierced by a door and smaller windows. The three central bays project a few feet forwards, and bear a pediment enclosing a terracotta relief of a sailing ship in an icy seascape. Beneath this are the largest mullioned windows, and lower still at ground level, the arched entrance, surrounded by alternating stonework with hidden courses.

There are innumerable details, from corbels supporting pilasters framing the big central windows, to dentilation about the eaves. At mid-elevation, from left to right is a prominent band of ornamental brickwork and terracotta coats of arms. When the town hall was built, the brickwork was there to see, but these days the entire front is painted in a cream colour that covers the terracotta designs, which came from the Skippers' old friends and suppliers at Costessey brickworks. The paintwork possibly offers some protection from the elements. The twelve heraldic panels, also painted nowadays, were those of significant Cromer and Norfolk families: Bacon, Cabbell, another Cabbell, Crowmere, Windham, Gurney, Buxton, another Gurney, Barclay, Weyland, Rede, Harbord.

During the time of construction, and for some years afterwards, the Skippers were allowed a room in the Town Hall, at a minimal cost of £10 per annum, from where they could supervise works all over Cromer. Joined to the rear of the building, and part of the plan, was a tall single-storeyed hall, used for many years as a theatre. George and his brother were summoned several times in the following decade to discuss small additions, mostly to the theatre hall. In 1930 the Town Hall buildings were for some reason found inadequate, and Cromer Council vacated the building. Now known as 'The Old Town Hall' it has had various commercial uses, and is now divided internally into offices. It remains a Grade II Listed building.

Back to the Grand Hotel in West Parade, or Runton Road, and the exposed building site facing the wind and waves. Skipper had won the commission to design the Grand Hotel in an open competition. Although George Godwin, the antiquarian writer-editor-publisher of *The Builder* had died in 1888, the wonderful weekly journal continued. It printed a lithograph of Skipper's Grand Hotel across two pages.

As Glenys Hitchings notes, the opening of the hotel on 15 July 1891 was celebrated with a dinner costing 7/6d exclusive of wine. Earlier in the day, the builders, Youngs of Norwich, gave their workforce of one hundred and twenty-five men a lunch in The Red Lion.

Building a hotel like that, on a gusty cliff top instead of a less-exposed site, was a considerable achievement, even for established and capable builders such as Youngs. Looking at old photographs of the building, it appears vast. Any photographer trying to step back to get the whole hotel in the frame could fall over the cliff.

The Grand Hotel was about the length of three cricket pitches with five-storeys, four connected mansard roofs clad with slate, and eight large chimneystacks with ten chimneys apiece. Built of red brick, offset by dressed white stonework around the very many large windows, it also had dormers, and a small white bellcote in the centre of the long, high roofline. The ground floor interior was big enough to accommodate large Drawing rooms, Writing Rooms, Smoking Rooms, Billiard tables, and the Dining Room.

To our modern view it was a bit of a beast, the equivalent of a high-rise block of flats in a dramatically elemental landscape. Ten years after its opening, the Grand was less of a novelty, as the investing syndicate led by Sir Kenneth Kemp were busy building other hotels. The Grand went into a slow decline and was sold in 1925. It limped on and was renamed 'The Albany' five years prior to a serious fire in 1970, after which the now-old Grand was demolished.

Pl. 39
George Skipper,
Architect, 1890–91,
The Grand Hotel,
Cromer.

Eighty years earlier, even as the Grand had been opening, the Skippers provided plans for the next hotel in Cromer. This was to be the Hotel Metropole, sited in Tucker Street, a less exposed side-street facing a churchyard. A report in The *Cromer & North Walsham Post* commented that there was 'nothing of a hurried or makeshift nature' about the Metropole's construction. (Was this an implication that the Grand Hotel had been hurried?) As with the Grand, Youngs were contracted to build the Metropole, completing in 1894.

Again, looking at the old photographs – if the Grand Hotel was a bit of a beast, then the Hotel Metropole was a bit of a beauty. Built of brick it was formed with gabled wings at each end, and in between a series of large arched windows, extending to the storey above. At ground level an arcade with six large arches opened to the street. Higher up, the two gables were defined with terracotta moulding, with finials on the sloping parapet, and extremely

Pl. 40
George Skipper, Architect, 1893–94, Hotel Metropole, Cromer.

ornamental brickwork, all of it from Gunton's at Costessey. There were more windows and dormers in the attic storey, hiding some of the green-slated mansard roof. At the summit a small cross roof carried another dormer beneath a tall finial. And that was the south-facing front – the other side, facing seaward, apparently had even more features. The extent to which Skipper was involved in the interiors of the hotels is not fully known. The Metropole was lavishly fitted, decorated and furnished; it possessed a fine entrance hall, leading to a stone staircase and the upper floors.

Sadly, this hotel did not survive either. If the Metropole had not been requisitioned by allied troops during the Second World War, it might not have been run-down and closed, and eventually demolished in 1972–73. And if that was not the case, we can be sure that the Hotel Metropole would have become a Listed Building, based on architectural merit and the name of the architect.

Following the Grand and the Metropole were a large amount of site-specific commissions for villas, terraces and shops in Cromer. These are to be seen in Alfred Road, Macdonald Road, Runcton Road, St Mary's Road, Mount Street and Bernard Road. Skipper bought up as many as fifteen of the plots himself, then made plans and contracted builders to follow them to completion. He had the capital to invest in the overall project he was engaged with.

Pl. 41
George Skipper, Architect, 1893, Kingston House, Cromer.

Among these lesser-known Skipper buildings was Kingston House, Numbers 30–36 Garden Street in Cromer, built in brick for Mr George Breese in 1893, with timber oriel bay windows and an octagonal turret with an ogee-shaped lead cap. As with the old Town Hall, the brickwork has been masked by cream-coloured paint. Another was odd Numbers 31-37 in Vicarage Road, a terrace of five houses adjacent to St. Bennets, built for Mr Samuel Jarvis, who was becoming more and more like a property developer.

The auction of plots had encouraged more than a few people to invest in houses. We must suppose that the purchasers approached Skipper after the auctions. As far as is known, George and Frederick Skipper still retained the room in the Town Hall and could sometimes be found in Cromer. Beyond this there was word of mouth recommendation, as well as national acclaim; the owners of the plots were keen to be associated.

A further motive was that Frederick Skipper was a surveyor, so the prospective investor could quickly assess the probable costs of actually building it. Cromer must have been teeming with labourers and craftsmen of every

Pl. 42
George Skipper, Architect, 1890–91, 31–37 Vicarage Road, Cromer.

description – there was scaffolding all over the town. All of the buildings required competent builders and used Skipper's preferred contractors and favoured materials, in particular terracotta and custom moulded bricks from Costessey brickworks.

A full list of Skipper's less public works in Cromer would be extensive. At the head of it would be St Bennets, Number 37 Vicarage Road, which is a Grade II Listed Building. The Listing authorities' description is thorough and

Pl. 43
'Cosseyware' Terracotta panel depicting fish and crabs, St Bennet's, Cromer.

Pl. 44
George Skipper, Architect, 1893,, St Bennet's, Vicarage Road, Cromer.

begins, 'The principal, west-facing, three-bay façade is dominated by a projecting three-storey porch which rises through the eaves and gives the impression of a battlemented gatehouse. It has splayed corners with quoins; slim pilasters on the outer edges; and prominent moulded storey bands'.

Again, Skipper's building showed historic features – the stepped parapets and finials at roof level, the pediments above both the door and the mullioned windows above it, and surfaces of knapped flint. The latter was last used in mediaeval times. The porch had two stained-glass transom windows and a terracotta panel inscribed St Bennets and Built AD1893. At first floor level and aligned with the tympanum above the front door, was a charming panel of Cosseyware terracotta tiles illustrating fronds of seaweed, fish, and crabs,

Pl. 45
George Skipper, Architect, 1896, St Mary's Road Cromer.

for which the town is famous. Behind St Bennets the other three Vicarage Road houses stretched down the street, all with two-storey bay windows, gables, and much use of knapped flintwork. Skipper was reviving the ancient craft.

Next door was Carlyle House, 39–41, Vicarage Road, built a year later in 1894, displaying many of the same features. Also developed by Mr Jarvis, it was, however, not necessarily connected to the Skippers. Other architects, especially Alfred Boardman and Augustus Scott, were at work in Cromer during the 1890s, and all of them could make comparable designs, or even consciously imitate his work. Another architect, Edwin Lutyens (1869–1944), visited the area in 1899, before drawing plans for Overstrand Hall, two miles distant.

One of Skipper's designs for larger private residences was Halsey House, completed a decade later. The elevation drawings that George Skipper had provided for Sir Francis Leyland Barrett in about 1899 were used in 1908, and apparently exhibited in the architectural section of the Royal Academy summer exhibition of 1910. A list of Royal Academy exhibits by George Skipper, the 'artist-architect', can be seen on page 235 of this book

Halsey House, Number 31 Norwich Road in Cromer, was originally known as The Red House. It is now a British Legion care home and has undergone a lot of modification, having started as a residence, before being a hospital during the First World War, subsequently a school, and then in MOD use during the Second World War. Surviving features recalling Skipper include dentilation and balustrading at the eaves, tall chimneystacks, eyebrow hoodmoulds and diamond-shaped flint patterns that stand out from the red brick walls. The terracotta details were extremely well made, in particular Sir F. Barrett's coat of arms, and in the courtyard entrance itself, a magnificent Baroque arched and hooded doorway in brick and 'Cosseyware'.

Aside of these properties about the town, the syndicate of investors wanted the architect to push on with more designs for hotels. The next to appear in 1895–96 was a rebuild to an existing building at Jetty Cliff, in the middle of the seafront and exactly above Cromer Pier, built four years later.

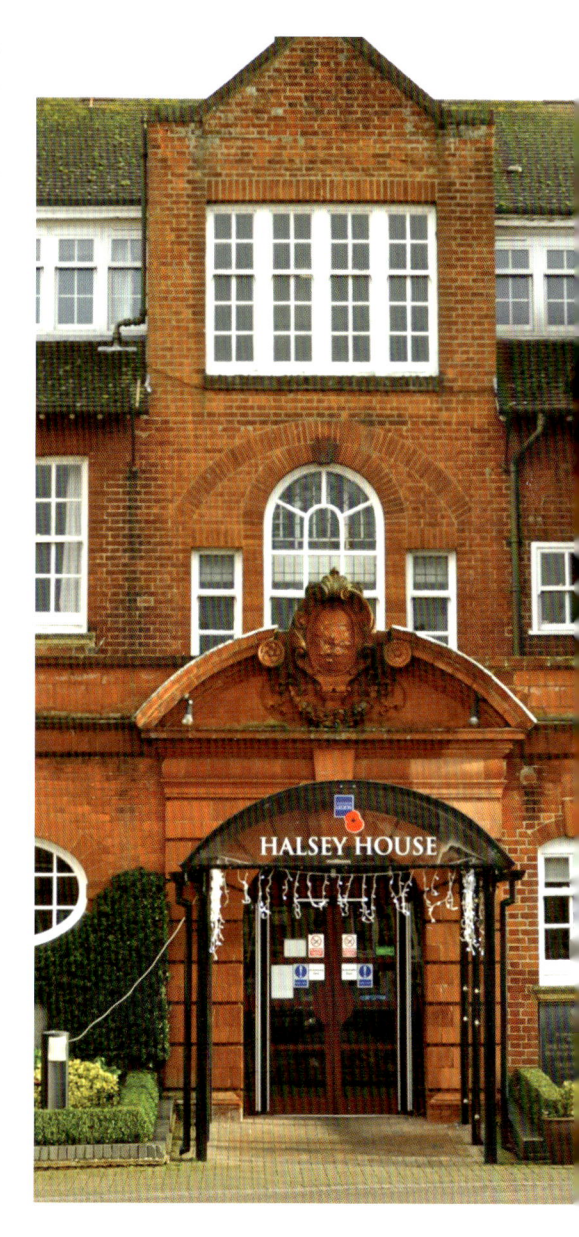

Pl. 46
George Skipper, Architect, 1900–08, Entrance to Halsey House,, Cromer.

Pl. 47
George Skipper, Architect, 1895–96, Hotel de Paris, Cromer.

Pl. 48
Mosaic floor at entrance of Hotel de Paris, Cromer.

This was the Hotel de Paris, which was put in place of four properties once belonging to the Harbords, Barons of Suffield and owners of Gunton Hall. These buildings had become a boarding house that had been purchased by a local man, Henry Soames Jarvis. Jarvis's son, Alex, asked for outside investment and the investors asked for another design from 'Cromer's architect'. George Skipper created a plan that enhanced the premium site, providing an impressive front, with smaller entrances at different levels from side streets to the rear. The builders, J.S. Smith's of Norwich started work straight away.

The Hotel de Paris was predictably large, with a wide front that is not straight, but has wings at either end inclining towards the sea at twenty degrees, like the claws of a crab. It was designed in a mixture of styles, an Edwardian – Queen Ann, if such a term is permissible. It had three towers that are 16th century in appearance; the central tower was five-storeyed and capped with an ogee-shaped cupola surmounted by a small bellcote. (This was exactly like the little feature he put on the roof of Cobden Terrace, the lowly terrace of workman's cottages in Street, Somerset, a few years earlier).

At the base of the central tower, (which reminded Pevsner of the Château de Chambord in the Loire), four Doric columns of Portland stone surrounded the arched entrance, its shape echoed in brick arches, pilasters, and balustrading on the storey above. The towers on the wings were smaller with a vertical series of bay windows, and capped by bell-shaped cupolae. The expanse of windows and brickwork across the front was enlivened by numerous details – flowers, classical ribbons, hood-moulds and mullions (ground floor only) – all enacted in 'Cosseyware'. Any architraving on the front-facing eighty (or more) windows also came from Gunton's brickworks.

Between the three towers were two gable fronts with bay windows on three-storeys. High on the decorative parapets on top of the two gables, where seagulls screamed and soared, two dormers peered out over the ocean. Behind these were pyramidal-hipped roofs, covered with dark slate and leadwork, emerging from the steep main roof. Between those angular brick gables were

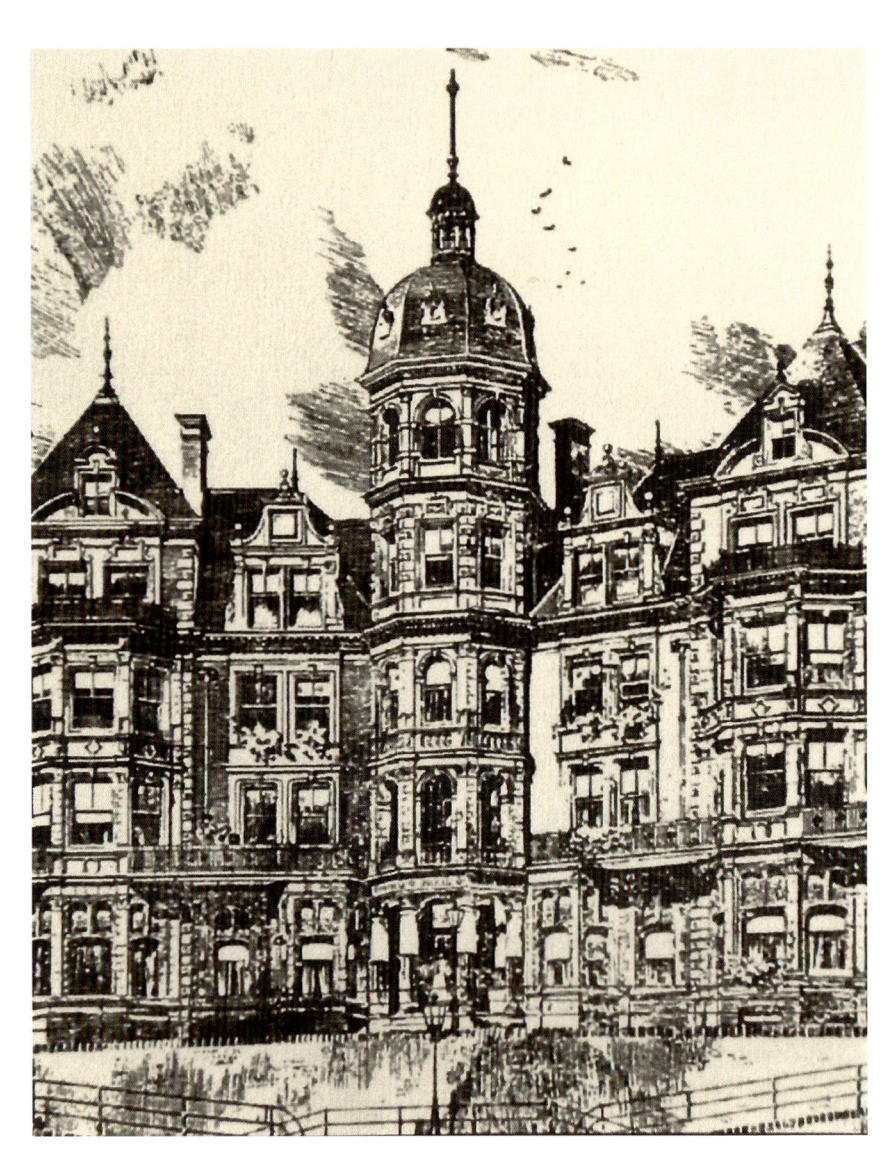

Pl. 49
George Skipper,
c.1894, (detail)
Monochrome print of
prospective
watercolour,
Hotel de Paris,
Cromer.

others, five in all, which were rendered white and shaped in a Baroque manner with finials, and a pair of casement windows.

The threshold at the front entrance, and around the rear doorway in the High Street, were decorated with pleasing mosaics in a combination of Classical and Art Nouveau styles, with garlands and the name, 'Hotel de Paris', picked out in capitals in a handsome font. The hotel was completed and opened in 1896. Its interior featured fine-painted plasterwork and stained glass windows, though this was not necessarily Skipper's doing. The hotel's appearance was much admired, though purists might be concerned at the mixing of diverse styles that, even to a critical eye, blend successfully at the Hotel de Paris. It is a Grade II Listed Building, and what is more, it has survived as a hotel, despite financial scares in the 1970s.

A few years after its arrival, the Hotel de Paris was considerably enhanced by the construction of a new pier beneath its cliff. Previous piers in that spot had been destroyed by storms; the last had been crashed into by a heavy collier in 1897. Investors gradually banded together to commission a new 450 ft long pier in 1902, using cast-iron framing and storm-proof piling. Renovated in 2012 the pier has an attractive arcaded entrance, while the pavilion at the seaward end remains a working theatre. The most popular view of the towering Hotel de Paris is from the pier below.

In the mid-1890s, with his office being built, George Skipper must have taken the train to Cromer many times. Conveniently the Midland and Great Northern Joint Railway Company had constructed another line from Norwich, via Melton Constable, Holt, and Sheringham, leading to a new and second station at Cromer Beach. As George alighted the train he could have walked in any direction to one of 'his' sites. There were at least ten Skipper buildings in the seaside town on the go at any time.

Aside of Cromer, with buildings still in construction, George Skipper and his brother had submitted a competition entry to design a Town Hall for Hunstanton, another coastal town thirty miles West of Cromer. The Skipper plan had been chosen among four entries. Building work commenced in early 1896, following the ceremonial laying of a foundation stone by Emmeline Le Strange, wife of Hamon Le Strange, Lord of the Manor and owner of much of the coastline. It was unveiled two years later by the Countess of Cottenham. Le Strange was enacting the vision of his father in establishing the resort.

Two surprises: firstly, that the East coast county has a West-facing coastline at Hunstanton; secondly, that despite hearing Norfolk has no rock, it seems it does have a stone that *can* be used in buildings (two if flint is counted, and actually three if clunch, or chalk block, is included). The Town Hall is built of Carrstone, a sedimentary sandstone conglomerate, quarried at Snettisham, five miles south of Hunstanton. Very striking in appearance, nicknamed 'gingerbread' and varying in colour from brown to dark chocolate-brown in colour, Carrstone was used with mortar either as rubble of different sizes, as in Hunstanton, or in beds of flat stones elsewhere.

Pl. 50 (detail) Carrstone corner of Hunstanton Town Hall, built in 1896,

Pl. 51
George Skipper, Architect, 1896, West elevation of Town Hall, Hunstanton.

Hunstanton Town Hall was a smaller version of Skipper's Town Hall in Cromer. Both Skippers were named architects on an inscribed panel dated 1896. It is a Grade II Listed building and the Listing authorities use the words, 'Late Victorian Jacobethan' in their description. A two-storeyed building, it had two brick chimneystacks on the ridge and a roof of tiles. Its West facing front had a wide gable in the centre, and single bay wings which were slightly recessed. The gable had a pediment and finial, with the town clock and carved ornament in the tympanum. Beneath this was a splendid window with stone mullions, pilasters to the ground level, and a white stone frieze carved with the words TOWN HALL. Below, at ground level, was the framed and arched entrance between two iron lanterns and stairs to and from an open expanse of seafront, known as 'The Green'.

The Town Hall had a single-storeyed adjoining hall, running at a right angle and facing South. Looking from the street, Greevegate, you saw the windows of the gable end of the main hall: next to this was a five-sided, two-storeyed porch with a conical roof, surmounted by a bellcote and weather-vane. This attached hall was for recreational purposes while the main hall housed the town's council and, nowadays, the Tourist and Information Service. It must be one of England's most attractive public halls, with a half-gabled entrance and a pediment in a chequered pattern. The chessboard effect was made by contrasting Carrstone squares with stone, resonant of the chequering on the Guildhall in nearby Kings Lynn, (though that was white limestone and knapped flintwork). The walls were buttressed, and the tiled roof topped by an angular wooden cupola, covered in leadwork.

Back in Cromer, where the appetite for hotels might have been sated by the Grand, the Metropole and the Hotel de Paris, there were four other hotels that George Skipper designed, or with which he was connected. These were the Imperial Hotel (1893–95), the Sandcliff Hotel (1897), the Cliftonville Hotel (1898) and the Lyndhurst Hotel, a few years later in 1904.

First of these, the Imperial, in Church Road, Cromer, was a building project for J. Young & Sons builders. As can be seen, Young's and Skipper had a reciprocal arrangement of sorts, whereby they called on the architect to supply plans and drawings for their projects and, conversely, Skipper would direct his patrons and clients to employ Youngs.

Pl. 52
George Skipper, Architect, 1896, South elevation of Town Hall, Hunstanton.

The Imperial was at one time a small Temperance establishment. Its three-bay redbrick front presented two gabled wings, lit by double-storey canted bay windows, and smaller casements overlined by distinctive radial-patterned lintels. The gables had lozenge-shaped brick finials and, behind them, tall chimneystacks and a pair of dormers on the roof. Beneath them, at ground level, were arched casements on either side of the arched doorway. The building ceased to be a hotel in the 1940s, and was divided into flats.

The Sandcliff Hotel, overlooking the sea on Runton Road, was designed by George Skipper for his client T.H. Wallis, using A. Fox builders. Continuing as a popular guesthouse in the 21st century, it was another red brick structure, with a pattern of squares, diamonds and X shapes in knapped flints which, as every Norfolk person knows, are broken and chipped flints with a flat face. Again the hotel is relatively small, with gable wings and bay windows. High up the gables are other windows, imaginatively placed between ornamental brickwork, and topped by a truncated finial with a diamond shape in knapped flint. The front entrance has a splendid arch in an impressive arrangement of 'Cosseyware', beneath three stained glass arched windows.

Pl. 53
George Skipper, Architect, 1897, (detail) Entrance to Sandcliff Hotel, Cromer.

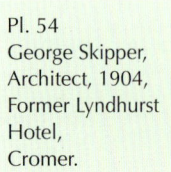

Pl. 54
George Skipper, Architect, 1904, Former Lyndhurst Hotel, Cromer.

The Lyndhurst Hotel, on West Cliff, now known as Alfred Road, was fundamentally similar to the Sandcliff and the Imperial, having three slightly projecting three-storeyed wings with canted bay windows. In between were, from the ground upwards, twin entrance arches, and pairs of windows on the two upper storeys. The gables and the parapet between them were all shaped in the Dutch or Flemish manner, with pronounced curves and finials, giving the Lyndhurst a distinct character. The little hotel was bombed during WWII, though the Dutch gabled front survived. It was never a hotel again, but was rebuilt to create three private houses, where the front wall was faced with flints in the round between brick piers and pilasters.

The Cliftonville Hotel, a successful hotel still in operation, was not designed by George Skipper. The plan came from A.F. Scott, a rival, whom we recall as the apprentice architect articled to his father some years earlier, who now held the position of Cromer's Town Surveyor. Scott's 1898 creation was a three and four-storey extravaganza on the Runton Road, using some the features that Skipper employed, namely a castellated tower at its centre (castellation no longer present), flanked by asymmetrical gables and a pair of octagonal four-storey towers.

Described by others as being in the Jacobean/ Arts and Crafts style, the brick front of the Cliftonville, now painted in a cream colour, was entered by a basket-arched doorway below two-storeys of canted bay windows. The hotel presented a second front, still unpainted, around the corner in Alfred Road, with identical gabled bays lit by bay windows. There are terracotta details in

Pl. 55
A.F Scott, Architect, 1898, (with additions by G.J Skipper,) Cliftonville Hotel, Cromer.

plaques and panels with relief moulding of leaves, flowers and grapes, all from Costessey brickworks.

Four years later in 1898, George Skipper was asked to supply plans for the western end of the Cliftonville's North front. He submitted a design with a stairway tower topped by an arcaded ogee-shaped lead cap. Also by Skipper was the complex stepped gable above two-storeys of larger canted bay windows. The Cliftonville is these days a Listed building, though it cannot be seen as a 'pure Skipper' design.

★   ★   ★   ★

Pl. 56
George Skipper, Architect, 1896. Office for his own Architectural Practice, 7 London Street, Norwich.

While these Cromer hotels and residences, all from Skipper's pencil, were being built, there were important developments twenty miles away in Norwich. Skipper's new offices had taken shape, and his team of draftsmen and surveyors moved into the Number 7 London Street address in 1896, though the building was not finished for another eight years. (Skipper would only ever use the upper two floors: the ground floor was occupied by Dry Cleaners and a tobacconist). The building work was essentially a new front elevation for the three-storeyed building. It was only two bays wide, and wedged in between Jarrold's store and a 17th century building that has since been replaced by a further extension of Jarrold's premises. Standing in front of Number 7 London Street today, the ground floor can no longer be seen, as Jarrold's now occupy the entire building. What a façade! The two upper-storeys were lit by a pair of oriel windows and, above these, by arched casements with 'eyebrow' hoods and dentilation. At the top of the building was a decorative terracotta parapet, mounted with three broad finials with domed heads, rising as octagonal buttresses from lower storeys. The two gable pediments were pierced by round windows, or oculi.

It is a Grade II Listed Building. The reason for Listing is the spectacular terracotta detail around the two oriels. They contained a total of eight large arched windows, and an upper tier of fourteen smaller ones. The mullions were made of Costessey brickworks' mouldings.

Beneath the windows were two horizontal panels, flanked by smaller square panels of relief mouldings, that give a biographical narrative. While James Minns and his son, as well as Fred Gunton, oversaw the making of the terracotta frontage of the office, they did not make all of it. It is easily noticed that the representational quality on these two horizontal panels is not the same as the rest of the terracotta work.

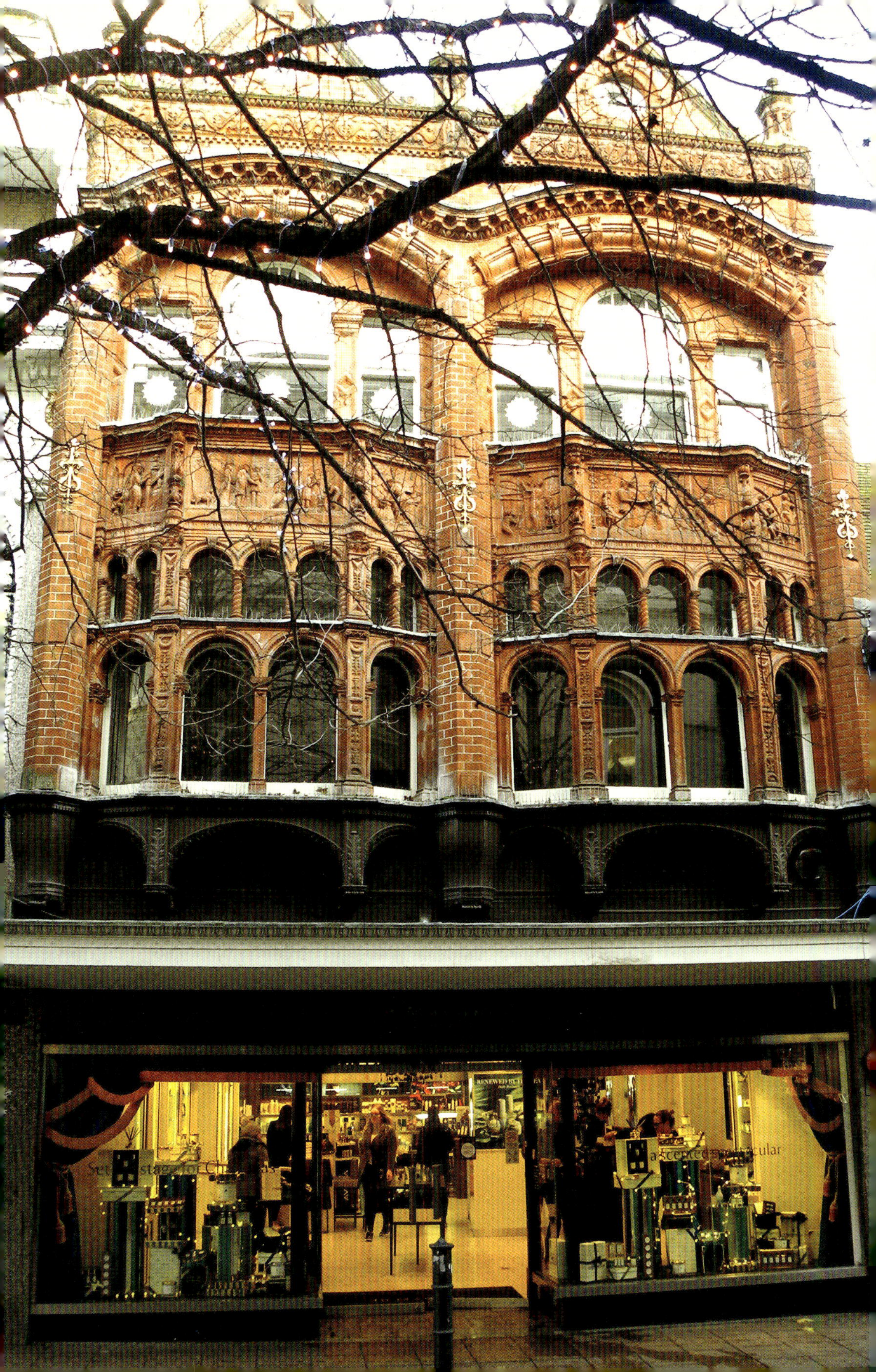

Pl. 57
George Skipper, Architect, 1896, Office at 7 London Street, Norwich. (detail) Left-hand panel in terracotta by Gunton's of Costessey, added c.1904.

Pl.58 *(facing page)* Right-hand panel.

The reason for this was unearthed by Faith Shaw in her 1971 research for her dissertation, 'An Introductory Study to the Life and Work of George J. Skipper, Architect of Edwardian Norwich and Norfolk'. She managed to find contacts who had known George Skipper in person. The most convincing of these was Henry Trueman (*c.*1884–*c.*1974) who worked under George and became his most dependable surveyor in later years. Shaw also discovered the elevation sketch for the office and discussed the terracotta frontage with Trueman. In her words, (and my italics) Trueman's brief explanation for the differing quality of the two large panels was a revelation:

'A master sketch was made by George Skipper to help joint sections, and ***everyone in the office shared in the carving***, but to George's design'.

This was highly unusual – the panels had been made by office-workers with penknives as well as expert artisan woodcarvers!

The left-hand central panel depicted George Skipper, about twenty inches tall, with his wife, Rachel Skipper, and behind them a little boy, Theo Skipper, with a dog. George wears a Top hat. He stands with a bowler-hatted client, and inspects an architectural moulding that a workman (Minns himself!) is presenting.

To the right of the same panel are two artisans of the Costessey brickworks. In the background are the faint lines of a classical building with a pediment and columns, and other buildings with towers, cupolae and Dutch gables. Significantly we can recognise the outlines of two of them: the one to the left shows Number 7 St Giles Street in the city, and the one on the right is Commercial Chambers in Norwich's Red Lion Street – both buildings that are still to be discussed. Their presence suggest that the panels were not finished, let alone assembled and *in situ* until about 1903–04.

The right-hand central panel depicted Skipper on site showing his plans to a client and his wife. Facing the busy street, the long panels were sixty-six inches wide, comprising three lines of six squares. The four smaller panels (of a better quality) were fourteen inch squares showing relief images of carpenters (upper left) making a staircase; foundrymen (upper right) casting iron with iron railings in view; bricklayers at work (lower left); stonemasons carving an architectural detail (lower right). All around the panels are moulded patterns, acanthus scrolls, little bearded faces, barley twist columns, and egg-and-dart braiding – no surface was undecorated.

It was a remarkable work, a celebration of Norfolk terracotta and specialist brick manufacture. An interesting observation made recently was that it was not permitted in the 1890s for architects to advertise; by placing the descriptive terracotta panels on the front of the office, Skipper was sidestepping the rule, albeit in good taste. The architect appreciated artist-craftsmen like Minns, partly because he was an artist himself, but also because he knew that the best architecture welcomes sculpture, and that these two art traditions were mutually beneficial.

Pl. 59
James Minns, c.1828–1904, Sculptor and wood carver.

George had known James Benjamin Shingles Minns (c.1828–1904) for many years, and his father, a contemporary, had known him even longer. Both Robert and George Skipper had bought hundreds of 'Cosseyware' items made by Minns at Gunton's, whether chimneys and mullions, or crests and decorative panels. George had commissioned a few of these, for example the panel in Cromer with fish, seaweed and crabs, composed of fourteen high-relief tiles. Minns lived in Norwich and gave his occupation for the Census Returns of England and Wales as 'Wood Carver' (1871), 'Sculptor' (1881), 'Carver' (1891), and again 'Wood Carver' (1901).

He was an artist and artisan too, but all the descriptions were true, because the technique of making terracotta details began with a woodcarving. At first Minns carved them in wood. From the carvings he took negative moulds into which brick clay was rammed; the resulting positive forms were dried and fired in the usual manner.

James Minns also carved angels in stone and others in wood, mostly for church interiors. However, for a period of about forty years, much of his work lay in woodcarving for the production of terracotta. He also taught woodcarving to artisans at the Norwich School of Art in the early 1890s, while Skipper's Cromer hotels were being raised. About the time Skipper's office in London Street was completed, James Minns died. He was succeeded by his son, John William Minns, also a woodcarver.

Pl. 60
Office staff at 7 London Street c.1899. George Skipper at centre in back row.

All of Minns's work for Gunton's of Costessey happened at the same time as discoveries in terracotta were being made by other artists and technicians. The medium of terracotta, or baked earth, was ancient beyond compare, with a history extending back beyond 25,000BC. For the purposes of sculpture, terracotta was used at a small scale in Roman, Mediaeval and Renaissance times. Europeans such as Bernini or Roubilliac made life-size busts in terracotta, while Canova used it for preparatory models. For British architecture, however, terracotta was an entirely new building material from about the 1860s. If it did not have great structural strength, it excelled as an economical decorative element.

Some exterior walls of the courtyard at the V&A Museum in London were decorated in the 1860s with terracotta details made by the artist Godfrey Sykes (1824–1866). With two assistants Sykes had a team who could sculpt a piece in clay, take a mould from it, then fill this with the right mix of clay before firing the result. He made decorative pieces, garlands and shields, to be fixed to the building, and items such as small columns, or pilasters, that added architectural quality.

Meanwhile, south of the Thames in Lambeth, a ceramic empire had risen up under Sir Henry Doulton (1820–1897), one of England's greatest manufacturers of pottery, whose name stands equal to that of Josiah Wedgwood, or Herbert Minton. Among Sir Henry's many feats, he had

Pl. 61
William Neatby, 1860–1910, Artist, architect and ceramicist.

Pl. 62
George Skipper, Architect, 1897–99. Side passage to White Lion Street, The Royal Arcade, Norwich.

encouraged art students and artisans to work for him. One such was George Tinworth (1843–1913) who had made terracotta panels and details, including a semi-circular tableau *c.*1870 featuring potters at work. This was to be seen outside Doulton's works, a precedent for the 'Cosseyware' panels outside Skipper's new office. A much earlier forerunner was part of Trajan's Column in Rome featuring artisans and labourers at work.

For Doulton, Art Pottery had two distinct branches, one of which was in unglazed earthenware, or *terra cotta*, and the other that was in richly glazed stoneware fired to a higher temperature, and this was known as faience. Doulton mastered the art of producing faience and at the same time acquired the skills of William James Neatby (1860–1910). Neatby had actually been trained as an architect, yet worked as a craftsman and designer for Burmantoft's in Leeds. He had joined Doulton in the late 1880s. After about 1900 he worked independently while still utilising the manufacturing expertise of Doulton. The ceramicist produced sculpture, tiles, murals, stained glass and enamels. He also made exquisite faience ornament for buildings. Doulton and Neatby's output was noticed by George Skipper, and when the prestigious commission for the Royal Arcade arrived, the architect made contact.

The commission came from Sir Kenneth Kemp (1853–1936), whom readers will recall as the leader of the syndicate of investors responsible for Cromer's hotels – the Grand, the Metropole and the Hotel de Paris. Kemp was an interesting figure, a cricketer, a soldier, a barrister and a banker, who had inherited the baronetcy from deceased cousins. His home at the time was in Erpingham, near Aylsham, though he owned land in North Norfolk, South Norfolk, and Norwich.

Kemp's activities in Norwich were enhanced by visits to Skipper's new office. Here they discussed the idea of creating an arcade of shops, and the possibilities of a site just around the corner, where an old coaching inn was in decline. It was a long narrow site, with an alleyway of stables for horses, adjacent to the Angel Hotel, running from Gentleman's Walk (at the eastern edge of the substantial Market Place) to the Back of the Inns, now know as Castle Street. The Angel Hotel had become known as the Royal Hotel in honour of the young Queen's marriage in 1840, and that is one source of the arcade's title, 'Royal'.

Equally, it was no coincidence that when Kemp and Skipper first discussed the idea of the Royal Arcade, the country celebrated Queen Victoria's Diamond Jubilee. Kemp had access to the freehold, he had an idea, and he was confident in 'his' architect. As for investors, he spent his life looking for them. Somehow the project took off, and Skipper began to plan the dream. Both men had seen Burlington Arcade in London, built in 1819, though it was probably Thornton's Arcade in Leeds, built in 1878, which offered more architectural information.

As it happened Sir Kenneth Kemp left for Africa a few months after attending the official unveiling of his Royal Arcade on 24 May 1899. He had already rejoined the Norfolk Regiment and went with them by ship to the Cape, where the British army were embroiled in the Anglo-Boer War.

George Skipper took Kemp's commission for the arcade with ease. The architecture was not complicated,

Pl. 63
Sir Kenneth Kemp, 1853–1936,, Soldier, barrister, banker — also Skipper's patron in Cromer and Norwich.

Pl. 64
George Skipper, Architect, 1897–99, The Royal Arcade, Norwich.

Pl. 65
George Skipper, Architect, 1897–99, (detail)
The Royal Arcade, Norwich.

and largely dictated by the linear site. It was entered at either end. Skipper more or less retained the old hotel front onto Gentleman's Walk and the Market, only making a three-arched entrance on the ground floor. The arcade was two hundred and fifty feet long. Once inside, a visitor was immediately aware of the marble floors and the two-storeyed interior space. Above them there was a long glass roof, with a large glass-paned lantern at its centre, and a pitched slate roof to one side and a traditional pantile roof on the other. The shop fronts were wood-framed bow and glass. The arcade 'jinks' at an angle of a couple of degrees, and there is a side exit towards White Lion Street. New flooring and a row of lamps were added in a restoration project in the 1980s.

In reality, the visitor hardly notices these ordinary features of the building. Instead they are dazzled by light, shining surfaces, expanses of green and cream coloured tiles, and a range of ornament from Doulton's Mr Neatby. These were primarily in faience, but also in stained glass images of birds and flowers. The faience was of the highest quality and proclaimed an English Art Nouveau in a special way. At the time of its opening the Royal Arcade was described in the *Norfolk Chronicle* as 'a fragment from *The Arabian Nights* dropped into the heart of the city'.

    The full effect, however, was and is best seen from outside the Castle Street entrance. The coloured ceramic covered pillar at the centre supported a frieze with faience lettering spelling ROYAL ARCADE in a font of the 1890s. Above this was a green and beige-pink balustrade, and above this an arched semi-circular stained glass window in a striped frame. The keystone of the arch rose and transformed to an emblematic angel in pale faience, its wings rising to the top of the gable, in a surround of honeysuckle buds on a blue background. The concave-curved gable is repeated at right angles above a sort of tower with a domed lead roof. A quarter-circle section of this tower presented three pairs of windows with mullions in faience above a treble band of bright red, green and blue tiles. Below this, but no longer present, was an unbelievably ornate stained glass window, in an even more ornate faience and brick clasped frame. In 1899 this was the saloon window of a public house, The White Rose, and above the faience tracery of the window frame were the words, Ales– Stouts– Spirits. This curve-fronted structure, masking a corner, also allowed a doorway to be placed on another elevation. It was typical of George Skipper, and a technique he had used from his earlier days.

Studded and bejewelled with Neatby's coloured shapes, the quarter-circled faience tower was a wonder to behold. It did not end there: the projecting wing of Skipper's entrance met the passing street with blue striped pillars. These supported a magnificent two-storey corner oriel, with an arcade of blue columns above, and a pair of four-light mullion and transom windows below. Exhausting as it is (even to see it), the description must continue, for the theme of the left-hand side, as you view the entrance, is almost mirrored on the right-hand side. There was another projecting wing, loosely described earlier as 'a sort of a tower', which had a curved front with a shop window below. Above this, the three thick bands of faience tiles continued and, above them, were another three pairs of mullion windows and the shallow dome of a lead roof.

It was extremely colourful and a marvellous sight, a credit to the architect, to the artisans, and to Sir Henry Doulton, who had died two years earlier in 1897. His company was granted the royal warranty at about this time, becoming Royal Doulton. Looking at this entrance to the Royal Arcade, the effect on a person, certainly for the first time, is one of awe and amazement, of being charmed by the building's decoration. It is a Listed Building, Grade II★, (a step up from Grade II), but one wonders who was the star – Skipper or Neatby?

Did George Skipper specify the shapes, designs and colours of these highly decorative architectural ornaments – or did the actual shapes come from Doulton and their chief ceramicist? Doubtless Neatby was responsible: nobody

Pl. 66
George Skipper, Architect, 1897–99, The Royal Arcade, Norwich.
(detail) Castle Street entrance.

will ever be able to answer the question – there is no reference in George's notebooks, or any record inside Doulton archives. Pevsner and Wilson, in *The Buildings of England Norfolk 1: Norwich and North East*, make the understatement: '...the Royal Arcade...stands as a high point in English Arts and Crafts'.

As for the end of coaching inns and the coming of horseless carriages, it was just about at this time that George Skipper purchased a motorcar. He was very proud of the vehicle, mildly boasting that he was the second person in Norwich city to own one of these new machines. Maybe it was a Humber, or a Renault, with which Skipper rammed the old Cringleford Bridge a little later. He was to pay for damages to the stone parapet of the bridge, a fine piece of architecture in itself. The irony of a lover of Tudor architecture damaging an early 16th century bridge was doubtless not lost on the embarrassed driver.

The Royal Arcade was a resounding success. What is more, close contact with Doulton enabled Skipper to facilitate another design, also to be built close by, just up Guildhall Hill at Number 7 St Giles Street. It was to be the offices of the *Norfolk Daily Standard*, a newspaper enterprise that began in 1885 and ended in 1905, only three or four years after this new building appeared.

Critics have questioned Skipper's originality, as well as his eclectic and revivalist tastes in architecture, but here is a building that flies in the face of such commentary. Norwich's Number 7 St Giles Street is original and eclectic, displaying a combination of revivalist style features covered in an experimental coating of honey-coloured faience. There is no other building like it.

It brings to mind Sir John Betjeman's much repeated quote of 1975, which he made in response to David Jolley's 'Architect Exuberant: George Skipper 1856–1948' exhibition. The poet and conservator of the built environment wrote to the curator:

> 'I am delighted to hear that you have arranged an exhibition of G.J Skipper's work. He is altogether remarkable and original. He is to Norwich what Gaudi was to Barcelona. It is so good too that the Norwich School of Art is behind this recognition of a local architect. The most effective way of saving a building from destruction is by getting people to look at it and see its merits for themselves. This you are doing for Skipper and just in time'.

A small digression: when Betjeman underlines 'just in time' we must remember that even as the exhibition was on display, workmen were still clearing the site of Cromer's demolished Hotel Metropole. From this point onwards, more and more buildings by Skipper were to be protected by Listing.

Back to Barcelona – Betjeman was not comparing Skipper with his contemporary, Antoni Gaudi (1852–1926), because of Gaudi's never ending cathedral, the Sagrada Familia, or his Park Güell on Carmel hill. He is pointing, instead, to the noticeably odd bits of architecture that you might come across as you walk about the Catalan city, for example the Casa Milà, an apartment

Pl. 67 *(facing page)*
George Skipper,
Architect,1899–1900,
Number 7,
St Giles Street
Norwich.

block with sinuous curves and wobbles, and the appearance of a colossal ant hill with windows. It is this quality that Betjeman refers to, of somebody walking around Norwich, or Barcelona, and suddenly being confronted by a special piece of architecture.

This is how a visitor to Norwich finds Skipper's buildings. Observing the flinty magnificence of the ancient Guildhall, with your back to the 1930s City Hall, you turn to the crest of the hill – and there it is, Skipper's extraordinary creation at Number 7 St Giles Street. You ask yourself, "What the...is that?"

It takes a moment or two to come to one senses and look at the components, and then to consider what they all add up to. The building is at the corner leading onto Upper Goat Lane. Skipper has clipped off the corner and placed the entrance on the diagonal. It is an archway, flanked on either street-front by much wider arched windows. To the left of the arched window is an ordinary doorway, and above this there are isolated slit windows and at the top, the highest part of the building, there is square campanile with a copper-clad pagoda roof and finial.

Readers will recognise this as a miniature version of Skipper's 1887 Clock Tower in Street, Somerset, at Clark's Shoe Factory. In fact the 7, St Giles Street building had a clock face beneath the campanile, though this has gone. It was lucky to survive the aerial bombings of 1942, when the adjacent building was hit. Besides, the faience clock tower could hardly have competed with the 150 feet tall clock tower attached to City Hall, erected across the road in 1938.

To see Skipper's campanile, of a shape seen in Austria or northern Italy, and immediately next to it, a substantial Dutch dormer-gable with a pair of windows and prominent scrolls, is to undermine the viewer's sense of reality. It is reminiscent of Portmeirion, the village in North Wales, built by the architect, Clough Williams-Ellis (1883–1978), in which Italian villas and Alpine cottages jostle with other architectural fantasies.

At the corner of the roof, next to the Dutch gable and slightly lower, was a round, domed turret. With six smaller arched windows above larger ones, it rose from an oriel below, composed of three mullion and transom windows over the main entrance. The St Giles's elevation had three arched windows with decorative spandrels at its first floor level, the side elevation had only one. Attached to the front were two terracotta portrait medallions, one of William Caxton, England's 15th century printer, and one of Daniel Defoe, the 17th and 18th century writer, poet and journalist.

The appearance of the former *Norfolk Daily Standard* building, already a concoction, was made much more unusual by being completely covered in Doulton's honey-coloured 'Carraraware' tiling and coping. The building was Listed Grade II in 1986. The Listing Authorities stated that it had a granite base, but above this, beneath the faience was brickwork and concrete. Over the last one hundred and twenty years the building has had a variety of uses. Most recently it has been a showroom for 'Fired Earth', selling ceramic tiles. In a building covered in Doulton's high-fired faience, this is very appropriate.

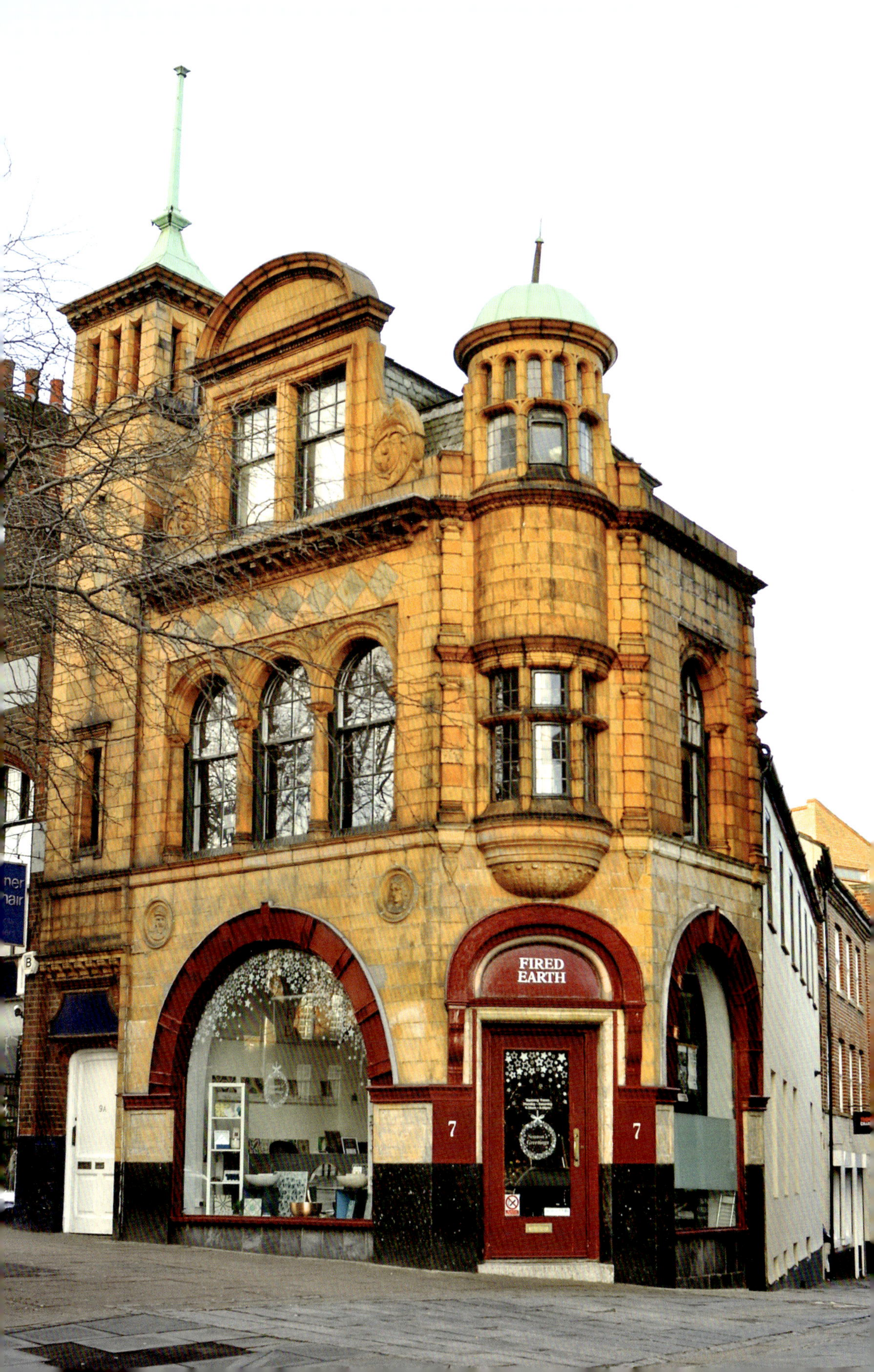
FIRED
EARTH
7
7

Pl. 68
George Skipper,
Architect,
1899–1900,
(detail)
Number 7,
St Giles Street
Norwich.

The *Norfolk Daily Standard*, and the *Norfolk Weekly Standard* had been founded in 1885 by Philip Soman (1834–1895). The proprietor of another newspaper, the *Norwich Argus*, he was also the owner of a publishing and printing works, to be known as Soman Wherry Press. Apparently Mr Soman's intention in starting the *Norfolk Daily Standard* had been to promote the Conservative Party cause for the upcoming General Election. It was to be a significant one, as it would be the first to follow the extended franchise and parliamentary reform confining constituencies to a single MP. In the event it was a loss for the Conservatives, with Lord Salisbury defeated by the Liberals under W.E Gladstone.

Undeterred, the *Norfolk Daily Standard* continued. The commission to design the office building came to Skipper either from Philip Soman, with a will to establish his son, or from the son, A. E. Soman, himself. The younger man, Asher Soman (1857–1934), presently publishing in London, would be returning to Norwich to run the newspapers in 1901. By that time Skipper's building at 7 St Giles Street was ready for him.

For every commission that George Skipper ever took, the architect made a note of the building's intended purpose. It would have been intriguing to have found his notes for the newspaper office in St Giles's. The building's purpose, we can only guess, was to amaze and amuse and charm, certainly to get a viewer's attention – it succeeded.

Interestingly, the Carraraware and other wall-facing tiles made by Doulton were actually invented by another Norfolk architect contemporary with Skipper. This was John Cockrill (1849–1924), nicknamed 'Concrete Cockrill'. The tile patent sold to Doulton in 1893 was for an 'L' shaped tile that was self-clasping to concrete and brick underneath: significantly the wall did not need shuttering, and was therefore easier and cheaper to raise than might be expected. The Royal Arcade, Number 7 St Giles Street, as well as Commercial Chambers in Red Lion Street, Haymarket Chambers, still to be described, and parts of other Skipper buildings – depended on these tiles, which were glazed by Doulton and marketed as new materials, including 'Carraraware'. In a Doulton advertisement for Carraraware we see that the tiles were used by the architect Thomas Collcutt (1840–1924) on the upper part of Savoy Court at The Savoy Hotel in London.

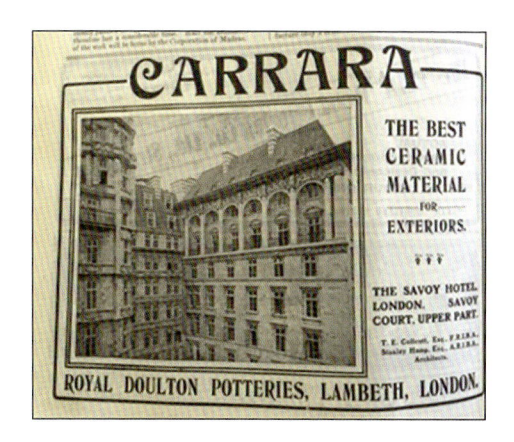

Pl. 69   Advertisement for Royal Doulton 'Carraraware'.

Pl. 70   Royal Doulton Potteries trade announcement for Cockrill-Doulton Patent Tiles, May 1900.

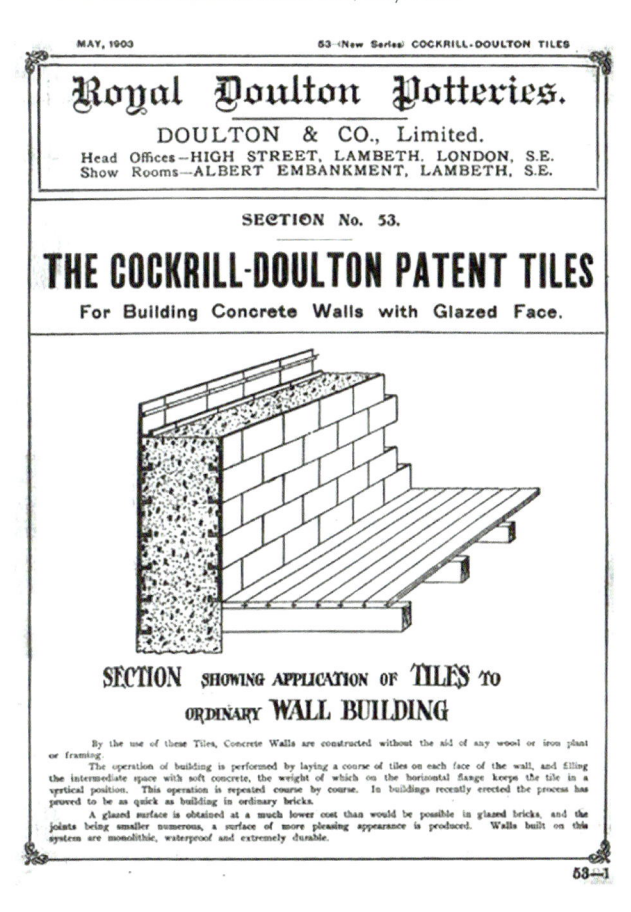

Concerning Concrete Cockrill, Borough Surveyor and Architect for Great Yarmouth, it seems there was a enthusiastic uptake for the new patented tiles in his own town. His son, Ralph Cockrill, also an architect, used Doulton's Carraraware to great effect in designing the 1903 purpose-built circus, The Hippodrome, also a Listed building. There is every reason to think that George Skipper and both Cockrills were in contact, and took an interest in each other's use of glazed tiles on exteriors.

The 1890s are often reviewed as a decade of stylish art and architecture. The 19th century came to an end amid hopes and toasts for the future, though the Queen was ailing and the country was at war. For George Skipper FRIBA, the 20th century and the coming Edwardian Age would be a continuation of his successes, he hoped.

Pl. 71
George Skipper, (signed GJS)
pastel drawing on two pages of his pocket sketch book,
13 September 1900, 'Old Shed, Snettisham'.
RIBA Collections.

CHAPTER FIVE

1900—1909

'But is was after 1900 that Skipper realized his potential as an exponent of Edwardian Baroque, to the extent that the Norwich Union building in Surrey Street may with reason be regarded as the best of its kind in the country'.
The Buildings of England Norfolk 1: Norwich and North East
N. Pevsner and B. Wilson

With hindsight, themes to George Skipper's life and works in the new century, become apparent. One impression is of his maturity, having been a busy architect for twenty years. Another is of his momentum, as the architect had already established a high-tempo work rate, overseeing several schemes at once, from the Royal Arcade in the city to the big hotels on the coast. An essential factor was money, and the new era was accompanied by an upturn in confidence, the confidence required by investors and patrons to spend a great amount of money on an expensive design by an architect, and probably an expensive building as well.

The Edwardian era is often depicted as the last sunset, as Britain entered the darkness of 1914 and what was to follow. Whether this is fanciful, or not, it was entirely true regarding money. Skipper's clients and patrons might not have commissioned handsome architecture, such as they did, if there had been less confidence.

In 1900 George and Rachel Skipper and young Theo were living at 59 Unthank Road. Two of his brothers were also in Norwich, with Robert at 17 Clarence Road, and Frederick at 112 Trinity Street. At the office fraternal eruptions of temper between the business partners were occasionally heard.

The Anglo-Boer War of 1899–1902 was reported in England almost daily. In 1900 it was two steps forward and two steps back. The news was a stream of engagements and incidents, reported in such a manner that readers at home could hardly conceive the ferocity of the action. There were a number of outcomes to the war, which was eventually won in 1902 by the British at a high cost in reputation, lives and morale. Chief of these was that South Africa's mineral wealth in diamonds and gold remained in the hands of Britain and her allies. Skipper's patron, Sir Kenneth Kemp, of Lacons (Lacons, Youell & Kemp) Bank finally returned from war in the Cape.

On 22 January 1901 the newspapers announced 'Death of Queen Victoria. Lamentation throughout the world'. The old monarch had ruled over a country

that nearly ruled the world. Feelings of optimism for the new king were tempered with news from afar of American and German imperialism, of famine in Bengal and dissent in Ireland and Russia. There were presidential assassinations, concerns about armaments and, of course, incredible inventions: the first airplanes, mass production motor-cars, radio receivers, gramophones, and cheaper portable cameras.

As always, a sense of the new was balanced by the same old ways. Skipper's shiny car, still slightly scratched from the Cringleford bridge incident, was stared at by countrymen bustling around the market. London Street was narrow and sometimes blocked for a few minutes while a lady descended from her carriage to enter a shop. Liveried servants held the horses; behind them drivers of heavier wagons and carts waited respectfully.

Looking down at the scene from the arched windows of the architect's office, Skipper's staff of draftsmen, clerks, surveyors and assistants, were working 'flat out'. By good fortune, and merit, a string of important commissions were reaching the office. In which order they arrived, it is hard to say, but they were completed in close sequence, with many of the projects overlapping and running concurrently. Most of these prospective buildings would be financial institutions.

Six of the works were within two minutes' walk from the office. But before these was the work which would be regarded as his finest, and that was a little bit further, perhaps a quarter of a mile away in Surrey Street.

Here was the site that had once been Surrey Court, a house belonging to Henry Howard, Earl of Surrey and the son of England's most powerful nobleman, the Duke of Norfolk. The site was on a mild slope and surrounded by historic buildings, all of which would be put in the shade by the building that George Skipper planned. Pevsner's *The Buildings of England* noted:

> Surrey Street is a Georgian street of distinction, though one may for a moment forget about it, knocked down by the smashing Norwich Union building which, without any doubt, is one of the country's most convinced Edwardian buildings. It is by G.J Skipper, here showing himself every bit as competent and inventive as any London architect.

Pl. 72
George Skipper, Architect, 1901, Copy of prospective (first) drawing: Surrey House for Norwich Union Life Insurance.
photo: Aviva PLC.

Pl. 73
The Builder, 'New Offices for Norwich Union Life Insurance Society'.

(Print of first drawing in Pl. 72).

The task was to plan a new head office. The client was Norwich Union Life Insurance Society, best known as 'Norwich Union'. Skipper won the commission through a competition. This was a blind competition, in which designs were not signed by the architects, and the commissioners could not see who the entrants were. It was convenient that the winning architect lived and worked in the city.

The client wanted a show of wealth and power. During its one hundred years history Norwich Union had accumulated several subsidiaries and hundreds of agencies and branches in Britain and her overseas dominions, as well as Switzerland, Greece, Turkey, and six branches in Italy. At some point it became the largest insurance business in the country. Using the emblem of the cathedral's spire, the company projected an image of provincial English stability and long-term security. Inevitably, as with most financial institutions, this sense of stability was implied in the use of stone.

Nominally the General Contractor was G.F. Hawes & Son of King Street, but Skipper was in charge of overseeing all matters of design, and picked nearly all the artisans. Moreover, in May 1902, the Skippers had issued Hawes with an eighty-seven page list of precise specifications, written in very legible longhand. For instance, just in case Mr Hawes, a well established builder, did not know what lime mortar was, the architect and his brother stated that they wanted:

Lime mortar to be composed of one part lime to two parts sand, one part cinder ashes and one part broken bricks ground upon a platform and then thrown into the mortar mill and then well ground up and incorporated with sufficient water and used fresh daily. The lime to be approved quality Kirton Lindsay Blue Lias.

Fatefully, the architect sub-contracted work to an impressive collaborator, who would, in turn, introduce Skipper to a number of extremely skilled sub-contractors and artists. Described as sculptors, marble merchants, stonemasons, marble decorators, and marble importers, this was Farmer & Brindley. It was a partnership between two stone carvers from Ripley in Derbyshire, the late William Farmer (1825–1879) and William Brindley (1832–1919).

Foremost of the pair was Brindley, not only because he was considered the better carver, but because he lived forty years longer than Farmer, and guided the company throughout those years. From the age of eighteen, Brindley had worked for Farmer on the decoration of churches. After another eighteen years the pair decided to establish their partnership and form a company, based at Westminster Bridge Road in London. They were very well respected by architects who employed them, significantly by Alfred Waterhouse, on more than a hundred projects, including the Natural History Museum.

It is worth remembering that George Skipper had been an apprentice under another architect who worked with Waterhouse – and so, by way of connection, the Derbyshire stonemason and George Skipper had already met. Another very well known architect, George Gilbert Scott, employed Brindley in the construction of the Albert Memorial in Kensington Gardens and thought very highly of him.

Brindley had realised that there was a growing fashion for coloured marbles for grand projects, and decided to go and hunt for the traditional sources of these stones. He visited ancient quarries, principally Roman ones, in three continents. He made enquiries about re-opening those that were closed, or forgotten.

"As my delight is in old quarry hunting and as I knew the high price fragments dug up in Rome fetched, I determined to try to find the lost quarries and see if they were worked out or not".

In this way Brindley established sources and contacts for marbles, for instance *Cippolino*, or *Verde Antico*, and extended the company's activities to supplying marble. He also studied geology first-hand, and made scholarly reports for RIBA on the subject of the architectural use of marble.

A significant client was J.F Bentley, the architect of Westminster Cathedral, who ordered twenty-nine weight-bearing columns and expanses of marble surfaces in various colours. Brindley then invited Cathedral representatives to see the columns being turned on lathes in his workshops, before his craftsmen

Pl. 74
William Brindley, 1832–1919, of Farmer & Brindley. photo: National Portrait Gallery Images.

spent several weeks carving the capitals. Both Bentley and Cardinal Vaughan, who founded the Catholic Cathedral, died before all the marble features were used in the various side-chapels. There were a few breakages and altered decisions, and a lot of valuable marble stock that was not used, and that was why, in the years of construction of the Norwich Union building, Brindley was able to offer Skipper quantities of the highest quality coloured marbles from overseas. Skipper persuaded the directors to extend the budget, and to accept Brindley's offer.

Brindley stepped back from managing Farmer & Brindley just when Surrey House was nearing completion, handing management to his son, Ernest Brindley, and his nephew, Henry Barnes. Writing in 2008 in the Westminster Cathedral magazine, *Oremus*, Patrick Rogers reported that Brindley then continued the search, travelling to Canada and USA, and visiting Japan on three occasions, still seeking marbles never seen before in Britain. He installed a marble museum at his workshops, and offered tours of the F&B premises to architects and geologists. The First World War effectively ended the brief cycle of architectural marble usage, and Brindley died in 1919. The company, without him, faltered on until the financial crash and depression of 1929.

George Skipper had also found another stone specialist, one who could supply the best building stone, and cut it with precision. This was Mr E.W.D Potter, whose stoneyard and machinery at 31–33 Chapelfield Road, was located close to J. Youngs builders. Starting in 1887 Mr Potter advanced stonemasonry from Mediaeval practices to modern times by utilizing electricity to power his cranes, drills, saws, lathes, planes, abrasors, scarifiers and polishers. Norwich architects and builders no longer had to work with Scotsmen and Yorkshiremen – they had their own well-equipped expert in Mr Potter.

Pl. 75
E.W.D. Potter, of Norwich, c.1860–c.1930
Monumental mason, sculptor and stone-merchant.

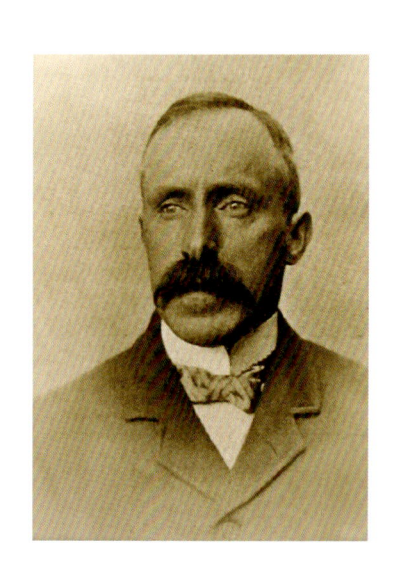

Edward and Wilfred Burgess, writing in *Men Who Have Made Norwich* in 1904 noted that Potter provided Skipper's Norwich Union building with £10,000 worth of work (calculated as over £2 million today). Although the front would be faced with Clipsham stone, Mr Potter's preferred material was Portland Stone. The Burgesses reported, 'Mr Potter has shiploads of Portland Stone brought direct from the quarries to Yarmouth'.

He had 200 tons of stone piled on the dockyard, and he had another 300 tons waiting at Norwich's Victoria station, from where it was a level half-mile journey by wagon to his premises in Chapelfield Road. Having begun as a sole trader in Coburg Street, Potter had built up his business and could now provide all the stonework for additions to Old Riddlesworth Hall, and even for the Duke of Grafton at Euston Hall. The monumental mason (as he described himself) had already provided dressed stonework for The Grand and the Hotel de Paris, and co-operated with Youngs and J. Smith's builders whenever needed. Potter could also obtain carboniferous limestone, or marble, from British quarries. And, should there be any doubt about the degree of handwork, as opposed to mechanization, a photo in the Burgess's book, published as Surrey House was being built, showed one of Potter's workshops with at least twenty men holding wooden mallets, bolsters and chisels.

By choosing E.W.D Potter, and Farmer & Brindley, whom he knew from London work nearly thirty years earlier, and whose advertisements were to be seen every week in *The Builder*, Skipper was able to handle prestigious commissions for stone-clad buildings with confidence. Starting with Surrey House, George Skipper's collaboration with both Potter and F & B would lead on to the bank in London Street, followed by another insurance company head-office in St Giles's, and then to the sumptuous country house and outworks at Sennowe Park. The involvement of William Brindley meant that Skipper had access to artists and artisans of the highest ability, particularly with marble.

George Skipper made the plan for Surrey House in three months over Christmas 1900/1901. Norwich Union announced the competition to select an architect on 19 November, sending invitations to a large number of architects. The closing date was 19 February. Skipper won the competition

Pl. 76
George Skipper, Architect, 1901, Front Elevation Drawing of Surrey House for Norwich Union Life Insurance.

Pl. 77
George Skipper, Architect, 1901–05, Surrey House for Norwich Union Life Insurance.
photo: 1905 postcard.
(Note that large statues of William Talbot and Sir Samuel Bignold have not yet been installed in niches)).

with his design, which he had named 'Utility'. The foundation stone was laid nine months later on 4 November 1901 by J. J Dawson-Paul, Lord Mayor of Norwich. Three years later it was open to staff, and then to the public on New Years Day 1905. An amount of extra work continued until summer 1908.

In considering Surrey House, the first thing to examine would be Skipper's original design of 1901, to compare with what was actually built. Apart from the frontage, as seen on Skipper's 1901 elevation drawing, there were others for North, West and East elevations, and floor plans for each level, a roof plan, and cross-sections.

The 1901 drawing of the front elevation of Surrey House showed a five bay building, focused on three central bays in three-storeys, with entablature and pediment supported by six Ionic columns. Behind the columns were taller windows with balustrades, a single curved pediment between two triangular ones, and smaller casements at the upper floor. Beneath, at ground level, was the arched doorway, with an arched window on either side, all surrounded by channel-jointed prismatic rustication, even at the quoins. The rough finish contrasted with the smooth surface of the columns nearby.

The first and last bays on either side of the Classical centre were flat roofed and of only two-storeys, with rustication up to the first floor's windows with their pediments and recessed arches. Below this the heavy rustication continued, and then turned at a right angle to project forward, as single-storeys with balustraded roofs. These terminated with street-facing niches, occupied by statues of robed dignitaries, and backed by balustrade and urns. In this way a small forecourt was created between the two advanced wings. The stone for the frontage of Surrey House was supplied and cut to requirement by Mr Potter of Chapelfield Road. Details to the stonework – the festoons, crests and cartouches were then carved by Brindley's men. This is specified in Mervyn MacArtney's piece in *Architectural Review*, but it would seem that E.W.D Potter's men had equal capability to add decorative detail.

It was the Classical frontage that won Surrey House many accolades, and the highest status of a Grade I Listed Building. Comparisons were made between the new building and the Amicable Society's Office in Serjeant's Inn, off Fleet Street in London, built in 1792 and acquired by Norwich Union in 1866. Another similar frontage was that of eighteenth century Houghton Hall, designed by architects James Gibbs and Colen Campbell. Skipper's Surrey House also bore a partial resemblance to the front of the Bank of England, by Sir John Soane, built in 1788, though that was much larger. Scale was and is an issue, as Norwich Union's Head Office seemed to have the atmosphere of a much bigger building. (Today it is diminished in appearance by the proximity of 1960s office blocks, also raised by the insurers).

The front of the building was actually only a little over 90 ft wide, though this appeared much wider because of the single-storey projections on either side that increased the width total to 124 ft, adding depth as well. The entire front was faced with Clipsham

Stone, first used to build Windsor Castle. Quarried near Oakham in Rutland, it is the hardest Jurassic limestone in England, varying in colour from light brown, or pale orange, to a smoky cream. Apparently Mr Potter had the quantities of Clipsham stone delivered from the quarry to his stoneyard.

The initial choice of stone cladding and the Neo-classical style were obviously symbolic of immovability and antiquity. All Insurance companies used blatant sculptural metaphors, for instance the parable of the vestal virgins, or winged hourglasses and the like. Some were imbued with symbols of freemasonry, since practically everyone in the ruling échelons and financial management was a freemason.

Where did George Skipper stand with freemasonry? It was universal and doubtless, he accepted it, despite being prohibited by his fundamental puritan faith. As for puritanism, Skipper was about to be responsible for a lustrous domed hall that would be the antithesis of the simplicity his co-religionists came to prefer.

Still looking at the carved details at the front, one saw from left to right a Vitruvian keyline running across the elevation at first floor level. On the walls of the first and last bay were two empty medallions, decoratively framed with an acanthus leaf, and a lion's head, its jaws gripping a furled shroud, or flag.

Over the entrance, where the door had large iron door-knockers in the form of lions' heads, was an ornamental cartouche in carved stone, draped with garlands of oak leaves. Not particularly large, it was the coat of arms of the Life Insurance company acquired in 1864, comprising the symbols used and reused by insurance companies, the winged hourglass, and the image of the handshake, encircled by a serpent devouring its own tail, symbolic of eternity.

Up at the top, the pediment stood over a frieze with the words NORWICH UNION LIFE INSURANCE SOCIETY, beneath egg and dart ornament and dentilation. An empty Baroque cartouche flanked by palm fronds occupied the tympanum.

Pl. 78
George Skipper, Architect, 1901–05, Surrey House for Norwich Union Life Insurance., (Aviva PLC) photo 2019.

The east, west and north elevations could only be partially seen, and were very much less notable. All three were faced with white brick. The east elevation was three-storeyed towards the south front, then two-storeyed to the north, with a large amount of casements, tall chimneystacks (since removed) and a slate roof, from which the glass dome roof of the main hall emerged. The west elevation was less nondescript, with a two-storey bow, arched casements and a projecting Dutch gable. The north elevation, recently put under a futuristic and practical atrium, was similar.

Entering the front door, the space opened to a large central hall, leading off to various offices on both floors. Originally, clerks working in the hall faced the door, with their backs to the clock. Middle managers used ground floor offices leading off the central hall, while directors were near luxurious boardrooms on the upper floor, from where they could watch those below from a balcony.

The interior of the central hall was first intended to be panelled in decorative plasterwork. In truth, once Mr Brindley's quantities of fabulous foreign marbles were added, the interior was anything but 'Utility'. On the

Pl. 79 George Skipper, Architect, 1901–05, Central Hall, Surrey House for Norwich Union Life Insurance.

Pl. 80 *(facing page)* George Skipper, Architect, 1901–05, (detail) Marblework in Central Hall, Surrey House, Norwich.

contrary, the design could have been renamed 'Opulent'. The central hall became The Marble Hall. Here were the relics of Brindley's Marble Museum, cut and polished surfaces prepared, and installed, by F & B's team. Among the artisans in the Westminster Bridge Road workshops were a group of Italian marble workers enlisted by Brindley. They all wore smocks and voluminous berets and worked together on the large items. More Italians were taken to Norwich to assemble the Marble Hall.

The sensation of entering Surrey House is visceral. Some say 'breathtaking', or 'stunning'. It is a shock, as if, by walking a few paces off the Norwich street and climbing six steps into the hall, the viewer has arrived in a foreign country. One's visual, spatial, and tactile senses are met with extraordinary colours, shapes and surfaces.

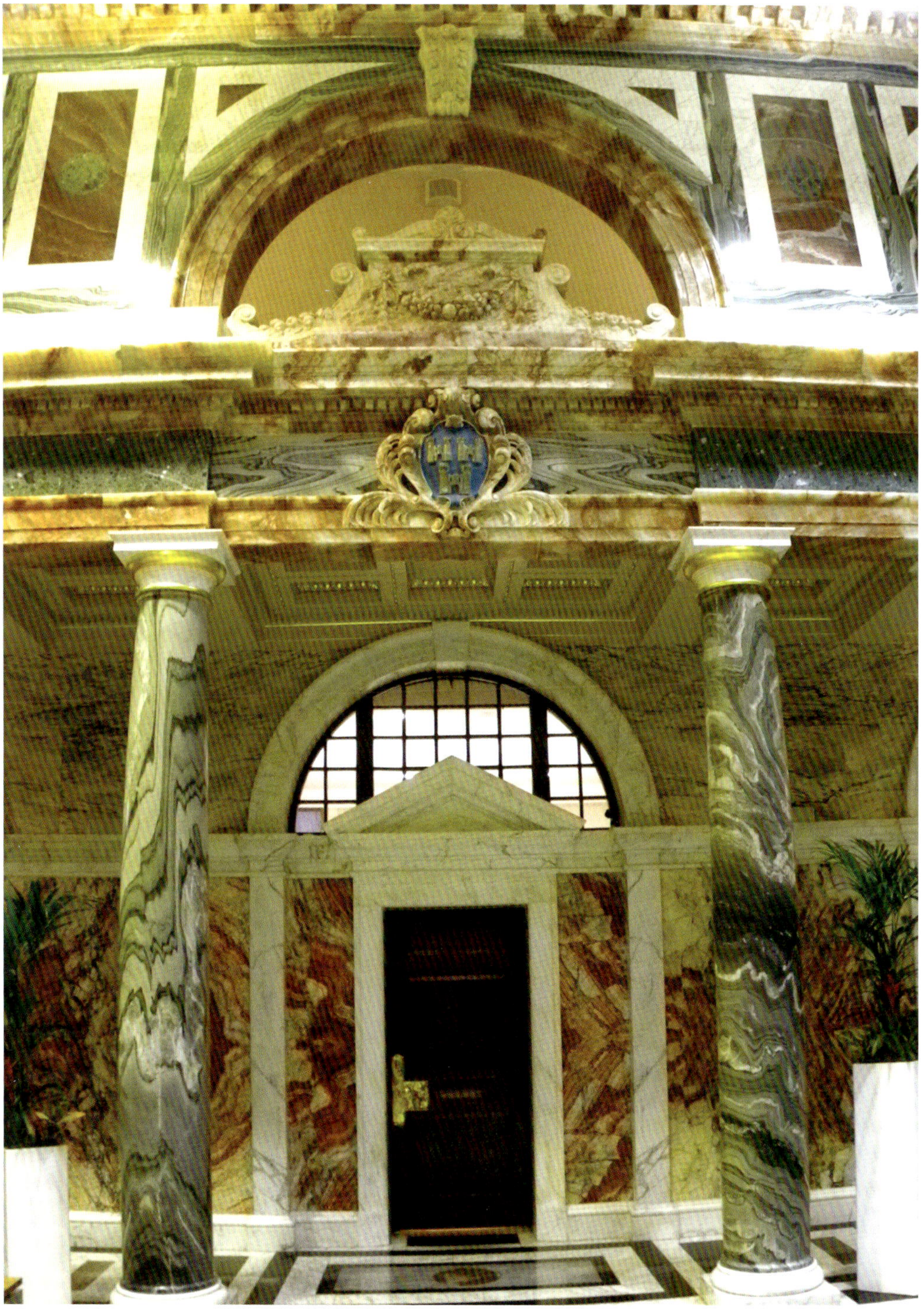

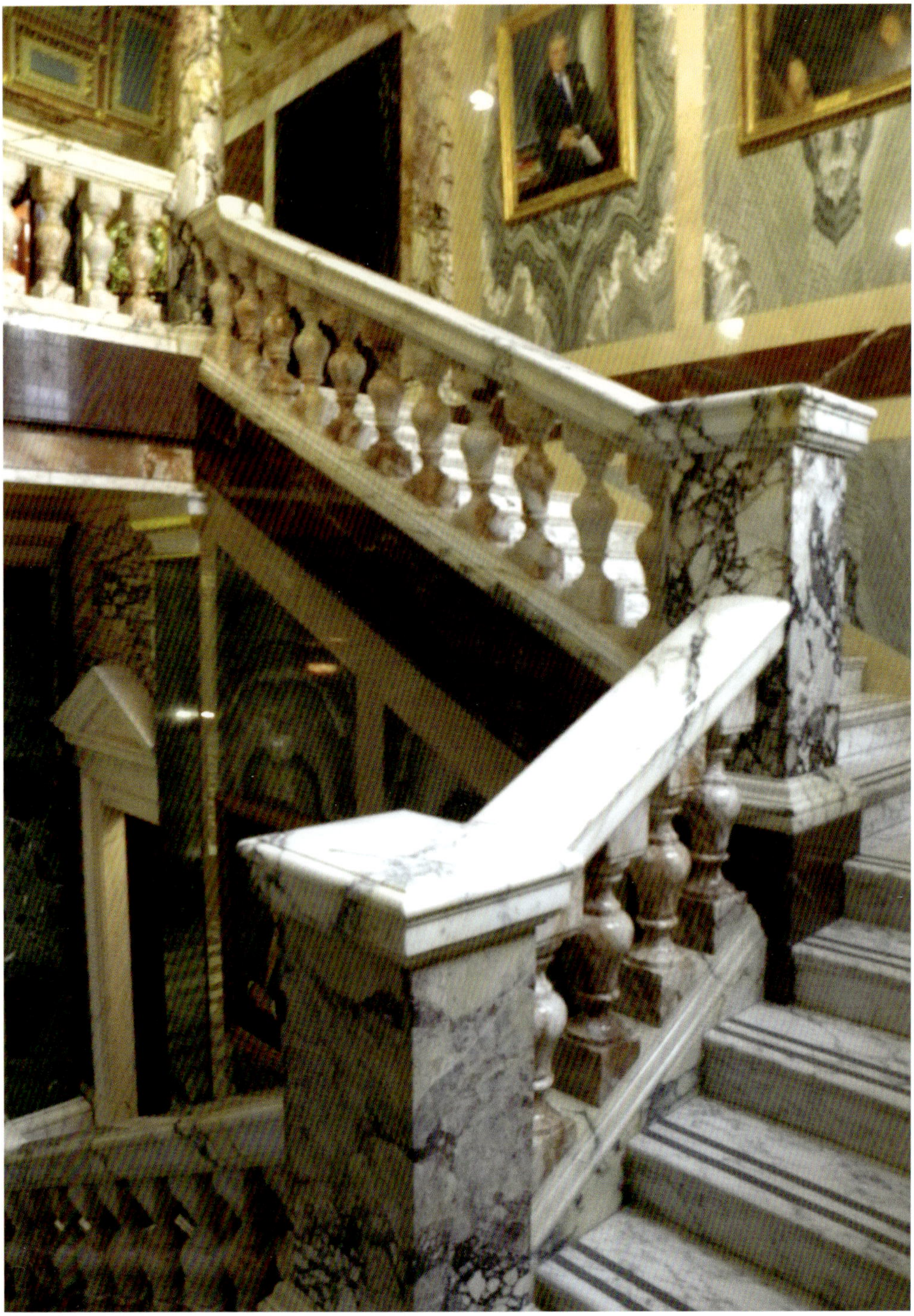

Skipper's design for the central hall, which might have appeared monumental in white marble, was almost lost in the swirling mass of colour. Around the hall lighter green *Cippolino* and darker green *Verde Antico* columns, forty in all, supported a succession of balconies and arches above. The walls were clad in marble, in creams and reds, with swirling patterns created by metamorphosis, heat and pressure millions of years ago. There are at least twelve doorways, with pediments and broad arches with lunettes. Above and between the ground floor arches were flamboyant cartouches resembling sarcophagi, magnificently carved in *Skiros Rosso*, a marble from Greece, where William Brindley had visited the quarry. As many as fifteen different types of marble were used in the hall. Some of the cornices and pediments were carved in alabaster.

The ceiling was a dome (Skipper's first) that was roofed and panelled, yet transformed halfway up to glass, over a simple web of steel supports, like a giant lens drawing in daylight. This was supplied by Messrs Homan & Rodgers of London. The floor was a chequered surface of black and white marble.

At the centre of the marble hall was something referred to as 'the font', though it was actually an 'air fountain' linked with an innovative heating and ventilating system. Whether or not this was part of Skipper's idea, it cannot be told. The item is disguised by more of F&B's marble; above it a large metal pendant is suspended beneath a canopy, surmounted by a bronze statuette of winged female figure, made by one of F&B's associates. This was the sculptor Henry Charles Fehr (1867–1937), educated at the RA Schools and responsible for the group, *Perseus and Andromeda*, outside the Tate Gallery.

Mervyn Macartney described the staircase in *Architectural Review*. 'It is entirely executed in marble, the walls being lined with *Cippolino* opened up, the handrail being of *Pavonazzo* marble, while the pedestals and columns are of a very choice *Breccia* marble'.

Ceilings above the majestic marble staircase were decorated with repeated patterns of doorways, female figures, and stylized plants, painted by an accomplished young artist. This was George Murray, who had very recently attended the Royal Academy Schools, where he had been awarded a scholarship and won prizes for his work. Other panels showed painted decoration,

Pl. 81 *(facing page)* George Skipper, Architect, 1901–05, Surrey House for Norwich Union Life Insurance. (detail) Marble staircase by Farmer & Brindley.

Pl. 82 George Skipper, Architect, 1901–05, Surrey House for Norwich Union Life Insurance. (detail) Painted ceiling by George Murray.

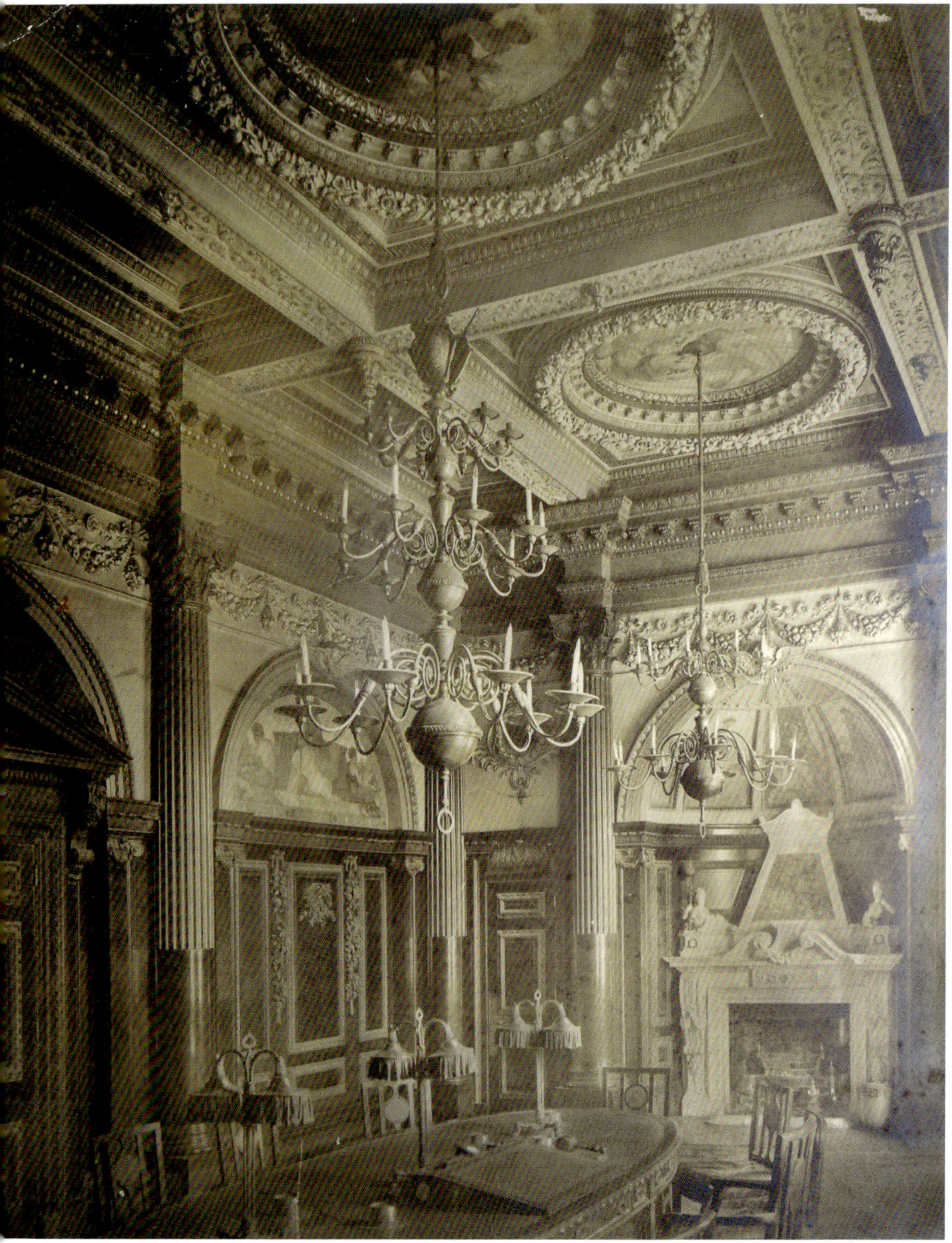

particularly in the Howard Room, by Skipper's associate, William Neatby. Mythical subjects, birds and creatures were painted with a texture to resemble tapestry work (these were covered over in the 1980s with plain panels and the Howard Room is no longer in use). There was also work by his first collaborator, James Minns and his son John, in the form of woodcarvings, described elsewhere as being in the manner of Grinling Gibbons (1648–1721). The budget of £6,000 for interior decorations was far exceeded. The use of marble added another £5,000, with a further £3,000 for labour. (Entire building costs were £71,800, and a further £12,200 had been paid in compensation to the girls' school that had occupied the site before building began).

Other sub-contractors to be named included George Crotch & Co of Norwich, producers of moulded plasterwork; H.H Martyn & Co of Cheltenham for wooden panelling and mahogany handrails; and The Artificers Guild, founded in 1901 by Nelson Dawson and chief designer, Edward Napier Hitchcock Spencer, who produced art metalwork, silverware, enamelled items and stained glass.

Outside the building were more sculptural works provided by Farmer & Brindley. Foremost were the larger than life-size figures of the founders, carved in Portland stone by Léon Joseph Chavalliaud (1858–1921). These were in the niches: that on the left (as you look at the building) portrayed William Talbot (1658–1730), Bishop of Oxford and leader of an incorporated Amicable Society, lending an air of ecclesiastical respectability. That on the right

Pl. 83 (facing page)
George Skipper, Architect, 1901–05, Surrey House for Norwich Union Life Insurance.
(detail) Director's Board Room. Vintage photo reproduced by courtesy Aviva PLC.

Pl. 84
George Skipper, Architect, 1901–05, Surrey House for Norwich Union Life Insurance.
(detail) Painted wood panel by W.J Neatby.
photo: Archive image NU 5257 reproduced by courtesy Aviva PLC.

Pl. 85
George Skipper, Architect, 1901–05, Surrey House for Norwich Union Life Insurance.
(detail) Statue of Sir Samuel Bignold by Léon Joseph Chavalliaud.

portrayed Sir Samuel Bignold (1791–1875), son of the founder of Norwich Union, secretary of the insurance business from 1815 onwards, and mayor of Norwich. Apart from Chavalliaud, the European sculptors employed by Brindley included Emile Guillemin, and the Piccirilli brothers. British sculptors working for him at the time were Charles Allen (1862–1956), and Thomas Tyrell (1881–1928).

Other sculptural items to the fore were six wrought and cast-iron grilles over the half-windows at ground level, lighting the basement. The ironwork of each one was formed by a row of three sea-wyverns, heraldic creatures, painted in gold. These were fabricated by J.W Singer & Sons of Frome, Somerset.

Just inside the entrance was a pair of bronze bas-reliefs entitled 'Solace' and 'Protection' by the sculptor Arthur Stanley Young (1876–1968). Known as Stanley, he signed them 'S. Young'. An angel appeared in each darkly mystical relief: bringing a cornucopia of abundance to a poor woman at her feet in one, and holding palm leaves protectively over two little children in the other. A young man, recently at the Royal Academy Schools, Stanley Young had interesting connections, as he was the son of Richard Young of H. Young & Co, whose inner-London bronze foundry was famous for casting large works and finely chased pieces.

The stone balustrade enclosing the forecourt was terminated by pillars. Serving as gateposts, they were draped with stone festoons and surmounted by urns. All the stone-carved urns were carved to Skipper's exact proportions, copied from urns he had seen, and drawn in his notebook, in previous months. Four tall bronze lamps stood on plinths along this balustrade at the front. With elegant glass shades and powerful clawed feet in heavy bronze, they too were signed by S. Young and made by Young's in London's Pimlico. (Although there may prove to be a family connection, Young's Art Foundry had nothing to do with J. Young's builders of Chapelfield, Norwich, who worked with Skipper on other projects).

Pl. 86
George Skipper, Architect, 1901–05, Surrey House for Norwich Union Life Insurance.
(detail)
Iron grilles over basement windows.

All this embellishment, and there was more, was undoubtedly more decorous than severe Palladianism would permit; far more too, than the architect had first envisioned. In case descriptions of gleaming surfaces lend the wrong impression, it should be stated that everything outside the front was well placed and to scale. Scale is critical and this aspect of its 'rightness' is touched on by Alexander Stuart Gray:

> 'Surrey House ... ... representing the high-water mark of Edwardian sumptuousness without vulgarity. Like Lord Burlington's villa at Chiswick, London, it looks larger than it is, the parts being in perfect proportion and the detail correct in scale'.
>
> A. Stuart Gray, *Edwardian Architecture – A Biographical Dictionary*

Respect, gratitude and praise for the design of Surrey House, which George Skipper received from all sides, was made sweeter with a cheque made payable to him for the sum of £4,264, a figure verified by Colin Skipper, grandson of his brother and partner, Frederick Skipper.

In the same turn of the century period, when his surveyors and draftsmen were engaged in so many significant projects, George Skipper received a kind of 'double commission' for a nearby site.

Due to the rearrangement of Red Lion Street, the road connecting St Stephen's with Castle Meadow, for the use of electric trams, the city-centre street was widened in July 1900. Everything on the south-east side of the street was rebuilt. One of these buildings was Number 11, destined to be the office of an accountant, to be known as Commercial Chambers when it was finished in 1903. The adjacent plot in Red Lion Street was vacant too, and had been purchased by the Norwich Savings Bank. The bank opted to utilize an architectural design by George Skipper that had previously been intended for a site in Magdalen Street.

This was how two George Skipper buildings were built next to each other at the same time. Officially the Bank was 5–7 Red Lion Street and Commercial Chambers were Number 11. Number 9 appears to be absent, but is in fact across the street at Burlington Buildings, impressively designed by J. Owen Bond, who had only recently been George Skipper's apprentice.

The two Skipper buildings are recognizably 'of a piece', but were not initially intended (at least not by him) to be together. Standing on the street, the right-hand site, grandly faced with stone, was much the wider of the two buildings. It had six bays, the first and last of which projected slightly. It is not a Listed building, one reason being that Barclays Bank, present owners and successors of the defunct Norwich Saving Bank business, made severe alterations to the ground floor exterior. The handsome doorway, arched and recessed with rusticated stonework, was replaced by a bland entrance with prominent commercial signage. The changes were mostly in simplifying the ground floor exterior to make space for 'cash machines' on the wall, while retaining four tall casement windows between the two doorways. The building has three-storeys, and the two upper ones are a matrix of grand windows in two rows of six, but with variation to the surrounds. Those in the lower row at either end (above the doorways) possess broken segmented pediments, and alternating bands of rustication.

The style of these windows was identified by David Bussey, the art historian most familiar with Skipper's Norwich works, as copies of those at the Palazzo Thiene in Vicenza, revised by the immortal architect, Andrea Palladio (1508–1580). In between were four equally-sized arched window surrounds with large keystones and carved swags, separated by pilasters with

Pl. 87
George Skipper, Architect, 1903, Norwich Savings Bank, (now Barclays) Red Lion Street, Norwich.

Pl. 88
George Skipper's prospective drawing of 'Commercial Chambers' in Norwich. Printed as a photo-lithograph by James Akerman in *The Building News*, 18 February 1904.

Reproduced by courtesy of the Norfolk Record Office.

Ionic capitals. The top floor's six windows were almost identical, though first and last were varied with the addition of scrolled pediments.

At roof height the bank had a level parapet and a shaped gable at one end, with a stone-carved coat of arms of the city of Norwich in a square frame. At the other end of the parapet was a low-arched gable with no decoration. Above it, according to Skipper's original plan, we might have expected a domed turret, but there is nothing there. The style of roof cannot be seen. The plan still sufficed, and besides, Skipper would have a little turret next-door on Number 11.

The reference to Andrea Palladio was a reminder that George Skipper had been acquiring a library of first and early editions of scholarly architectural books. Skipper's bookshelves held publications by architects such as Colen Campbell, William Chambers, James Gibbs, William Kent, James Leoni, and Domenico de Rossi. The editions by Palladio included *The Four Books of Architecture*, printed in 1738.

As it happened, it was the other work, the slender office next door, that was designated to be a Grade II Listed Building. It certainly had historic interest, being a combination of Skipper's architectural ideas and Neatby's artistry, backed by Royal Doulton.

William Neatby had already worked with Skipper at the Royal Arcade, and at Number 7 St Giles Street, where the ceramic tiles covering the building were Doulton's 'Carraraware' faience, sometimes known as 'Lambeth faience'. Though of a different shade, almost everything on the only elevation of Commercial Chambers was made of the same material. It was a glazed stoneware with a dull eggshell-like surface. Where the tone at Number 7 St Giles Street was honey-coloured, Commercial Chambers were sandy-buff and grey tones. On first impression a visitor might easily think it was stone. The team who assembled all these 'Carraraware' details at Number 11 Red Lion Street were J.S Smith and Co, who were later absorbed into Youngs, Skipper's preferred builders.

Skipper's design was pleasant in every way, packing a lot of features into a narrow span, a mere two bays (Pevsner states 'only one window-bay wide'), or about twenty feet in width. The ground floor frontage is not as it was on plan, with the shop front showing a new expanse of glass and signs, and an additional modern door. Above these, still on the ground floor, but supporting a balcony cornice, were three life-size sculpted figures of children in buff-grey terracotta, not quite *putti*, but an Edwardian equivalent, cheerfully guarding the entrance. These are significant works of art, and despite the investigations of art historians over a number of years, there has been no clarification about who made them. I have an idea it was the sculptor at work in Surrey House.

Pl. 89
George Skipper, Architect, 1902–03, Commercial Chambers, Red Lion Street, Norwich. (detail) One of the Terracotta figures above doorway.

Pl. 90
George Skipper, Architect, 1902–03, Commercial Chambers, Red Lion Street, Norwich. (detail) Terracotta figure on roofline.

Pl. 91 *(facing page)* George Skipper, Architect, 1902–03, Commercial Chambers, Red Lion Street, Norwich.

The two figures on the right appear to support the scrolled consoles above Skipper's original doorway, an intriguing and beautiful arrangement in playful Baroque style. Separating these larger than life-size sculptures was a recessed oculus with a curvilinear wrought-iron screen. Between the brackets that the two figures stand on was an elaborate floral cartouche all in marble, framing a sphere, bound with two ribbons inscribed COMMERCIAL CHAMBERS.

Looking at this building, the eye roves over features, from the ground to something very interesting and odd at the top. In this written account it will take some time to reach the top, as the next two-storeys cannot be described in a few words. Both were filled with recessed bowed mullion windows, with twelve-light stained-glass panes, and separated by swags and small cartouches; one contained the city's coat of arms, the other a rearing horse. These windows were framed by emerging pilasters with Ionic capitals; the pilaster on the right appeared to stretch wider to cover the inner stairway, lit by very narrow windows.

Were they pilasters or not? Stephen Thomas, the guiding light to this study of Skipper, described them as 'disappearing pilasters'. Moreover he noted that the first use of disappearing pilasters was attributed to Lutyens (at Heathcote in 1906), by the architectural writer, Gavin Stamp (1948–2017), in *Edwin Lutyens Country Houses*. In fact Skipper's use of them at Commercial Chambers predates Heathcote by three or four years.

However, we are still climbing. The marvels of Skipper's plan rose above the prominent bow windows to the top of the building, where an entablature supported an unusual mix of features. This is so far up that it is not easy to see, although the view is rewarding, and what might be referred to as 'classic Skipper'. A recessed segmental arched window, or lunette, was surrounded by banded crossettes and, at the centre of these, a keystone stretched up to merge with a sculpture of a seated figure. Behind the figure, like a finial on a shaped gablet, is an obeliscal spike, in his first-time use of this feature. To the right is an arcaded turret with a domed copper roof.

Looming over the pedestrians far below, the sculpted figure is a source of fascination. It has been neither identified, nor attributed. Nobody has been up to the narrow ledge to examine it.

Intriguing questions about the identity of the sitter have been asked. The first clue we have shows Skipper's first artwork of the building, in which the seated figure at the top appears to be of a young woman. In the event, however,

GALLYONS
COUNTRY LIFESTYLE CLOTHING

Pl. 92
George Skipper, Architect, 1902–03, 'Commercial Chambers', 11, Red Lion Street, Norwich. (detail) Pair of terracotta figures above entrance.

the figure is that of a seated bearded man, looking downwards in a pose that implied concentration, as he stares at paperwork. A plan perhaps? Art history savants are divided: some think this alluded to a scribe, or clerk, a reference to the accountant and client, Charles Larking. Others, and I will add my name here, think this was a terracotta figure of George Skipper himself. It certainly resembles him, bearded and with a mane of hair, as seen in photographs of the period. If the statue was a fond memorial to the architect, it represented a second portrayal of George Skipper on the front of one of his buildings, the first being on the front of his own office.

Around the time when Commercial Chambers was in preparation, when entire walls, features and details were being fired in faience by Royal Doulton,

Neatby ceased to be a direct employee of the Lambeth pottery. He set himself up with an architect, E. Hollyer Evans, and a Mr Eddison, in a company called Neatby, Evans & Co. It was an innovative design studio, with showrooms in London, functioning from 1901–1908. Was it Neatby's new company that undertook, among other things, the manufacture by Royal Doulton of the four terracotta figures attached to Commercial Chambers?

Both the seated man on the high parapet, and the three Edwardian children acting as caryatids by the front door, I tentatively attribute to the sculptor, Henry Charles Fehr, (1867–1940) (see Pl.128). Fehr was very highly thought of: at the age of twenty-five his work was purchased by the RA's Chantrey Bequest and presented to the Tate Gallery. He had also modelled terracotta figures on the front of the Hotel Russell, in London's Russell Square. The sculptor was already working with Skipper at Surrey House, and would continue at Sennowe Park. Fehr had young children at the time, which probably helped in the modelling. The whole arrangement at the entrance of Number Eleven is an instance of architectural sculpture at its best.

Plans for Commercial Chambers had been submitted to the City Engineers on 20 January 1902. There were minor hold-ups, with amendments, mostly surrounding any rainwater downpipes, which Skipper wished to hide inside. There were lengthy discussions with Arthur Collins, the City Engineer, with whom the architect got on very well. These centred on the arrangement of the doorway, with the terracotta figures on their protruding brackets. Collins protested that they would project out into the street, where they might contravene regulations and even obstruct the highway. The architect was quick to respond, with questions about the true line of the pavement in relation to the newly widened road. Referring to the complicated stone brackets as corbels, Skipper wrote:

> I further send you herewith the clay-sized drawing of this corbel, with the marks put on it. As you are probably aware we have to make all our details to this clay-size, which is greatly in excess of the work when it is shrunk, and come out of the kiln. You will therefore see we laboured under this difficulty as well as the difficulty of the uncertain pavement line. I have marked on the drawing a few comparative figures as to the amount Mr Larking would give and as to the obstruction caused. I certainly had no idea of disregarding the recognized rule, and had in my mind all the way through that we should be conferring a public benefit to the city of Norwich.

That last sentence of Skipper's letter said it all! Commercial Chambers was completed and officially opened on 12 October 1903. The *Eastern Daily Press* reported that a celebratory dinner was held in the Orford Arms Hotel, for office staff, builders, workmen and guests. Of particular note was the attendance of Frederick Skipper at 'the convivial and jovial meeting', and it was he who accepted the 'Toast to the Architect'. George never attended these gatherings, because of his adherence to Brethren customs and abstinance from alcohol.

Since they were accountants, Larking's retained clearly written receipts of the amounts they paid out. They are not aggregated and so a total sum is not shown; nor is the architect's fee listed. One figure that does stand out was £478 to Royal Doulton for tiles and terracotta. Another shows £138 paid to G.E Hawes builders, for building walls and chimneys. The work of general building and applying the Doulton 'Carraraware' tiles was done by J.S Smith & Co, who were paid £2,204. (Despite being a public benefit and a Listed building, the present-day City Council have located a modern bus-stop in front of the doorway, all but hiding the entrance and attendant sculptures).

For George Skipper in 1903, Norwich was becoming like Cromer had been a few years earlier in the 1890s, with multiple concurrent constructions. In the same early Edwardian years Norwich Union Insurance Company, in addition to the prized head office in Norwich, had commissioned a major branch for Cambridge, facing Emmanuel College. Construction took place in 1903–04 at the site in 30 St Andrews Street, and went round the corner into Downing Street.

All in rusticated stonework, the St Andrews Street frontage in Cambridge centred on a gigantic niche, a sort of inverted portico three-storeys tall. This was the main entrance at ground floor and, above the niche, at the eaves of the mansard slate roof, were plain oversailed chimneystacks, and dormers in the form of three large oculi. The one in the centre was beneath an open-bed pediment, the other two were hooded with scrolled pediments; all three were topped by urn finials. Other windows on the elevation were three sashes with fifteen-lights. Those on the second floor were arched.

The theme continued along the Downing street façade. As he did so often, Skipper had placed an entrance at the corner, and above this an oriel window, and a pair of over life-size cherubs, carved in stone, holding a globe, or medallion between them – a Baroque delight from Skipper's newly found suppliers of architectural sculpture.

RIBA records state that the building was demolished in 1975. It was replaced by a brick and concrete office, with one or two features badly copied from the original. As a structure the replacement does nothing but detract from the atmosphere of Emmanuel College, built in the 17th and 18th centuries, some of it by Christopher Wren. How wretched it is to mourn for a demolished building!

At the same time as Skipper's Norwich Union office was being raised in St Andrew's Street, the architect was also engaged in the first stage of an extension to the University Arms in Regent Road, Cambridge. A description of the hotel and Skipper's extensive alterations will follow in a chapter tracing the architect's work in the 1920s, at which time the second stage of Skipper's planned changes were being enacted.

Back in Norwich, where George Skipper could walk in any direction from his office to see one of his buildings gradually materializing, we come to Number 11, The Haymarket. Contemporary with Commercial Chambers, no more than a hundred and fifty yards away, the Haymarket building was another 'one of a kind'. It too had relevance to Norwich's financial institutions, and it too used Doulton's wares to create tones and shapes of colour on its façade.

Pl. 93
George Skipper, Architect, 1903–04, Norwich Union Life Insurance offices, Downing Street frontage, Cambridge. DEMOLISHED 1975.

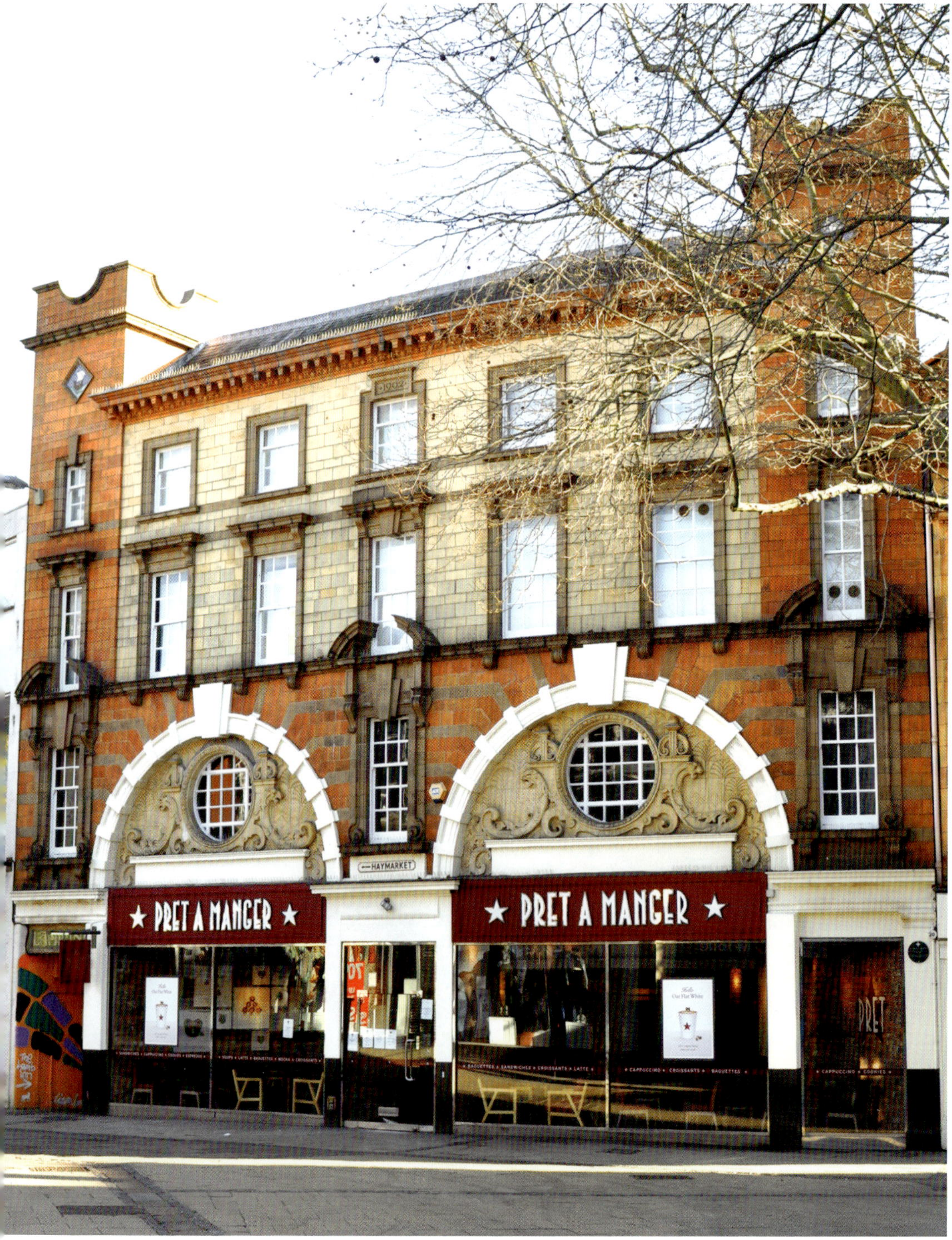
1902
HAYMARKET
★ PRET A MANGER ★
★ PRET A MANGER ★
PRET

Among many descriptions it is regarded as 'the best building in Norwich *not* to be a Listed Building'.

The first occupant of the upper floors was the Norwich Stock Exchange, a short-lived enterprise. The only stocks familiar in that part of Norwich were associated with a pillory and whipping post, removed from the Market Place more than a hundred years earlier. Nevertheless, George Skipper's overall contribution to Norwich's financial district included two banks, two insurance companies, a stock exchange, and an accountancy.

Haymarket Chambers, in the old Haymarket, an extension of Gentleman's Walk, was a building that evidently gave its architectural progenitor and generations of Norvicensians a good deal of pleasure. The front is slightly convex, and symmetrical too, with towers at either end of a flat roofline, and an enormous pair of white arches at first floor level. Another first impression was of its colouring, with a palette of soft reds and creams.

The architect's first watercolour of the building, a charming image retained by RIBA, was actually dated 1896. It depicts a cream-coloured horse pulling a trap at the trot past the Haymarket building. I think it is the best of all Skipper's prospective drawings, or paintings, with a hint of Munnings in the depiction of the horse. Alfred Munnings (1878–1959) was nearby at the time, finishing at Norwich School of Art and exhibiting in the city. Skipper's watercolour also shows a tall chimneystack at the centre of the roofline, though this is no longer present. The ground floor was at first an upmarket grocery, a business owned by J.H Roofe. It is nowadays a modern expanse of glass and doors, rented to 'Pret a Manger'.

Examining the front of Number 11 Haymarket, the components of the design become clear, though there was artifice as well. It was four-storeys

Pl. 94 and Pl. 95
George Skipper, Architect, 1901–02, Haymarket Chambers, Norwich.

high and seven bays wide. The first and seventh bays were defined as towers that emerged from the top of the elevation. Close to the summit of each were terracotta medallions with bas-reliefs of sailing ships, symbols of commerce.

The 1902 Haymarket building provided a demonstration of a practical use for polychrome, or coloured surfaces, in architecture. Skipper wished to give a sense of volume, or at least depth, behind his façade. One way was to project a bay or wing, as he usually did; another way was by change of colour, in particular between the towers in a reddish hue, that contrasted with the pale tones of the adjacent surface. The perceived projections of the tower bays were entirely an illusion.

The top two floors were taken up with two rows of sash windows. Larger sashes on the first floor elevation accounted for much of the building's character. The end bays and the centre have prominent keystones, flanking pilasters, and broken segmental pediments.

At first floor the remaining bays, to left and right, were framed within two large Florentine arches lit by oculi. On either side of the two round windows were ornamental details in buff-coloured terracotta, the work of William Neatby, showing sinuous wyverns and the faint outlines of an Egyptianised landscape, with dunes and palms. David Bussey provides the comparison with Palazzo Massimo alle Colonne, in Rome, by the High Renaissance architect, Baldassare Peruzzi (1481–1536). Skipper's building offered more; every part of the front of Haymarket Chambers had passed through Royal Doulton's kilns.

This was one of Skipper's creations that emanated a sense of wellbeing and refined good cheer. Again one thinks of Skipper's critical query, 'What is the building's purpose?' Surely it was to convey a sense of confidence.

George Skipper, his brother Frederick and the team of draftsmen were at full stretch, providing drawings, elevations, plans and specifications for so many city-centre buildings in progress. Office procedure was for George to sit at his desk and summon the different clerks of works for each of the concurrent Norwich projects. One by one they were questioned and instructed by Skipper, who took note of arising problems and made plans to overcome them. But there was far more new work to come, and not all of it was in the city.

Amid the major works, smaller requests came to the office. Among these was one in 1902 for a floor plan and garden design for a Doctor Allen of Norwich. This and other ideas are first-sketches in his notebook and no more – some will have materialized as professional plan drawings, and then as buildings – others will remain only as pencil marks on a small page.

Skipper's notebook for 1903 contained a sketch plan of a farmhouse for Sir Kenneth H. Kemp. His old patron, the likeable cricketing colonel, had houses in South Norfolk at Mergate Hall, his principal home by then, as well as Gissing Hall, Flordon Hall and more properties in North Norfolk. The location of the farmhouse that Skipper planned for Kemp is not known.

Pl. 96   George Skipper, 1896.
Prospective watercolour of Haymarket Chambers prior to
plan, or construction five years later. RIBA Collections.

Pl. 97
George Skipper, Architect, 1902–03 Royal Norfolk & Suffolk Yacht Club, Lowestoft.
Vintage photo by Donald Shields in 1910.

There is also notice of a 1905 plan for additions to the Centre Cliff Hotel at Southwold. This was not one of the architect's big hotel plans, and had originally been a Georgian house on the clifftop, to which a new wing was added. It is no longer a hotel, and there is no recognizable feature from Skipper's intervention.

There are other documents in the Norfolk Record Office (NRO) that testify to George Skipper's new and increasing interest in town planning. The city of Norwich was increasing in population and area. New roads into less-developed districts would be needed, and some of the surveying and planning work was passed to the Skipper brothers. One of these was in 1902 on the edge of Mousehold Heath, involving plots in Branford Road, Churchill Road and Crome Road. Another, in 1904, involved plan and section surveys for a proposed extendsion of Glebe Road, to join it to a new road, Recreation Road.

A significant prize won by George Skipper was the commission for a yacht club on the East coast. This was the Royal Norfolk and Suffolk Yacht Club, which had been founded in Lowestoft in 1859 by a number of interested gentlemen, with Colonel Wilson of Beccles elected first Commodore. After a few years, the club had contacted the architect, Edward

Boardman, to provide some sort of scheme for its clubhouse, dedicated to the needs of its members, to include accommodation and provisions. Boardman's building, begun in 1884 and completed in 1886, was a clapboarded structure secured on an iron frame; its appearance was functional and members described it as 'a timber shed'.

That description was at variance with the town's altering status. An old borough and famous fishing port, Lowestoft had attracted the attention of Sir Samuel Morton Peto (1809–1889), one of Britain's most successful railway entrepreneurs. He extended the railway to Lowestoft and developed the dock facilities; he built smart town houses and hotels overlooking the sea, intending the place to be both a European port and an English resort. Peto lived nearby at Somerleyton Hall, which he rebuilt at great expense. A decade later his finances crashed and he left.

But the die was cast and Lowestoft had new classes of persons living and working in the town, and visiting in the summer. Sailing was popular, either inshore, or inland to the Norfolk Broads, a journey to an unspoilt silent world. The yacht club itself was popular, and gained in membership and prestige, so much so that the existing 'timber shed' was deemed too small. The commission to design a new building had been offered in open competition.

Pl. 98
George Skipper, Architect, 1902–03
Royal Norfolk & Suffolk Yacht Club, Lowestoft.
photo 2019..

Pl. 99
George Skipper,
Architect, 1902–03
South aspect,
Royal Norfolk &
Suffolk Yacht Club,
Lowestoft.

Pl. 100 *(facing page)*
George Skipper,
Architect, 1902–03
(detail) East face,
Royal Norfolk &
Suffolk Yacht Club,
Lowestoft.

Skipper's winning design was, as the Listing authorities at Historic England note, 'A very advanced design for its date'. The yacht club is highly rated and Listed as a grade II★ Historic Building. The early 1900s design was contemporary with Arts and Crafts style, but had strong hints of the 1920s and 30s. It contained references and influences of other proponents, such as the architect, Charles Voysey (1857–1941), or Erich Mendelsohn (1887–1953), referred to as an 'expressive modernist', and responsible for the 1935 De La Warr Pavilion at Bexhill-on-Sea.

At the eastern tip of England and looking across Lowestoft's outer harbour, where chains rattle and mast-pennants flutter, one sees the clear outlines of the RNSYC house on Royal Plain. To the fore is a hip-roofed extension with render-over-brick painted walls, with its east-facing front pierced by a very large arched segmental sash window, and above this three large oculi, better described as portholes.

The roof incorporated a triangular window at its peak. Behind this was the three-storey, three-bay main block, surmounted by a 'Look-out' room, glazed

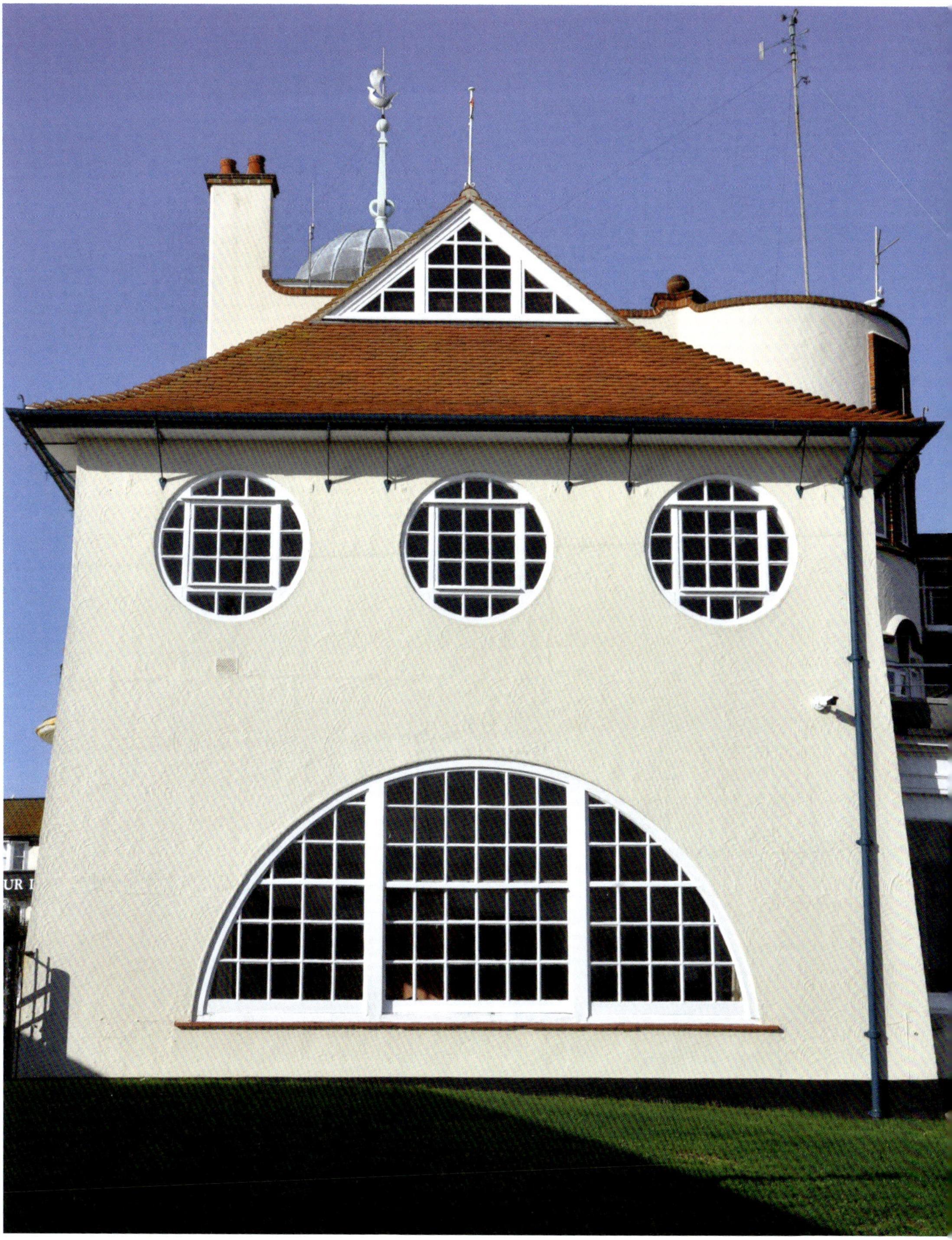

Pl. 101
George Skipper, Architect, 1902–03 (detail) East face, Royal Norfolk & Suffolk Yacht Club, Lowestoft.

Pl. 102 *(facing page)* George Skipper, Architect, 1902–03 (detail) terracotta ship design on South face, Royal Norfolk & Suffolk Yacht Club, Lowestoft.

in all directions, and roofed with a lead-covered dome. The entrance porch was on the south side of the building, between another pair of semi-circular arched casements. Above the doorway was a window opening about fifteen feet tall, containing two windows, one above the other and, in between them, a terracotta sailing ship in a panel. Around the corner, the block structure presents its west-facing wall, which was a large rendered expanse with five insignificant casements and one porthole beneath the glass 'Look out'.

Still looking at the building from the direction of the sea, Skipper's plan is easy to read. In essence it was 'L' shaped and he designed a short tower that engaged the two arms of the 'L' shape. The architect did this regularly, hiding corners with entrances and stair towers. The yacht club's short tower can no longer be seen as it is contained within a long verandah. This is now weather-proofed with glazing and roofing sheets, but it was originally unglazed and covered by a first floor in the form of a thoroughly nautical wooden deck. The tower emerges (from the present-day roofing) and is lit with large casement windows and, on the storey above, by a bay window in between two wood-framed portholes. The north-facing wing, the other arm of the 'L', was of the same dimensions as the east facing one, the only difference being the upstairs windows, which are three square casements, instead of portholes.

136

I fear my architectural description will not convey the 'rightness' of Skipper's design in its seaside setting. Perusing views of all of Skipper's buildings, the Norfolk & Suffolk Yacht Club building stands alone. The use of oculi, and of towers and entrances to mask corners were part of Skipper's palette. On the other hand, the yacht club's rendered walls, semi-circular windows, bonnet roofing, (whereby the lowest part of the roof is at a shallower pitch than the upper portion) and ship's decking, were comparative novelties. The overall appearance is rightly referred to as Arts and Crafts, an entire movement in art and design, but there was something of the Garden City ideal as well. In due course Skipper would be part of this new movement and was soon to plan rural village housing that would seem 'at home' if seen in Letchworth, or Welwyn Garden City.

On the days when the sun did not shine in Lowestoft, club members could retreat from the verandah or upper deck. The inside of the clubhouse was spacious, comfortable and warm. From the central hall part-glazed French doors led to the restaurant, or the North room, where armchairs were placed around a fireplace and overmantel. The first floor was mostly missing, creating an octagonal open space that overlooked the hall, as if it was a ship's hold. The staircase and wooden rail, enhanced with tapering newel posts and dished finials, was another sign of Arts and Crafts style.

Any mention of the Arts and Crafts Movement must lead to William Morris (1834–1896). It was Morris who saw mission and purpose in handcraft and made Britain reconsider standards of design for textiles, furniture, and much else, including buildings. To what extent was George Skipper influenced? A comparison might have been made between the building referred to by Cromer folk as The Red House, actually Halsey House, designed by Skipper in about 1899, and William Morris's 'Red House' designed by the architect, Philip Webb (1831–1915).

Webb's 'Red House' for Morris had been built in Bexleyheath, outer South London, in 1858–59, and displayed features such as oculi, turrets and a bellcote, all in red brick and tile. Skipper used these and other features repeatedly. More

Pl. 103
George Skipper, Architect, 1900–02
Swonnell's Maltings, Oulton Broad, Lowestoft.

Converted to residential purpose in 1980s.

pragmatic, he also took advantage of Mr Potter of Norwich's electrically powered stonecutting machines, as well as the industrial output of Royal Doulton. Undoubtedly influenced by Morris in the 1880s and 90s, new commissions took Skipper in other directions; he would return to aspects of Arts and Crafts later.

The RNSYC house was not his first building in Lowestoft. At the time of the yacht club's building at the harbour, the architect had a much larger project underway in Oulton Broad, just inland from the town, though still with access to the sea, and westwards along the river Waveney. This was a six floor maltings and factory for S. Swonnell & Son to be built at the waterside on land that had earlier belonged to George Borrow and his wife.

Malting from barley grain was extremely big business. Basically brewers had made beer close to centres of population, where they had barley delivered by wagon, and made their own malt. Increased traffic, railways, urbanization and demand caused brewers to understand the advantages of building malt

Pl. 104
George Skipper, Architect, 1900–02, Swonnell's Maltings, Oulton Broad, Lowestoft.

Photo taken in 1942 after aerial bombing.

houses, or maltings closer to the fields of barley. George Skipper had grown up with maltings in Dereham, some of them built by his father's teams using Skipper's bricks. He had made a specific study of the architectural requirements for malting, and had made plans for alterations to a malt house, for Mr Leeds at Wells-next-the-Sea on the North Norfolk coast (demolished 1977).

George's handwritten notes on maltings were full of measurements:

> PARTICULARS OF MALTING HOUSES
> That designed for S. Leeds Esq., of Wells had the following measurements.
> Ground floor to 1st floor – 7 ft 4½" incl 7½" joists
> 1st floor to 2nd do – 6 ft 10½" incl 7½" joists
> 2nd floor to 3rd do – 6 ft 10½" incl 7½" joists
> 3rd do to underside of beam 6ft and from underside of beam to top eaves 9".
> Windows 2' 6" from floorline, to Ground floor 2ft 6" x 2ft 6" in size.
> 2' 4" above other floor levels by same size (2' 6")
> Doors about 4ft wide, 6' 9" or 7' 0" high
> Windows in kiln about 4' 6" from floor level 3'3" wide x 3'0" high,
> and those in Malt and Barley stores 3'0" x 3'0" in size.

> Kiln drying floor is always in modern houses 17 ft above ground floor and to the top of the kiln roof above drying floor about 26 ft, generally gives ample roof for pitch for draught.
> PROPORTION OF AREA CONTENTS:
> Working floor 180 ft sup' to 1 quarter
> Kiln floor 27 ft sup' to 1 quarter
> Steep floor 4½ft sup' to 1 quarter
> Malt Store floor 16 ft sup' onto Ground floor
> Barley Store floor 8 ft sup' on Ground floor
>   or 10½ cubic feet to 1 quarter.
> Note – The proportions both of Malt Store and Barley Store are not always the same but vary according to the Maltsters' requirements. These proportions however are about right.

Swonnell's were a larger operation. They moved their business up from Nine Elms, near Battersea in London, to Oulton Broad in order to collect barley grown down the Waveney valley and send it to London in the form of malt. Large coal-fired burners were installed for the complex roasting and drying processes.

In time Swonnell's extended the buildings to handle larger quantities, but Skipper's 1900 plans continued to be at the core. The photograph provided shows the waterside view of Swonnell's maltings, just after they had been bombed in 1942; some of the inside of the stricken factory can be seen.

It was large and built on the waterfront. In the photograph we see the end of the building, where loading and unloading took place. Cliff-like expanses of brickwork formed two gabled wings. One of these has been ripped open by the explosion, exposing vast drums, tanks, drying floors, and iron girders. A variety of windows, some arched, some narrow, and some round, were interspersed over the elevations. The roofs were clad with slate, their profiles hidden by emerging ventilation shafts, with pyramidal roofs and elegant finials. A taller tower stood to the rear, covered in clapboard, and topped with another pyramidal slate roof.

Following the wartime destruction, repairs were made and the maltings were soon back to full production. However, in 1965 Swonnell's were bought by R.W Paul (Maltsters) Ltd., who decided to move production to Grantham in Lincolnshire. The maltings were left empty for fifteen years from 1968–1983 before some of the brick buildings were converted for residential use. They were granted Grade II Listing from English Heritage, although this was reversed when it was agreed that they had been substantially transformed, and no longer resembled George Skipper's plan of 1900–1902. Students of architecture will note that Skipper was capable of making technical designs for specific industrial buildings. Most of his architectural peers, who could design hotels and mansions, were not able to plan a malt house.

If malting barley was big business, so was wool production, nowhere more so than in Australia. Through connections, Skipper was asked to draw up plans for a large country house for Albert Augustus Dangar, at one of his many livestock ranches at Gostwyck, 48,000 acres near Uralla in New South Wales. George was obviously not going to make a site visit. He engaged his mind and put pencil to paper.

The design for 'Gostwyck Grange', seen in the RIBA Collections, Ref: PA246/29(4) shows all elevations. From the East elevation, the building would be symmetrical. There would be outlying towers at either end (four in total) with arched and pedimented windows below ogee-shaped roofs and finials. The entrance was to be at the centre, with a rusticated arch beneath a pediment, an enormous window and an elaborate gable. On either side of the entrance Skipper drew a pair of gablets with 18-light bow windows that would stand out against the steep roof, and beneath these further bays to illuminate the large mansion. Balconies were indicated at first storey level, and three tall chimneystacks stood proud of the long roofline. The story stopped there – Dangar presumably paid for the plans but did not take up the design, and indeed there was never a Gostwyck Grange built. RIBA captioned the style as 'Jacobean Revival'.

⋆   ⋆   ⋆   ⋆

George Skipper's next assignment was for the immediate neighbours in London Street. In fact the commission was conceived earlier, in 1896, as soon as Skipper moved into his London Street office. The Jarrold family could clearly see that they did not need to look further for someone to enable the extensive rebuilding of their department store.

With the commission a situation arose whereby George Skipper's character was tested. The circumstances are best described by Pete Goodrum in his book, *Jarrold 250 Years – A History*, published in 2020:

> '… … Local builders Thomas Gill had won the contract, and at £7,174 their price was competitive, although it was still a significant amount of money. Managing the project now became a balancing act. On the one hand there was the need to keep the store as operational as possible, while on the other the work had to be carried out. Equally, there were issues about just how much of Skipper's proposals the Jarrolds were prepared to accept, aesthetically and financially. The original design had featured a dome, on top of the sweeping bay-windowed frontage at the corner of London Street, but the Jarrolds thought it was a step too far, so Skipper demurred.
>
> The relationship between client and architect was also proving to be a challenge. Initially at least the project was not running on time. Skipper wasn't even punctual for meetings, let alone for delivering the overall scheme. Flamboyant as ever, he was regularly on site though: with his office next door, it was easy for him, but his presence was not always welcome. William Jarrold found it difficult and when Skipper's attitude offended him, he took action and wrote to Skipper's brother, Frederick. The Skipper brothers were partners, but it was a tense relationship and constantly on the point of fracturing. Despite that, William Jarrold wrote to say that if George Skipper 'repeated his conduct' then the Jarrolds would reluctantly bar him from the premises'.

Pl. 105
George Skipper, Architect, 1902–03 (and second stage in 1920s), Jarrolds, Norwich.

The whole Market Place in Norwich sloped down to Jarrold's corner, where Skipper's original design offered extra height. We know of Skipper's fondness of turrets and cupolae from his designs for Crispin Hall and Cobden Terrace in the 1880s, with ten more in Cromer in the 90s, and still more in Norwich, Cambridge and Sennowe Park. They served a purpose in raising height, providing a focus, or even to cap a stairwell. If the overall plan was not approved, new elevation drawings would have had to be submitted for approval. However, building work started straight away in May 1903.

The cancellation of the uppermost feature could not pass without George responding in a way liable to offend. Concurrently involved with eight or nine important Norwich construction sites at the same time, he regarded himself very highly, and this may well have irritated Mr Jarrold. Furthermore, before any work had started, there was an issue, because Skipper's office was next door, and that was being refaced too. Skipper submitted through Gill's, the builders, his plans (Number 5523, addendum 5) for extensions and alterations to Jarrold's and plans for alterations to his own office. The properties were to be extended and newly faced conjointly. Skipper applied to the Norwich Urban Sanitary Authority for the 19th century equivalent of Planning Permission. Skipper's first Notes of Intention to Erect New Buildings, submitted on 4 April 1903, dealt specifically with the shared wall between Jarrold and Skipper. The 'straight, solid party wall boundary to the two properties' needed to be made secure in new brickwork straight away. So Skipper was not just the architect, he was the neighbour building his own frontage too.

Whatever had taken place, GJS was used to being at the centre; he was also hardened from a life's contact with builders. There is no excuse for bad manners, but there was another side to the story of the missing turret and its domed copper cap. Much of the matter was about George's character, and explains something about who he was.

There is the belief that an artist-architect, who has laboured to get a design 'just right', does not deserve to have the design altered. The tricky situation of satisfying a client, as if 'the customer is always right', must be balanced by the knowledge that invariably the customer does not know best. Designs are either approved or not. To have the domed turret erased from the design must have been infuriating. He was too proud to lower his head, and tacitly accept a decision made by people not conversant with architecture or aesthetics. Some sympathy must go to George, who had to see the altered design every day for the rest of his life; doubtless some architects who hear of this will understand his frustration. Turrets and cupolae in Norwich were cancelled at 30 London Street and at the bank in Red Lion Street at near enough the same time. It is extremely fortunate that the omissions of towers to all three buildings were not immediately noticeable, and did not overly detract from their architectural quality. Or so we like think.

As a final remark about the domed tower, it appears that Jarrold continued to print and publicise George's sketch of his plan, titled, 'Looking Forward', depicting the corner view of 'The House of Jarrolds' – including the domed tower – for several more years.

Pl. 106
Publicity material: *"Looking Forward"* 'A sketch by Mr G..J Skipper depicting the completed elevation of THE HOUSE OF JARROLDS'.

George was already known to have a temper, invariably in connection with his work. He could be acerbic or abrupt with workmen, even downright furious sometimes, and with good reason. In all the architectural projects discussed it was his name, and his good reputation, that hung in the balance. He did not want or permit substandard work, and he needed this to be understood. He found a truth in William Blake's idiom, 'The tigers of wrath are wiser than the horses of instruction'.

A very amusing anecdote was recounted by his family: many years later, knowing that George Skipper could be bad tempered, a Miss King, possibly the Skipper's housemaid, had advised him to consider a homeopathic remedy. So George had purchased some of a particular medicine. However, on returning home, he presented the curative pillules to his wife, thinking that they might help *her* to deal with someone with a short fuse!

Jarrold's new building, once in place, was likened to a tiered wedding cake (not necessarily a derogative) with so many columns that could be icing sugar. Another impression was of a cream-coloured edifice with balconies in the old quarter of New Orleans, or even the upper decks of a Mississippi paddle steamer. It is a Grade II Listed Building.

The frontage incorporated the end of London Street and curved round the corner of Exchange Street. The layout was such that a view of Jarrolds is invariably of the corner. Rather than pausing at each stage of construction, spread over twenty years, let us view Jarrold's as it stands today. The large structure is four-storeyed throughout, and all surfaces are rendered and painted. The roof cannot be seen. There are 5 bays in London Street, a corner bay, and 7 bays in Exchange Street, which was the part that was renovated later in the 1920s.

Jarrold's London Street elevation's has plain 20th century shop windows at ground level. The first floor frontage presents two large arches containing windows; in between sits an elegant oriel, flanked by Ionic pilasters and framed with dark red columns of polished granite. At second floor level there is a continuous arcade of white Ionic columns before recessed plain windows. The third floor is a line of large oculi and scrolls and, above them, a flat parapet, punctuated by regular antefixa with acanthus leaf designs. There are urns at the roofline's corner, where the domed turret had been intended.

The Exchange Street elevation copied and extended the theme, the only difference being the addition of five two-storey arched windows at ground floor, separated by tall Ionic pilasters.

Everything happened at the corner bay that linked the two street elevations. Here was the main entrance, recessed behind Doric columns that provide the suggestion of a balcony above, where the curved frieze is embellished with egg and dart key lines, and the family name is picked out in gold paint.

Skipper's design had a gracious air – it was a brave and ingenious scheme. How did the architect know it would succeed and even win the affection of all classes? Above all he was placing his design in a significant site, where it would have to compete with powerful architecture from every era surrounding

Pl.107 *(facing page)* George Skipper, Architect, 1902–03. (detail) Entrance at corner of Jarrolds.

JARROLDS

Pl. 108
George Skipper, Architect, 1902–03, (detail) Balcony on London Street, Jarrolds, Norwich.

the open Market Place, famed throughout England. Skipper's building could not possibly have been more different to the very nearby Guildhall, a fortified flint-clad building from the days of King Henry V and Agincourt. Jarrold's premises mark the corner of the entire Market Place area. In an instance of genius Skipper had put a curve on the building, just where it mattered. If architectural historians can see precedents to some of Skipper's other designs, was there a forerunner to Jarrold's building? Was there something in the architect's private library to compare? Nothing comes to mind. The style, to my untutored eye, was a mélange of Neo-classical and Baroque.

Interior spaces of the store have been altered again and again. Progressive additions have extended Jarrolds premises to north and east frontages in

Bedford Street and Little London Street, though these are functional and mostly featureless in the 20th century manner.

It is fitting that people can see plaques and inscriptions near the main entrance. They are picked out in paint, and refer to authors, mostly forgotten, who once graced the lists of Jarrold Publishing. It is a link to the family's other businesses, as printers, booksellers, binders and stationers, and publishers. The list of names includes Dr C. Brewer, F.J Gladman, Maurus Jokai, Saunders Marshall, James Spilling, W.K Farnell, and Mary Sewell, who wrote *Homely Ballads for the Working Man's Fireplace* and *An Appeal to Englishwomen*. Mary's daughter was Anna Sewell, who had died when George Skipper was working in Dereham in 1878. Nothing could have prepared Jarrolds Publishers for the success of the book submitted to them by Anna Sewell.

Black Beauty, was the story of a black horse that is sold and resold, and mistreated, before being found again. Profoundly influential, it was told in the first person, from the horse's mouth. The equine had thoughts, described injustice and emotion. It was published a year before the author's death and has been sold in many editions to a total of more than fifty million copies, making it the sixth best selling book in the English language.

Skipper's building for Jarrolds is the only one of the architect's well-known works in Norwich to have remained in the hands of its original owners. The building is well maintained, and on winter nights, illuminated with floodlighting that defines Skipper's exterior, a welcoming sight.

The gradual stages of Jarrolds' alterations were not fully completed until 1923. Even then there would be more changes to come, when the ground floor of Skipper's offices, previously occupied by Smith's Dyers and Cleaners, and Salmon & Gluckstein, tobacconists, were converted to 'The Red House Tearooms' in about 1935. Many years later, after Skipper quit in 1946–47, the upper two floors of his office at 7 London Street were finally incorporated into the extended department store. Nevertheless, for Listing and heritage purposes, Jarrolds own two Skipper buildings.

At the time, in May 1904, George Skipper, was again thrown into grief. His wife Rachel died. She was his partner for thirteen years and the mother of his son Theo, then aged ten.

Five weeks later, George's father, Robert Skipper, died on 23 June 1904. In practice Skipper senior had been a guiding light for George in the 1870s and 80s. It had been he who had determined his son's life in architecture. Almost eighty when he died, Robert Skipper had been living with his wife, Caroline, at 68 Clarendon Road in Norwich, having dispersed his properties and brickworks. Subsequently Caroline, George's stepmother, also changed address, moving to 92 Park Lane, quite close to George's first (and last) home in Mill Hill Road.

Having left the Mill Hill Road house after his first wife died, George and Rachel, and young Theo (with the dog seen in Minns's panel on the front of the office) had been living in 59 Unthank Road.

Following Rachel's death, George and his son moved away again. At a later census in 1911 he would be back at the city end of Unthank Road, at Number 39. But, for at least some of the period 1905–1908, George and Theo lived at Number 432 Unthank Road. We know this because he wrote it at the head of letters, some from the office, that he sent to Henry Bulwer of Heydon. (Bulwer had been thanking him for supplying a carved coat of arms, and Skipper promised to inform the craftsman, Mr Potter, of Bulwer's praise).

Pl. 109
George Skipper,
Pencil sketch,
5 November 1905,
RIBA Collections.

Pl. 110 *(facing page)*
George Skipper,
Architect, 1905
Canterbury House,
Norwich.

This address has added interest because it was next door to a particularly handsome property, 'Canterbury Villa' that George Skipper designed for Mr E.W.D Potter himself. Of the same vintage as George's father, Potter was a master-mason (and a monumental mason) who intended to build to Skipper's design and then sell. Building took place in about 1907, though the original conception was George's first sketch, made on 5 November 1905. It appeared in his sketchbook, roughly drawn, to be followed by proper elevation drawings and floor plans. These were not altered: the original sketch and what Mr Potter built were identical.

'Canterbury Villa' (now known as Canterbury House) was a two-storeyed redbrick building, with a tiled roof, and two ordinary-sized brick chimneystacks, originally tall, but nowadays lowered. The south front, which was separated from the road by a front garden and driveway, was a symmetrical arrangement with stone-mullioned windows, and what might be described as a tower-porch rising from the ground to above the eaves. It was bow-fronted and chequer-patterned, with 1 ft squares of limestone ashlar alternating with brickwork.

This chequered finish lent an antiquated air, and covered the ground floor entrance, recessed behind a pair of Doric columns. At the first storey, an eight-light bow window, surrounded by the chequer-pattern and stone quoins, rose to a small parapet with a pair of tapering finials. The west front has a similar bowed bay, with windows at both levels, and a small balcony and balustrade. Mr Potter had spared no expense. The grounds contained a small range of outbuildings, all contemporary with the house, including a small coach house, stables and loft. A wrought-iron gate to the garden was suspended between stone and brick piers with overthrows and globe finials. One can only assume Potter sold at a good price.

It is not known precisely how long George and his son lived at Number 432 Unthank Road. Nor is it known what the living arrangements were, or whether Theo was sent to board at school. A drawing in his sketchbook of a young lady, captioned 'Billie', might refer to either a family member, or a governess. Undoubtedly he was helped in bringing up a motherless son. Having experienced the loss of his own mother, George was acutely aware of Theo's position.

Despite the loss and upheaval in Skipper's private life, important commissions continued to arrive. One of these came from his enduring contact with Sir Kenneth Kemp who, in his capacity as a banker and lawyer, had friends on the board of directors of several businesses. A major work, undertaken when the Norwich Union building was approaching completion, was for a design for another insurance company.

Norwich and London Accident Insurance Association, (founded in 1856 as the General Hailstorm Insurance Association), had from 1876 occupied premises in Numbers 41–43 St Giles Street. Skipper's task was to entirely recreate the building. He must have consulted his private library of architectural titles. The overall result, emerging behind scaffolding two years later, appeared to have been transported from 18th century Vienna, Milan, or St Petersburg. It was, Pevsner commented, '. . . very Baroque indeed'. Colin Geoffrey Skipper, George's great-nephew and a Chartered Surveyor, called it 'a Chatsworth in miniature'. The architectural critic, Ian Nairn (1930–1983) visited Norwich in the 1970s and was very impressed by Skipper's work. Having seen Surrey House he visited St Giles Street and pronounced it, 'another firework by Skipper . . . smaller but if anything even richer'.

It would be perverse not to enthuse about this continental palace that George Skipper teleported to an English mediaeval street. Some would say that it was not authentic, though it has existed for over a century. All would agree that it was an object of beauty, and that it deserved its status as a Grade II ★ Listed Building.

Following his work at Surrey House, it was Mr Potter who procured the honey-coloured Bath Stone and the white-grey Portland Stone. F&B supplied more marble columns. It was to be a magnificent façade, a Baroque expression of Classicism, cleverly designed and executed in the best materials by the best craftsmen.

Standing on a marble-faced plinth course, Skipper's design was for a three-storeyed building, seven bays wide, with the first, fourth and seventh bays projecting about three feet forwards, to add depth.

Pl. 111
George Skipper, Architect, 1904–06, Former Norwich & London Assurance Company offices, (Now St Giles Hotel) Norwich.

The fourth bay at the centre would seize any viewer's attention. The entrance, a rusticated arch between pairs of Doric columns, was no ordinary doorway. The columns supported a curved and scrolled broken pediment, its raked sides clasping an ornate sphere, surrounded by floral swags. Suspended from this, and above the archway, the carved stone arrangement lowered to the head of a woman crowned with a laurel wreath, and surrounded by palm fronds, symbolic of honour and peace.

The window above this central doorway only added to the effect of architectural magic. It was deeply recessed and surrounded by a Classical arch, rising to another pediment, this time open bedded, the available space filled with keystones and adjacent wedge-shaped voussoirs merging with the rustication.

The advancing first and last bays featured tall sashes at ground floor, with scrolled brackets supporting small balustraded balconies above. They stood before similar windows and were flanked by pilasters decorated with intricate mouldings of shields, swags and ribbons. They also supported entablatures inscribed, between coronals, FOUNDED MDCCCLVI on the left wing, and REBUILT MDCCCCVI on the right wing. Outside of the pilasters were polished Cornish granite columns, running from ground through first and second floors. The third floor front of these bays, featuring smaller arched

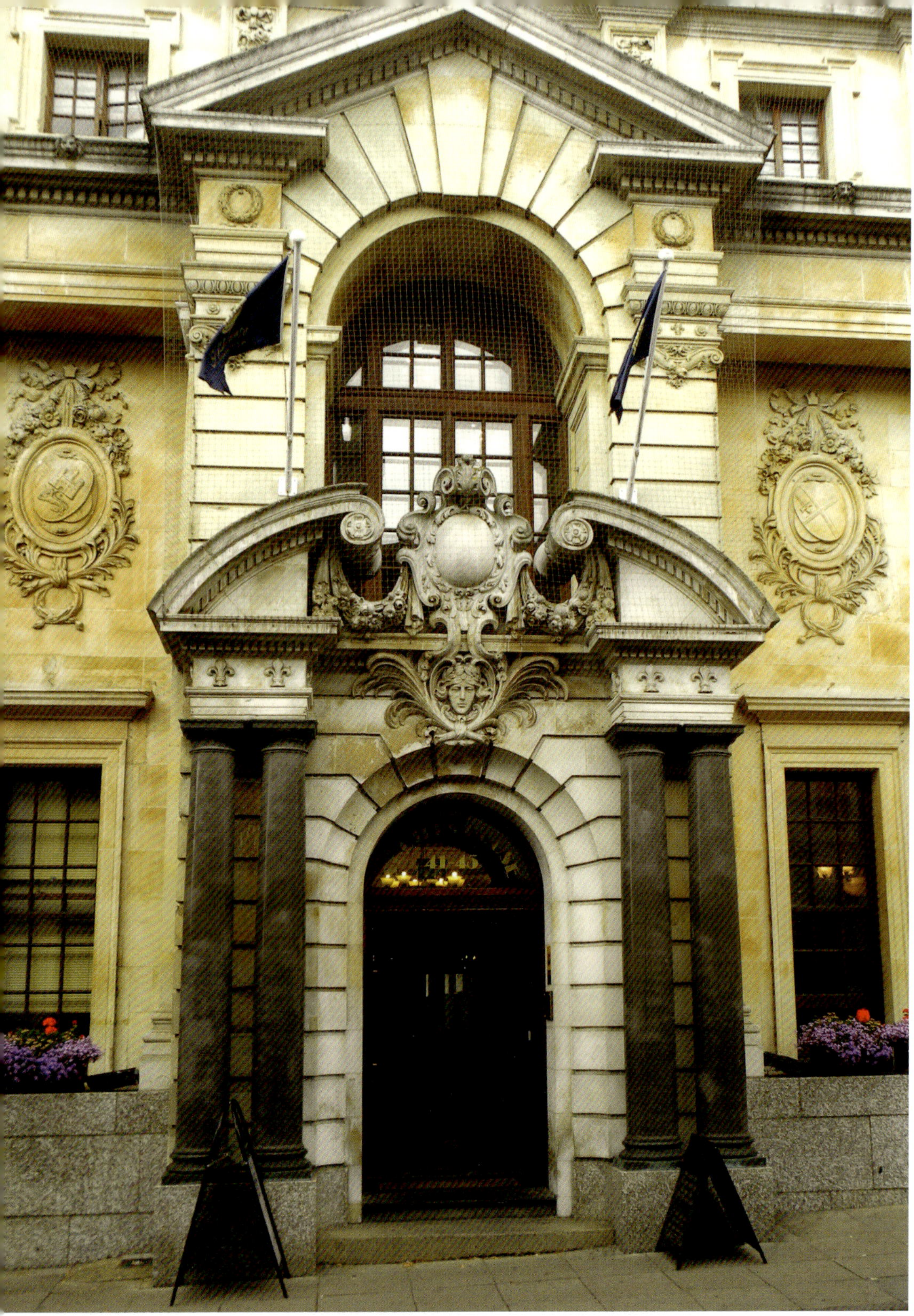

windows and more stone swags, rose to a balustrade parapet interspersed with Portland Stone urns. There were sixteen of these, reminiscent of Blenheim Palace's roofline.

The receding double-bays, the second and third, plus the fifth and sixth, were bisected by further white granite columns. In the place where further sashes might be expected, were two oval cartouches: one represented the city's coat of arms, the other was that of the Guild of St George.

How good were Skipper's collaborators? The answer is 'very', in fact Benedict Read, writing in his masterpiece, *Victorian Sculpture*, makes the point that Farmer & Brindley 'represent a significant phenomenon in the development of architectural sculpture'. Moreover, Read quoted the remark of the very well known architect, Sir George Gilbert Scott RA (1811–1878), who said that William Brindley was 'the best carver I have met with, and the one who best understands my views'. Mr Potter, the mason with 'shiploads of Portland Stone' had the highest standards in stone carving as well.

At St Giles House, in addition to the interplay of advance and recede, there was an attractive tonal contrast. The façades were made of Bath stone, its warm colour distinct from the grey Portland at the centre, or the substantial white columns. All these architectural tricks supplied a depth to the front that was needed because, unlike Surrey House, there was no forecourt between the building and the street. A final contrivance was that the top floor, with its balustraded parapet and urns, appeared to recede even further. The entire front was cleaned in 2003, enhancing the soft hues.

The interior was fairly lavish too, with marble pillars, a stone pediment over the fireplace, and a domed ceiling. Beneath the rebuilt mansion-offices were the remains of a 15th century undercroft, in an early use of brickwork.

Only three years after completion, The Norwich and London Accident Insurance Association was bought out by Norwich Union in 1909. Skipper's building was sold to the GPO and became the Telephone Manager's office for the Norwich area, though the actual exchanges were in peripheral locations.

Pl. 112 *(facing page)*
George Skipper, Architect, 1904–06, Main entrance, Former Norwich & London Assurance Company offices, (Now St Giles Hotel) Norwich.

Pl. 113
George Skipper, Architect, 1904–06, (detail)
Urns on parapet, former Norwich & London Assurance Company offices.

Pl. 114
George Skipper, Architect, 1906–08
Putti and decoration at entrance to former London and Provincial Bank, Norwich.

Pl. 115 *(facing page)*
George Skipper, Architect, 1906–08, Former London and Provincial Bank, Norwich.

The only recollection of this period lies in the name 'Telephone House', which remained. After the Second World War it became the offices of Norwich City Council's education and treasury departments. Modern and nondescript extensions were made to the rear. Many years later 'Telephone House' was converted into a small and luxurious hotel, and subsequently renamed 'St Giles House'. It is always remarked that the very old street of St Giles is too narrow to allow a viewer to step back in order to admire the quality of Skipper's Norwich 'Palazzo'.

Another observation from Pevsner was that the house two doors down, the Masonic Hall, by the architect Albert Havers (1864–1930) was built 'in Skipperish mode', as it showed obvious similarities, and was built of Bath stone just one year after St Giles House.

Another stone façade was George Skipper's design for the London & Provincial Bank in Number 30 London Street in Norwich (eventually Barclays from 1918). This was his response to a direct commission, with the client doubtless impressed by the architect's achievements. Another contributory factor to the bank's selection could have been the close proximity of Skipper's office, five seconds' walk from the site.

Construction took place in 1906–08. The bank, which had three-storeys and four bays, had only the street-facing elevation, and was built of Portland Stone. The ground floor wall was lined with channelled rustication, and pierced with four arched openings, three of which were recessed windows with keystones that reached up to a beautiful wave-scrolled key line. The fourth, on the right hand side, was the doorway, flanked by dark marble columns, and capped by a broken pediment. Rising from this doorway, there was a cartouche, surrounded by scrolls, between a pair of over life-sized cherubim. It bore the face of a woman with curling tresses and a hairband, an echo of Ancient Greece or Rome, who stared straight out onto the street to meet the eye of anyone entering. It was a powerful doorway, obviously inspired by the Italian Renaissance. The building is now The Ivy Norwich Brasserie.

The cherubim appeared to support a balcony at the base of a recessed and bowed bay window, beneath a small curved pediment with ornament, reaching

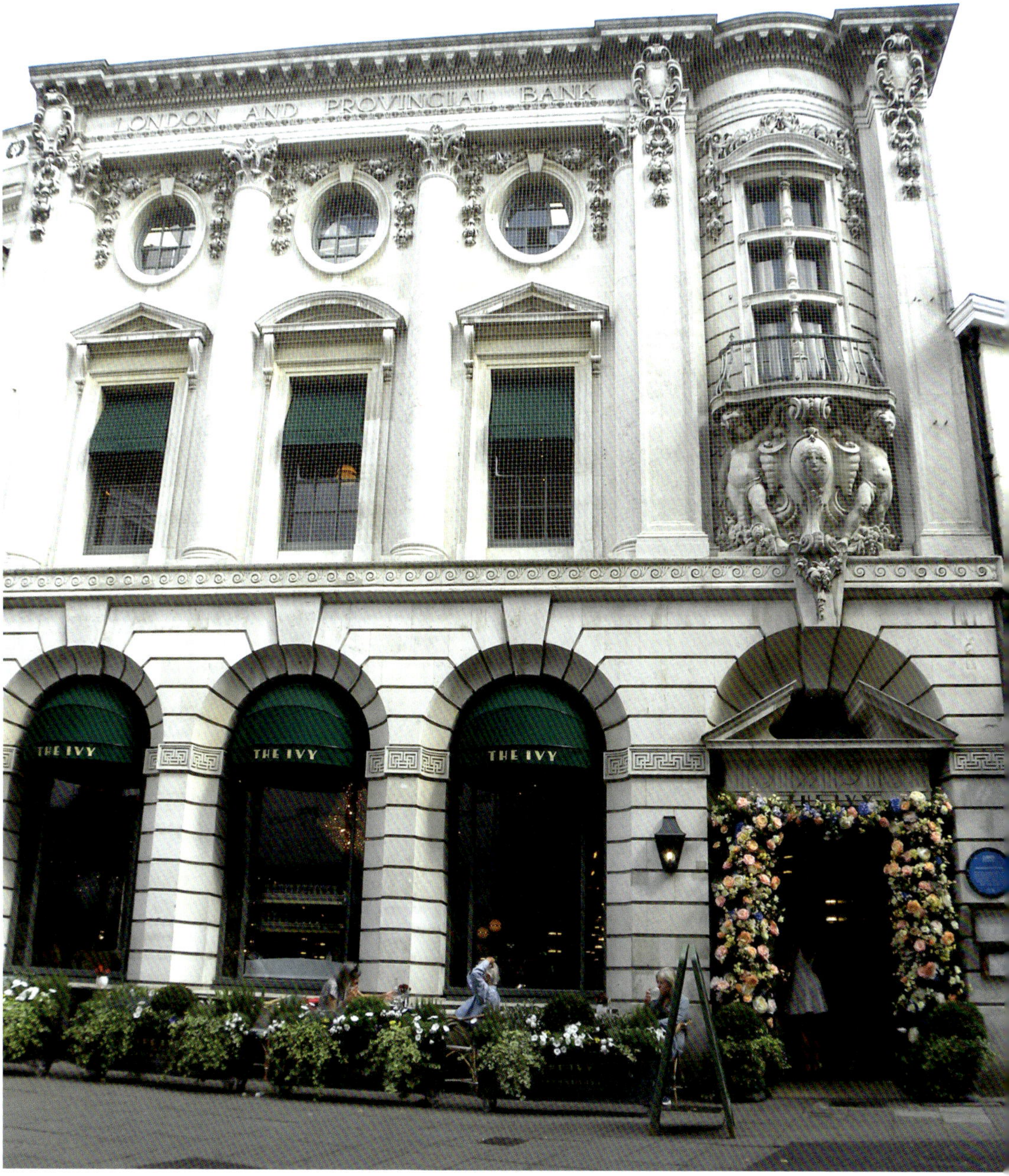
LONDON AND PROVINCIAL BANK
THE IVY
THE IVY
THE IVY

to the eaves. The roof could not be seen. The fourth bay, with its doorway and two-storeyed bow, was intended by Skipper to have a domed turret at the top. This bay was also at odds with the rest of the upper storeys, which presented three tall casements with classical pediments that almost touched three large oculi above. These round windows are separated by four Corinthian columns and surrounded by garlands. Still higher a cornice fascia was inscribed with the name of the bank between two cartouches, flowing with floral ornament.

The absence of the tower is not immediately noticeable, but there was an extraordinary interplay between the fourth bay and the other three. It is better described by Stephen Thomas:

> 'Coming off the columns or pilasters in this fourth bay, sections of the entablatures break across the rest of the façade as string courses uniting the main elevation. The rest of the façade often appears set back, suggesting a different classical origin from that of the entrance, as if two elevations have been smashed together in a play of advance and recession. All of this is done with classical detailing around windows and with deeply carved decoration in a Mannerist style'.

Incidentally, very nearly identical cherubim, without doubt from the same hands and chisels, were above the entrance of the Cambridge office of Norwich Union Insurance, designed by Skipper and built two years earlier.

A postgraduate thesis by Dr John Booker, conducted in 1984 at the Institute of Advanced Architectural Studies in York explored the subject of 'The Architecture of Banking – A Study of the Design of British Banks from the 18th century to Modern Times'. He observed that from the 1840s an Italianate style was found increasingly appropriate, while philanthropic Savings Banks found Gothic and Tudor designs preferable. From the 1860s, however, the overall banking business of the UK was reorganised, with the advent of national branch networks. Booker noted that there was a confusion of styles around 1900, with 'the first signs of environmental concerns, the influence of aesthetic movements, and the gradual evolution of the 'Queen Anne' style, which was to develop into the safe Neo-Georgian of the 1920s'.

Published later under the title *Temples of Mammon – Architecture of Banking*, it had clear relevance for Norwich, which had a number of banks in the middle of the city, all of which were well designed and built. Some of them, for example the National Provincial (National Westminster) Bank, also in London Street, designed by the bank's in-house architect, Frederick Charles Palmer, in the 1920s, were extremely elegant. Pevsner described the tower on Palmer's National Provincial as 'Wrenian'.

However, since Booker's study and the latest Pevsner edition a huge change has taken place in Britain, with a powerful effect on towns and cities everywhere. The final three or four 'high street banks' began quitting the high street from 2015 onwards, preferring to use computers at distant locations. Leaving aside the social implications, this leaves thousands of significant buildings redundant with an uncertain future, though a lot of them are Listed. Many have become restaurants or wine bars.

Away from the city, it was probably in 1904 that George Skipper was approached by Mr Thomas Albert Cook for a design for a grand country house at Sennowe Park in Norfolk. A Georgian house had been built in this place in the late 1770s by the Wodehouse family, and leased out during the 19th century. The landscape had been improved with plantations, a garden area in front of the house, and a wooded drive. After the last of the Wodehouse lineage died, the trustees briefly engaged the famous architect, Decimus Burton (1800–1881), to make alterations to the house before selling. These amounted to adding in part an upper storey, and an iron-framed verandah around the south and east fronts.

Pl. 116
George Skipper, 1904, Prospective watercolour of Sennowe Hall in Norfolk for Thomas Albert Cook.

The Sennowe estate was sold, and sold again in 1899 to Thomas Albert Cook (1867–1914), (known as 'Bert'), third grandson of the first Thomas Cook, who had started the vastly successful eponymous travel agency, nearly sixty years earlier. Bert sold his third of the business, leaving his brothers to manage. His interests were in shooting and the sport of carriage driving, and that was why he had purchased the 160 acre estate, adding a further 8,000 acres in 1904.

Oh to be an architect in the grand old way! Skipper would attend to all aspects and outworks that could be viewed from the house. Sennowe Park would be a first for him. It was also, in a way, the last, and has been named as such, for it was the last grand country house to be built in England. After Sennowe, a place of optimism, came the war and after that a time when many country houses would be demolished, burned, or left to dilapidate.

The circumstances of the meetings between architect and client, and the precise orders left by T. Albert Cook, are not known. After giving instructions and, presumably, some advance money, Bert left for a round the world voyage, with all travel bookings taken care of by the family firm. Equally unspecific was the order of command. Was Skipper in charge? Was this a repeat of the Surrey House situation, where he was not only the designer, but the contractor as well? If so, Skipper had an extremely skilled and able team of associated artisans. There was Potter with his electric machinery, Brindley and his Italian marble men, Neatby with his Doulton tiles and paintbrush, and others still to be named.

How was George? It seems remarkable that the architect was able to oversee so much at Sennowe Park, let alone the major Norwich sites. At roughly the same time he became a widower again, responsible for his child, and was moving home as well. Another impression was of his journeys to Sennowe, conducted over a period of four years: each was a trip to the country and old home territory. The train service from Dereham to Wells-next-the-Sea was good, running across the estate to the little station at County School, remembered from his father's days. On other days George brought out the motorcar, setting out from Norwich on the open country road to Sennowe, roughly twenty miles distant.

Pl. 117
George Skipper, Architect, 1905–09, Ryburgh Lodges, gatehouses to Sennowe Park, Guist, Norfolk.

Regarding the question of overall responsibility, Bert's descendant and the present owner of Sennowe, Charles Temple-Richards, said:

> "I think that Bert was very much in the hands of Skipper in the design of Sennowe, although he returned from a long world tour to see the results of the work with the remark 'and where is my ballroom?' One can imagine Skipper slapping his forehead in dismay. An enormous cast-iron conservatory with a fountain, known as the Winter Garden, was added to make good this omission, although I doubt it was ever used for dancing, as with the fine marble floor and all that glass it must have been echoey and cold".
>
> The English Home UK, 30 June 2019: 'The Guardians of Sennowe Park').

For Skipper in the 20th century, as with architects of grand country houses in earlier centuries, there was a requirement for diversions, whether fountains, Greek temples, towers, or grottoes.

At Sennowe, the architect's 'To do' list of works extended from the house, to new gardens, to temples and balustrades and terraces, to a stable block, a tall belfry with an interior staircase, a bridge, a boathouse, an identical pair of lodge houses, and a second pair of gatehouses. And a lake!

The environs of Sennowe, in particular the drives, were thickly planted with deciduous trees, that have matured and block the modern-day sounds and sights of the Norwich to Fakenham road along the north-east edge of the park. This protective screen of woodland all around gives the house and park a strong sense of belonging in the English countryside. Most of the plantations along the drive were made before T.A Cook arrived, but more trees were added.

To arrive at Sennowe Hall a visitor enters one or other of the gateways to the estate. Both entrances – one on the quiet Ryburgh road, and the other on the busy Norwich road, are overlooked by pairs of lodges, or gatehouses.

From the first moment one is seeing signs of Skipper. Both pairs of twin lodges are among the finest, not just for architectural historians, but for anyone with an eye. In a masterful two-part review of Sennowe Park in 1981, the writer, Clive Aslet, later editor of *Country Life*, wrote 'A hint of the scale on which work was undertaken is given by the two sets of unusually imposing entrance lodges, eclectic Jacobean in style'.

There are reasons to believe that one of the pairs of elegant gatehouses, or lodges, was among the first of the 'outworks' to be started on. The Ryburgh Lodges, on the S-W side of the estate, needed to be ready for the return of T.A. Cook himself. When Bert returned from his travels in 1907, Sennowe Hall was not even near ready for him. The owner and his wife and son started living in the South Lodge, the one on the left, if seen from outside the gates.

Though the Ryburgh lodges were similar, the left-hand house had four more rooms than the other. It had been in existence already, and Skipper's design was built over and around it, to match the other. Both lodges had three-storey central tower-houses with wavy crenellation on the parapet. Like smaller versions of Skipper's Mancroft Towers, the elevations featured two-storey canted bay windows, and twin casements above, all with dressed stone mullions. There were stone consoles, heraldic cartouches, quoins – all of which stood out against the red brick walls. A large stone cat, a squirrel and an imperious owl sat on the parapet, looking down at the roadway. Joined to outer sides (away from the gate) of the 'fortress' fronts, were two-storey houses, with pitched slate roofs and three chimneystacks apiece. On the inner sides, towards the gates, the lodges had further canted bays with stone mullions.

Most noticeable, and adding a distinctly historic air, both buildings were given external staircase turrets. These were crowned by circular platforms that

Pl. 118
George Skipper, Architect, 1905–09, South Lodge, Ryburgh Drive Gates, Sennowe Park, Guist, Norfolk.

Pl. 119
George Skipper, Architect, 1905–09, Norwich Drive Lodges, Sennowe Park, Guist, Norfolk.

were surrounded by eight-column colonnades, and topped by cupolae, finials and weathervanes. One can imagine standing up in one these 'crows nests' and seeing a carriage and four coming from the hall at high speed! Were the gates open?

At ground level, on both sides, a short arcade wall reached to stone piers that were carved with niches and shields, and surmounted by heraldic beasts. The piers served as gateposts for the large wrought iron gates over the drive. These too were made to a design of Skipper's that included an ornate metal overthrow. Beneath the stair turrets the two lodges faced inwards to the gates; these elevations contained the working doorways towards the gateway, and are lit by additional canted bays. The Ryburgh Lodges are Listed Grade II buildings of historic interest, as are the ones built later on the other side of the estate.

It is interesting to recall that when George was a young apprentice, articled to John Lee in London, Lee himself assisted and associated with the architect, William Eden Nesfield. Nesfield had made lodges at Kew and Regents Park and elsewhere. His single lodge for Cloverley Hall, near Ightfield in Shropshire, built in about 1870, could be compared to the Ryburgh Lodges, though it did not have a tower.

The Norwich Drive lodges at Sennowe, built later in about 1909, were identical to each other, though not the same as the Ryburgh Drive pair. Square in plan, to one side they had red brick towers with dressed stone quoins and copper roofs. Unlike the other lodges' towers, these did not feature open colonnades, or platforms, instead having a single blank oculus on two faces. At the peaks of the overhanging copper roofs were wooden lanterns, with finials attached to tall weather-vanes. At ground level these towers contained outward and gateside entrances beneath arches. Higher up, stone stringcourses and mounted shields stood out against the brickwork. The rest of the lodge houses were less ornate, with four-light bay windows and casements above, all with stone mullions. The hipped slate roofs had only single chimneys.

The superbly elaborate wrought-iron gates of the main entrance, designed by Skipper, were suspended from square-section stone piers, decorated with lion's heads and mounted crests. Above them was an overthrow of curlicues and shapely leaf patterns. The handsome gates were used by visitors from the world beyond Sennowe, and the lodges housed two families who guarded the entrance. There were several more wrought-iron gates at the Hall, all of exceptional quality. The designs were all Skipper's, but credit must go to the unnamed blacksmiths.

Once inside the gates, a journey of several hundred yards up the drive brought one to the East front of Sennowe Hall. If seated in a carriage, it would be driven carefully by the coachman, who turned the leader with the reins and guided the vehicle in a tight loop, bringing the team to a halt in the Carriage Porch.

There was nothing particularly wrong with Sennowe Hall as it was, but Cook wanted to entertain and enjoy his country life. Skipper's design was to

Pl. 120
George Skipper, Architect, 1905–09, Norwich Drive gates, Sennowe Park, Guist, Norfolk.

Pl. 121
George Skipper, Architect, 1905–09, East front, Sennowe Hall, Guist, Norfolk.

Pl. 122 *(facing page)* George Skipper, Architect, 1905–09, (detail) Central bay, East front, Sennowe Hall, Guist, Norfolk.

envelop, mask, and add to the Georgian building. The architect achieved this so successfully that though the original building remained in evidence, it was a new house, an Edwardian Baroque mansion, with elevations that bore no resemblance to the original. Skipper would be credited rightfully as architect of Sennowe. It would be a transformation.

His method of hiding the older house, by refacing its white gault brick surfaces with mathematical tiles to perfectly simulate regular brickwork, by repeating its projecting bay, by drawing attention to his new and exceptionally elegant bowed bay, and by adding about ten bays to double the length of the building – was ingenious.

Skipper's new east front had seventeen bays. From the left, or south of the elevation, the hall began with the new carriage porch, built in stone, either from Lincolnshire or Somerset. In one of George Skipper's first images of Sennowe, a soft-toned watercolour, the porch was shown with a domed roof, but this idea must have been dispensed with. Its third arch, facing to the front is now glazed, but the rest of the porch was enriched with columns, rustication, and carved swags and garlands. Stone urns festooned with flowers stand on its flat roof. Up above, where the old house projected, Skipper had disguised the original windows with stone surrounds, cills and heads. The third-storey of

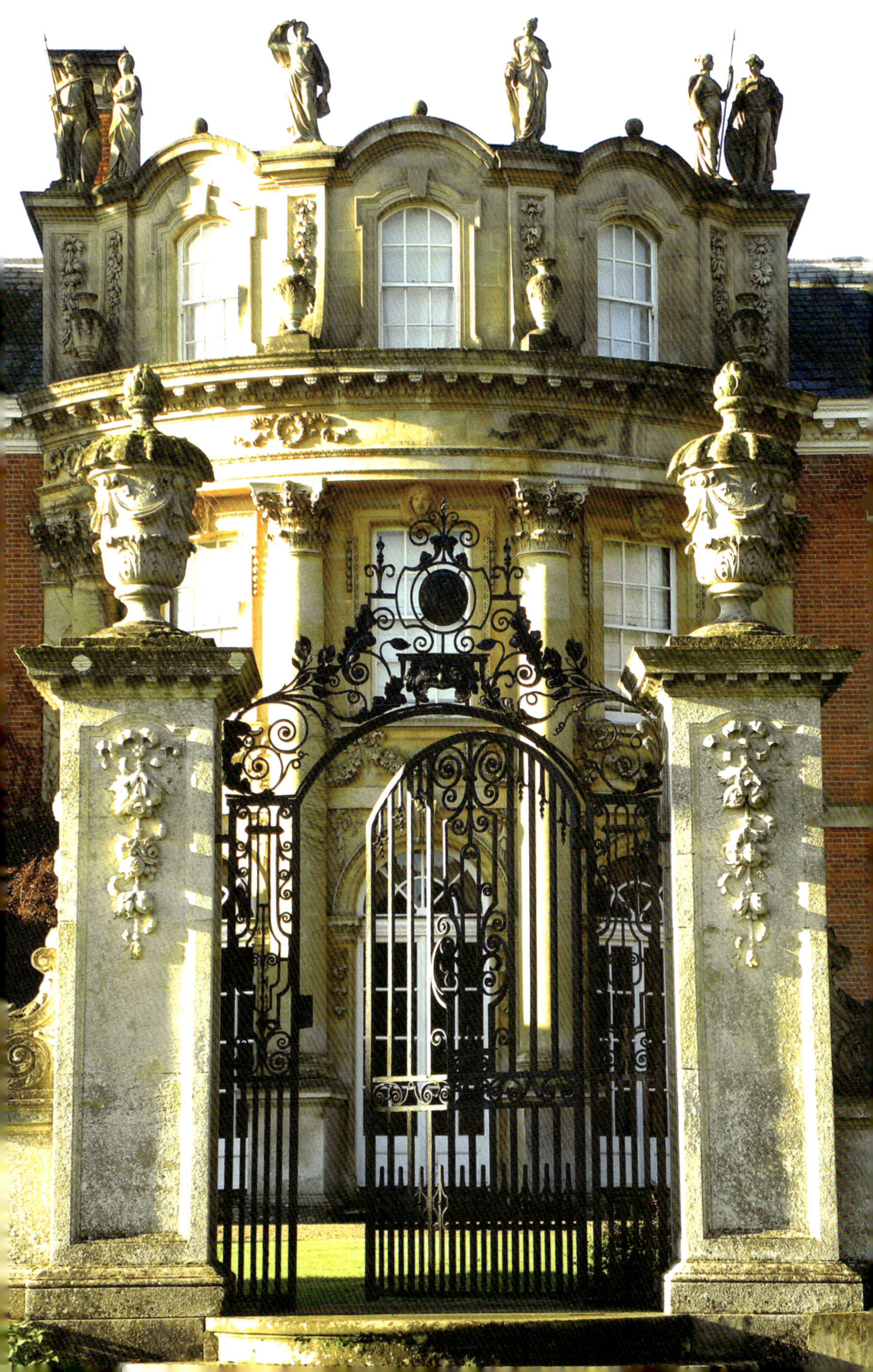

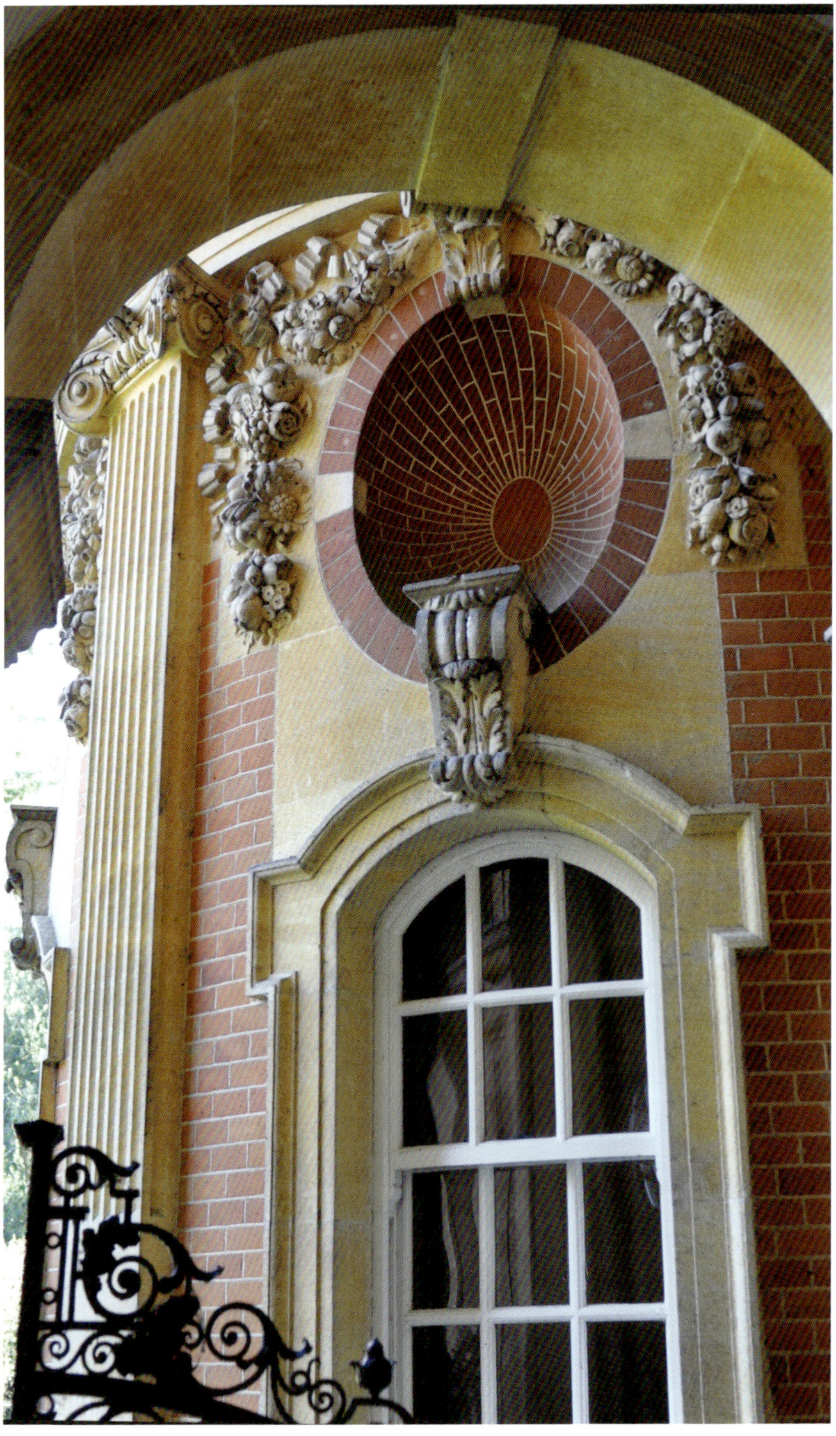

this bay emerged from the slate roof as an octagonal tower, to which Skipper added a balustrade between piers mounted by urns. The three windows at this stage are oval in shape and surrounded by distinctly Baroque stonework, with projecting keystones and curved hoods.

Those three projecting bays (3,4,5) are mirrored in every way in bays (13,14,15) at the other end of the elevation, creating symmetry. In the central three bays (8,9,10) Skipper created a graceful and complex three-storeyed bow, an architectural *piece de resistance*, as Baroque as it could be, that recalled the architecture of palaces in France and Italy. Clive Aslet referred to its 'un-English richness'.

Four Corinthian columns around the bowed bay separated three arched French doors, with lunettes at ground level, and three straight-headed windows above. Rising to the third floor, the columns supported a decorated and curving frieze, and above that an attic, with arched and hooded windows. Finally, above the attic, gazing out over the parkland and all the way to Aegean, stood a curving line of three-quarters life-size stone statues, six in all, female and male figures in classical dress, including two holding spears.

There was a vast amount of detail, with garlands, amphorae, egg and dart patterns, classical heads, wreaths and ribbons – all crisply carved in soft-toned stonework. All the details contrasted with the very regular pointing in between the mathematical tiles. Their appearance was that of ultra-consistent stretcher bond brickwork.

Regarding the division of labour between the two talented teams of stoneworkers, the figures on the roof were said to be have been made by Brindley's Italians, while all the carved architraves and urns were cut by Mr Potter's men in Norwich. The large Corinthian columns might have been turned on the lathe by either firm, equally competent. In truth, the statues could easily have been bought by Farmer & Brindley from Italians in London. More unusual was their presence on the roofline: it was something a man on the Grand Tour might have seen in Rome. Few places in Britain had such figures apart from Houghton Hall in Norfolk, Blenheim Palace, an Oxford college chapel, or Alnwick Castle.

In all it was a complicated skyline. In his *Oxford Dictionary of Architects,* James Stevens Curl offers thought-provoking definitions of the word 'Baroque'. Among them, he notes:

> '… theatrical and exuberant it employed convex-concave flowing curves in plan, elevation and section, optical illusions, interpenetrating ellipses in plans that were often extensions of the centralized type, complicated geometries and relationships between volumes of different shapes and sizes, emphatic overstatement, daring colour, exaggerated modelling, and symbolic rhetoric'.

Away from the eye-catcher that was the central bow, the east front ended to the North with a returned two-storey bow, decorated with festoons, and

Pl. 123 (facing page) George Skipper, Architect, 1905–09, (detail) North end return of East front, Sennowe Hall, Guist, Norfolk.

Pl. 124
George Skipper, Architect, 1905–09, (detail)
Recessed oval niche in gauged brickwork, Sennowe Hall, Guist, Norfolk.

Corinthian pilasters in an echo of the main bow. From there an arcade led to the carriage entrance, still to be discussed. However, on the bow, and on the back wall of the arcade was another phenomenon in the form of recessed oval niches in gauged brickwork. Of a quality unmatched anywhere, they had a use as places to stand lanterns along the arcade, but even empty they are attractive. George Skipper had provided drawings for the brickmakers and skilled bricklayers to follow: the resulting features are works of art.

The south front of Sennowe Hall was unaltered, apart from the removal of all the cast-iron framing of the verandah created by Decimus Burton: these were replaced with a roofed colonnade composed of Ionic columns. This continued around the next corner, to face West, where Skipper had made a large conservatory with fine windows and a marble floor, to be known as the Winter Garden. The rest of the west front was a kitchen courtyard, leading to the north front presenting a small two-storey wing, and a long arcade linking to the back of the carriage and stables block.

The interior of Sennowe Hall retained a Georgian air, with comfortable and elegant reception rooms. It is less obvious today which parts Skipper was responsible for, though there were marble columns on the landing, marble fireplaces, and three archways by the large wooden staircase, made of three flights of panelled joinery. Skipper's sketches show that he was happy to draw every detail of baluster and rail; no aspect would deter his self-reliance.

A room inside the south front served as the library, beneath a vaulted barrel ceiling, reminiscent of the late 16th century, and decorated with exquisite plaster moulding. This was just the sort of 'Jacobethan' feature Skipper might have attempted. A sketch of a vaulted barrel ceiling existed in Skipper's sketchbooks. The salon, a very large room made by combining two large rooms of the original house, had a vast fireplace in Neo-classical style, with marble columns to the ceiling and entablature in brown marble. Another fireplace in the dining room, again with marble columns, was noted for its scrolled pediment, carved with garlands and game birds.

Pl. 125
George Skipper, Architect, 1905–09, (detail)
Photograph of interior in 1909, showing staircase in background. Sennowe Hall, Guist, Norfolk.

The full extent of Skipper's interventions at Sennowe Park, and at other sites is not easy to gauge. Did he plan everything? The real answers to all the questions about Skipper's projects – the approved plans, elevation drawings, letters and lists, specifications and prices for work were in plan chests in the office in Norwich. For reasons to be explained in a later chapter, these did not survive.

As recounted earlier, Bert Cook came home in 1907 from his circumnavigation. Apparently pleased (certainly not displeased) with all works in progress, Bert confronted the architect with the question, 'Where's my ballroom?'

Was that on the list?

1. A pair of lodge houses.
2. A second pair of lodge houses.
3. Sennowe Hall.
4. New terraces and gardens.
5. Stable and carriage block.
6. Belfry tower.
7. Lake and Boathouse.
8. Bridge.

There had been no mention of a ballroom. The remedy, we are told, was the immediate construction of an iron-framed, de-luxe conservatory, or orangery, with a bowed glass roof. Skipper added a marble floor and solid fuel heating. It would serve as a ballroom. At the front of the Winter Garden, as it would become known, Skipper designed a pedimented doorway with its head

Pl. 126
George Skipper,
Architect, 1905–09,
(detail)
The Winter Garden
Sennowe Hall,
Guist, Norfolk.

Pl. 127 *(facing page)*
George Skipper,
Architect, 1905–09,
(detail)
Interior of the Winter Garden,
Sennowe Hall,
Guist, Norfolk.

and entablature supported by Ionic columns. Double bays on either side conformed to the design with two more columns and arch framed windows. Two more urns sat behind the single pediment.

In this atmosphere of marble surfaces and streams of light and shade, a central well and a small fountain was sunk. Around it, a circle of green marble columns with a cornice and an open roof formed a delightful surround to the fountain. At the centre, standing on a tall plinth was a statue, a small bronze female figure by H.C Fehr, titled 'Spirit of the Waves', first exhibited in 1903. Hearing of more marble columns, it will be obvious to readers that the supply of Brindley's marbles, whether intended for Westminster Cathedral, or not, was not exhausted.

From Bert Cook's time, Sennowe Park accommodated a variety of animal sculptures, from heraldic lions, cats and eagles at the gatehouses and garden terraces, to the figures on the roof, and marble dogs on the fireplaces. There was also a larger than life-size stone lion on a large plinth in the S-W of the park, inscribed, 'I was erected 1909 by T.A. Cook Esq., to guard Sennowe Hall'. These works cannot be attributed with complete certainty.

There was, however, a sculptor on the premises, in the person of Henry Charles Fehr. The very fact that he was at Sennowe, just after his sculpture had been placed inside the Marble Hall of the Norwich Union office, proved that Skipper's team of associated experts and artisans went from one site to the other. Fehr had attended the RA schools and 'won every prize there was to be won'. Subsequently he trained under Thomas Brock, and gained a reputation based on sensual ideal works, city-centre statues of great men, and architectural sculpture. Within a few years he would make sculptures for eleven First World War memorials, among which was the near-erotic figure of 'Peace' in Leeds, suffused with meaning, and glowering with dark emotion.

Fehr's allegorical statues of 'Morn' and 'Evening' at Sennowe were to be found on the south front colonnade. There were other figurative works by him, including particular pets and creatures carved on fire surrounds and, it is suggested, some of the heraldic emblems mentioned earlier.

Regarding the garden terraces, it must have been immensely exciting for George Skipper to be entrusted with the gardens, which he established in a

Pl. 128
The sculptor,
Henry Charles Fehr,
1867–1940,

formal manner. To the South of the house, overlooking the falling slope towards the river, Skipper envisaged an Edwardian garden, comprising an upper terrace and lower terrace confined by a substantial brick retaining wall, with bastions, balustrade and quoins.

At a halfway point, marked by stone staircases, and a balustrade with a picturesque three-arched *loggia* underneath, the terrace drops to a lower level. Aligned with this division, the lateral North-South enclosing walls on either side were enlivened by tall open-sided rotundas. Described by Pevsner as pavilions, and by others as temples, they were formed with Tuscan order columns and a domed roof, and surmounted by stone eagles. Adjacent staircases allowed persons to exit to the sloping parkland. Still on the terraces, Skipper positioned four larger urns on bases, at the corners of an invisible square on the flat lawn. There was a degree of geomancy to the arrangement, for it was made on a plan.

The urns, incidentally, were large, and not the same as those on the roof of the hall. All of them were made in the same way as the numerous stone urns at concurrent projects in Norwich, at Surrey House and St Giles House. In fact there had been a plethora of urns, deriving from George Skipper's own designs, shown in sketches in his notebooks. The urns, in total approximately fifty or sixty of them, were cut from Portland Stone by Mr Potter's masons with their electrically powered machines, before hand carved details of festoons and ribbons were added. The quantity of 20C carved stone urns, amphorae and gigantic basins in the garden were another Skipper phenomenon.

Some of the terraced area was planted with roses, shrubs, laurels, and a few small yew trees, but mostly the terraces were lawn, which 'set off' the south-facing prospect of the house behind, with its arcade and Winter Garden practically part of the terraces.

In describing Skipper's works for T.A Cook, the current owner of Sennowe Park remarked:

> 'Skipper added an elegant stable block to house Bert's carriage horses and no expense was spared. The tiling in the stables is as extravagant as a Turkish bath and there were more radiators there than in the house. He could also not resist the indulgence of an enormous and elegant tower for the water supply. It was built in the style of an Italian campanile, and dominates views of Sennowe from all around. It houses a belfry, which chimes the quarter hours night and day'.
>
> Charles Temple-Richards, *The English Home UK*, 30-6-2019:
> 'The Guardians of Sennowe Park'.

Pl. 129
George Skipper, Architect, 1905–09, Pavilion, Sennowe Park, Guist, Norfolk.

Pl. 130 *(facing page)*
George Skipper, Architect, 1905–09, Entrance to stable / carriage yard, Sennowe Hall, Guist, Norfolk.

The magnificent stables and carriage courtyard was entered by an arch at the end of the east front, which a visitor would see even before arriving at the house. Needless to say, with Bert's interest in four-in-hand, the equine accommodation was as good as it got. The walls were faced in sea-green and cream glazed Doulton tiles. The ground-plan was not exceptional in England,

Pl. 131
George Skipper, Architect, 1905–09, Staff quarters in carriage yard, Sennowe Hall, Guist, Norfolk.

because a good many other grand houses, for instance Chatsworth, Wentworth Woodhouse, Hackwood House, or Ragley Hall, had carriage yards and stable blocks, invariably four-sided on plan and approached by an arch. The difference at Sennowe was that the courtyard for horses and carriages was built in the 20th century, after the moment motorcars arrived, though the client had a garage built as well.

The entrance to the carriage and stable block was ornate. Centred on the broad arch that ran twenty-five feet as a tunnel towards the rectangular quadrangle inside, it projected five or six feet in front of the building range. The entrance was framed by a pair of Tuscan Doric columns, imitated further outwards by pilasters that framed flat arches around the recessed windows. These side entrances had added gravity with rusticated stonework, quoins, large keystones and voussoirs.

The central arch had a double keystone that reached to the cornice where two stone dogs, probably carved by Fehr, sat on guard. Held between quoins and dark stone consoles, the wall's brick courses were channelled to imitate the rusticated stonework, and rose to stone festoons surrounding an oculus. Still higher, above another cornice was a pediment forming the gable end of the attic storey. The tympanum contained a blank shield and palm leaves, decoration also carved on the Norwich Union building. Behind this, and astride the ridge was a small copper-covered clock tower, topped by a domed lantern.

Walking through the arch and turning about, one saw the inside of the entrance. It was almost exactly the same as the outer face. On the other side of the courtyard was a house with an entrance behind an open colonnade of Doric columns. It had an upper storey, and above this a full-width tympanum, containing a central cartouche, surrounded by the now familiar arrangement of festoons and garlands. On the north side of the carriage-yard were the centrally heated and extravagantly tiled stables, referred to earlier, comprising eleven loose boxes under a pitched slate roof. The carriages, originally twelve in number, were kept in open-lots on the south side.

Set in a brick wall in the courtyard was a stone drinking fountain, where water once flowed from a bronze lion's head beneath an oyster shell in an arched niche. It had a fluted circular basin and a stone surround that was relief-carved with swags and bows. (For afficianados of old drinking fountains, Skipper's design, carved either by Potter's men, or Brindley's Italians, is a delight).

Looking at Sennowe Hall's East front from certain angles it appeared as if the end of the building had a turret, though this was an illusion, because the freestanding tower was behind the stable block, separated by about fifty yards. Referred to as a clock tower, it did not have clock face, or dial, and the passing of time is noted by a bell. As

Pl. 132
George Skipper, Architect, 1905–09, Drinking fountain in carriage yard, Sennowe Hall, Guist, Norfolk.

Pl. 133
George Skipper,
Architect, 1905–09,
The Clock tower
(actually a
bell tower),
Sennowe Hall,
Guist, Norfolk.

well as being a belfry, it also contained a slender tank of water for maintaining water pressure in the Hall.

The tower is instantly recognisable as a work by Skipper and, though not identical, readers will be reminded of his first tower for Mr W. Clark in Somerset. The second tower, for Mr Cook in Norfolk, had a few 'extras' and has been awarded an Historic England Grade II★ Listing. As befitted the differing outlooks of the two clients, the Sennowe Park tower was far more ornate than the one in Somerset. Both were about 60 ft tall with weather-vanes adding to their height.

Sennowe's tower was built of brick and dressed stone. It had a rectangular floor plan with a front and back door. Three-storeys of brickwork were pierced only by windows with stone balconies, and a further three narrow windows, one above another, up to the fourth floor level. The bricks gave way to a few courses of dressed stonework with another three narrow windows facing North and South, (only two on East and West sides).

Above this the cornice projected, creating a square platform, or balcony, around the eight-sided, arcaded belfry. Adding a blue-green hue, it was capped by a conical copper roof with an iron weathervane. Also on the balcony, at each corner, were stone pedestals mounted by obeliscal spikes with ball finials, ornamental devices from Elizabethan times. It was a complex arrangement, described as Italianate, though it appeared 'very Skipper' and quite English. The tower was surrounded by plantations of trees that have matured and partly hidden the view of the tower, diminishing its impact on the landscape. The bell itself is in good order, striking four times an hour.

The lake in Sennowe Park was situated on the other side of the field below the south terraces, and on the north side of the river Wensum, which feeds the lake. It was about seven acres, calculated as the work of 100 navvies working non-stop for two years (or 200 men in half the time). The worksite could be accessed either by the river, rail, or by roads from the hamlet of Broom Green, coming from North Elmham and Dereham. The navvies, tough men who were used to canal and tunnel work, were accommodated locally in combination barns and farm buildings, or ferried in by train. The Great Eastern Railway line from Dereham to Fakenham and Wells-next-the-Sea ran through the Sennowe Park estate, with nearby stations at Ryburgh and County School.

Pl. 134
George Skipper, Architect, 1905–09, The boathouse, Sennowe Park, Guist, Norfolk.

It would have been logical for much of the excavated soil to have been carted up towards the house to make the level terraces on the slope. If George is to be credited for supplying a lake, it would doubtless have been one of his clerks who negotiated with the navvies' foremen. Pleasantly irregular with two or three islands, the lake was intended as a duckshoot, rather than a place for recreation. Skipper supplied the design for a large timber-framed boathouse with red-pantiled roof, upstairs rooms, and a lunette window. Renovated in 1960, it was built at the water's edge to the South of the lake's eastern end. Reached by an outside staircase, it had a covered balcony on wooden stilts overlooking the lake on three sides. A tall brick chimneystack of the sort Skipper favoured emerged from the roof.

It may come as a surprise for readers, but George aspired to be a poet. Among several poems he wrote, there was one inspired by the joys of spring, which he dashed off after a day at Sennowe. (Later on he added self-deprecating comments beneath and around the sonnet, jibing at his own romanticism).

Springtime
(Written on returning from Sennowe)

Where pure white blossom of blackthorns may
With purple trees in background lay.
And birds' clear notes melodious fill
The fragrant air of fair April.
When sprouting buds of tender green
Midst grey-brown branches, here unseen,
On which as yet no leaves have shown
Beneath bright grass just freshly grown.
A pale blue sky: a gentle breeze
Brings doves' soft coos from thicket trees,
And lambkins' bleat from rounding hill
And noise of water in the rill.
These woodland sights, sweet nature's sounds
The spring time yields – the earth abounds
With pure delights – Life's hidden glow
Afresh invests all things below.

GJS. 23 April 1907

All the building at the hall and the outworks lasted for some years, and were not announced in *The Builder* until 22 September 1911. One of the last on the list of Skipper's works at Sennowe Park had been the bridge. Built on a straight section of the Norwich Drive, about a third of a mile from the gates and lodges on the Norwich road, it was sited at a point where another trackway and watercourse crossed, and this was sunk, so that it passed under the bridge.

It would be easy not to notice the bridge, even when passing over it. It was flat and at least 45 ft wide and 80 ft long. Standing on the drive you would see on either side a balustrade between a pair of square-section pillars with ball finials and carvings of coronals and lions' heads. In truth the bridge was unnecessary, and could be viewed as a sort of folly, a costly ornamental structure with an excuse for a purpose. The only possible advantage could have been that when Bert was tearing up the driveway with four spirited coach-horses and a light open carriage, there would be no dip in the landscape. The drive was where he exercised his four-in-hand skills. He wanted it long, straight, smooth, and wide.

The bridge was an afterthought, built in 1909 or 1910, when Bert had returned from his world tour. It was elaborate, made of brick and dressed and rusticated stonework, and it featured three large arches with huge double keystones. The vaults passing underneath the bridge were constructed with concrete. The architectural style was English Baroque, in keeping with the Sennowe Hall's magnificent new stables and carriage house. Historic England, recognizing the architectural quality, added the bridge as a separate item to the list of protected buildings at Sennowe Park.

David Jolley's text accompanying the *George Skipper – Architect Exuberant* exhibition at Norwich School of Art in 1975, and reprinted in Edward

Pl. 135
George Skipper, Architect, 1909, Bridge on the Norwich Drive, Sennowe Park Guist, Norfolk.

Skipper's *Celebrating Skipper 100* in 1980, assessed the significance of Sennowe Hall and Park for the architect:

Pl. 136 George Skipper, Architect, 1909, Arch and balustrade of bridge on the Norwich Drive, Sennowe Park Guist, Norfolk.

'The client's trust in his architect was splendidly repaid … … It was not only Skipper's most extensive undertaking, it virtually brings to a close the most significant period of his output: for with the First World War all but essential building programs were halted, and thereafter – with scarcely an exception – the opulent commissions, which brought out his qualities so well, were not to be obtained. And in a very special sense, Sennowe is particularly moving, for it offered the romantic and exuberant in Skipper's nature at long last unrestrained freedom of expression. Sennowe, relaxed and expensive, and the Norwich Union Office, compact and tightly designed, are twin peaks in his architecture'.

I imagine George Skipper driving the motorcar away from the hall at this time, crossing his bridge and reflecting on the completion of everything at Sennowe, and all that had happened in the Edwardian decade. He had been phenomenally busy during those years.

CHAPTER SIX

1910—1919

George Skipper's time up at Sennowe Park, engaging with interesting and cultivated artists and artisans, while constructing a home with urns and pavilions for a wealthy client, was detached from what was happening elsewhere. Beyond the graceful gateways, the world streamed by. By this time there were over 100,000 motorcars in Britain.

King Edward died in May 1910, and was succeeded by George V, a relative youngster of forty-five years old, who would reign for another twenty-five. A popular monarch in difficult times, he was more modest in his outlook than his father. There was a General Election in 1910, won by Herbert Asquith's Liberal Party. Within months there were workers' strikes.

It is hard to ascertain what was going on with Skipper, because the flow of work slowed up. This may have been his choice, especially after the unbelievable pressure of so much work in the previous fifteen years. The architect was re-arranging his office. The biggest change was that the Skipper brothers' working partnership came to an end by agreement in 1911.

Faith Shaw, the first researcher (1971) in what I refer to as 'Skipper Studies', offered this later insight (guided by Edward Skipper) into the somewhat one-sided relationship:

> 'F.W' as he is known from plan signatures had not had the hard competition experience of his brother, nor was he trained at all as an architect. It seems likely that much of his work consisted of meeting and entertaining clients and finalizing structural details on the design plans, and he himself has said that sometimes he was only an office boy.

The reason for Frederick's departure was not what Edward Skipper described as their 'imcompatible temperaments'. In fact Frederick wanted to leave his brother's practice to enter a Surveyor's partnership with his eldest son, Reginald Skipper (1891–1983). This was not possible, as they were not Chartered Surveyors, though Reginald qualified later. Fred would partner his second son, the architect Eric Hayward Skipper FRIBA (1897–1982).

George's own son, Theo Skipper, was sixteen years old in 1910 and considering medical school and the dentistry profession. According to the 1911 census, Theo and his father were then living at 39 Unthank Road, their third change of address, all in the same road, within five years. Reasonably tall, dark haired and with a pleasant countenance, Theo seems to have been a well-adjusted young man, despite losing his mother. He had not been forced to take up with the Brethren, though he was doubtless acquainted with their practices and had, through his father, met a number of them.

One evening in September 1911, Theo came home and chatted with his father. He mentioned that while dining with the parents of a friend of his, he had been introduced to a young widow, a schoolteacher from Wales. Theo was very impressed and moved by her story, and by her beautiful singing voice, hinting that one day he would like to marry someone of that sort. George was attentive to what Theo was saying because a few minutes earlier he had been sitting with his copy of the *Norwich Mercury*, (16/9/1911) and had read a report on what had happened, only two weeks earlier, to the husband of this young lady.

Her name was Elizabeth Alice Charter (née Roberts), the widow of James Ord Charter. She was always known as Alice, and James, who was known as Ord, had been her teacher in the John Bright County School in Llandudno, Caernarvonshire. They had married in about 1907 and had a child, Ralph Charter, born in 1909. Mother and son were now staying with Ord's grieving parents, Mr and Mrs Charter, in Newmarket Road, Norwich.

The circumstances of James Ord Charter's death, along with his cousin, in a boating accident in the Dee estuary, were reported in the newspaper. Ord had gone with his parents to visit his married sister, who lived at Heswall in Cheshire. This is on the South side of the Wirral, overlooking the river Dee and the shoreline of Wales, about three miles away. The Dee estuary could be a difficult stretch of water, with an undertow, sandbanks, and the chance of heavy weather blown in from the open sea.

Also staying with the family was a student, Mr Stephen, who went out into the estuary in a rowing boat, accompanied by two children on Friday 1st September. He crossed over to the Welsh shore, but had blistered his hands, and decided to leave the boat on the shore and return to Heswall by train. In order to retrieve the boat, Ord Charter's father and Stephen rowed across the estuary, but conditions were bad, so they turned back. The next day Mr and Mrs Charter and Stephen returned to Norwich, leaving Ord and his cousin (by marriagre), Frank Todhunter, to deal with the missing dinghy. Both men were strong and capable with boats.

That evening Ord and Frank set off from Bagillt, Flintshire, heading for Heswall, Cheshire, in the abandoned rowing boat, though fishermen had advised against it. They might have tried to turn back for the Welsh shore, because conditions became impossible. Both men drowned. A gale had blown due North at 11.30pm when they were at sea, and there was a nineteen foot tide at 12.15am.

James Ord Charter's body was found by a fisherman and his son, at a location eight miles North of the Welsh coast. The empty boat drifted ashore at Prestatyn four days later. Further reports in *The Flintshire Observer* of 29/9/1911 bore the headline TRAGEDY OF THE DEE and related that both men had been cautioned by a collier on the Cheshire shoreline before they set out. The witness said that he had told Ord and Todhunter that they would not be able to turn back from the Welsh shore. For both families it was a terrible loss.

A little later in Norwich, Theo met Alice Charter again, and invited her to Unthank Road, where she met his father. The course of this meeting, and subsequent ones, will have to be imagined. Alice was conversant about buildings: her father, by then deceased, had been a builder and stonemason in Llandudno. She had been brought up by her mother, Sarah Ann Roberts, a strict Methodist and a member of the Women's Temperance Society. Mrs Roberts managed her husband's building firm, so Alice had things in common with Theo and his father.

The outcome of these meetings was a surprise to some because, after a year or so, George Skipper and Alice became engaged. There was an age difference of thirty years, but this was not an obstacle. In fact Alice's deceased husband had been much older than her, and George's first two marriages had been to women older than him.

George and Alice married in Conway, Wales, in 1913. It was to be a happy marriage, although its course was doubtless affected by the coming war. Many years later Alice was asked why she had married George, and she had replied, "For security". But this is not to say that security was the be all and end all. Once married, George and Alice, with her son Ralph Charter, only four years old, moved back to Skipper's own house, 'Kingsley Villa' at 50 Mill Hill Road, which had been rented in the interim. It was a reasonably large and comfortable home for the couple and generations to come.

Looking after her son, Ralph, Alice could count on the support of Ralph's grandparents, Mr and Mrs Charter, in Newmarket Road. There were also other Skippers in the vicinity, including George's stepmother, Caroline, now in her eighties. George's youngest brother, John Skipper, had died in Dereham in 1901 at the age of thirty-eight. If George was in contact with his second-youngest brother, Richard Skipper (1861–1957), it was not recorded. Nor are there signs that he had much to do with his eldest brother, Robert, who had married Agnes Peacock in 1891. They had two children, Evelyn Mary Skipper, and Gilbert Wilemer Skipper, who was roughly the same age as Theo and also intending to become a dentist.

At the time of his marriage in 1913, George Skipper was actually quite rich, as a result of relentless work over the previous twenty years. The residue of fees paid in Somerset, Cromer and Norwich had aggregated to a sum of money, which if invested, could provide an income.

Regarding investments, there was a shark in the waters. This was Arthur Burr, a speculator convinced (and convincing) of the untold wealth of the Kent coalfields. Coal had been discovered in East Kent many years earlier, but Burr formed the Kent Coal Company in 1896, with a view to exploiting what he claimed was a vast resource. Shakespeare Pit at Dover was the first to be dug, but water was found at 366 ft. Test borings were made as the search for coal seams moved around East Kent. Five more pits were opened, though none of the collieries produced commercial quantities of coal until 1912.

Burr tried to keep up an air of optimism for the benefit of prospective buyers of shares, but started a process familiar to the modern-day world of business. He formed over twenty new companies that would operate only one part of the mining process, whereby each of his companies would be working for his other businesses. He moved money around between his companies, and to sustain the constant loss of money, he sold shares, but the more shares he sold, the lower their value became. Burr himself had been honoured at Dover Castle in 1913 by a dinner, with a speech by Sir Arthur Conan Doyle who predicted that Dover would grow to be one Britain's greatest cities. Only a year later Burr was called a confidence trickster. Brought to court for fraud and financial irregularity, the judge called him "a dangerous rogue". Burr was bankrupted and divested of the companies. He died five years later, with numerous court cases against him still in process.

How much money George Skipper had invested in the Kent Coal Company will never be known. Apparently he had also bought shares in a French vinyard and Brazilian railway stock, both of which declined in value during the 1914–1918 period. It would seem that Skipper's personal losses made the difference between being comfortable, or not; between possibly retiring from his practice, or not. It was a hard blow. Hundreds of Kent Coal Company shareholders had to write-off their losses, or even go bankrupt themselves, but it was not the end of the story for the architect.

Burr's activities had brought other industrial ventures to Kent. The Chislet Colliery, near Canterbury, had been bought by the Anglo-Westphalian Coal Syndicate, managed by a German citizen. Since this was May 1914, it was only a matter of time before the manager was interned for the duration of the First World War. When the war ended, the Chislet Colliery Company needed three hundred houses for its miners, who had come from Wales. Skipper would design the houses in a newly created village. However, this would be in the future – George and Alice were still to endure the war and all its implications. However, they had significantly less money than if the architect had never heard of Arthur Burr and the Kent Coal Company in the first place.

Everything seemed held in suspense for the 1914–1919 duration, notably the Suffragette Movement, seeking to extend the franchise to women. Another ongoing project on the side of fairness was the gradual move towards municipal housing and, after the war, social housing with the advent of council houses.

The Housing and Town Planning Act of 1909 prohibited the construction of the old Victorian 'back-to-back' terraces, and authorized local councils to prepare schemes for building streets and houses. The law established town planning, previously a concept, and encouraged practitioners. The Local Government Board would employ a Town Planning Inspector, and in November 1913 an association of Town Planners was established. This was the Town Planning Institute. Among its aims was 'the scientific and artistic' development of towns and cities. George Skipper applied to join the institute, and before long was adding the initials MTPI after his name as well as FRIBA. He was positively enthusiastic about town planning, and I believe his motorcar had something to do with it. He could see the increasing traffic in the narrow streets and knew that something would have to be done. He planned new routes that he would later suggest to Norwich City Council.

There was increased contact with the City Council. Skipper had for many years been establishing groups of houses and terraces, for instance a terrace of houses in Ella Road in Norwich in 1887, though these were for private builders and developers. However, his 1904 project in Recreation Road had involved the City Council. In the future, as well as planning new roads, the local authorities would buy Skipper's designs for new houses, to be built at a fixed price, for renting to families and, in due course, as 'homes for heroes'.

Skipper's last private commission before the war was for Colin McLean, at a property known as 'The Heath' in Dereham. The client was a game farmer, and subsequently president of the Norfolk Naturalists Society. Shortly afterwards, McLean enlisted and left for France, where he was seriously wounded in 1916. The commission was for Skipper to supply designs for a

Pl. 137
George Skipper, Architect, 1913, Front elevation drawing for 'The Heath', East Dereham. Image: Norfolk Record Office.

new wing that would contain a dining room and servants' quarters. A transfer copy of Skipper's design drawing for MacLean is held in the Norfolk Record Office and reproduced here. 'The Heath' was eventually demolished and its large grounds developed into a housing estate, served by two new roads, Heath Road, and Colin McLean Road. After work at 'The Heath' there was no work commissioned, or conducted, for the next five years, apart from alterations to Number 7 Pottergate, Norwich, where the architect added a timber-framed east gable.

The Great War began and its effect on people's lives was absolute. There is no record of how George and Alice lived through these years, where hardship and dismay dominated almost every facet of existence.

George's brother Frederick lived nearby at 15 Ipswich Road. He too suffered the loss of his wife, Harriet Amy Skipper. Within months he married a much younger wife, Catherine Julier, from Norwich. Frederick's son, Eric Hayward Skipper, the architect, became an Able Seaman in the Royal Navy, serving for the duration of the war.

Interestingly, the *Architectural Association Journal* carried the banner:

JOIN THE ARMY AT ONCE.
If you are not free to do this, or are otherwise incapacitated,
then JOIN THE VOLUNTEERS.
The 4th BATTALION "ARCHITECTS"
CENTRAL LONDON REGIMENT should be your corps.

'Rouse ye, ye builders! Cannot you hear the crumbling and cracking of the doomed walls of nations? Fling from you till a more fitting time your T-square and the tools of your trade, pick up the spade of the sapper, learn to pontoon the flowing river for the advancing hosts of your brothers-in-arms; by such engineering will you ensure the stability of the walls of our Empire'.

Pl. 138 *(facing page)* Family portrait, c.1916: George Skipper, Theo Skipper, Alice Skipper and her son, Ralph Charter.

George's son, Theo Skipper, volunteered to join the Royal Army Medical Corps in 1914. He served with the RAMC for the full length of the war, firstly as a Private (No. 26936) and later as a Sergeant (No.2060). Theo's enlistment was later to become crucially significant for his father.

Theo's duties were those of a non-combatant. The RAMC, founded in 1898, provided the army with nursing, ambulances, surgeons, field hospitals, and arrangements for evacuating the injured soldiers. They were assisted by the Red Cross, St John's Ambulance, Voluntary Aid Detachments and innumerable charitable and private associations.

When it became obvious that the war would not be over by Christmas, the War Office shifted from raising an army of volunteers to compulsory conscription in 1916. This presented a problem for a number of religious groups, to include Methodists and even some Anglicans, but principally for the Christadelphians, Quakers, and Jehovah's Witnesses and, of course, the

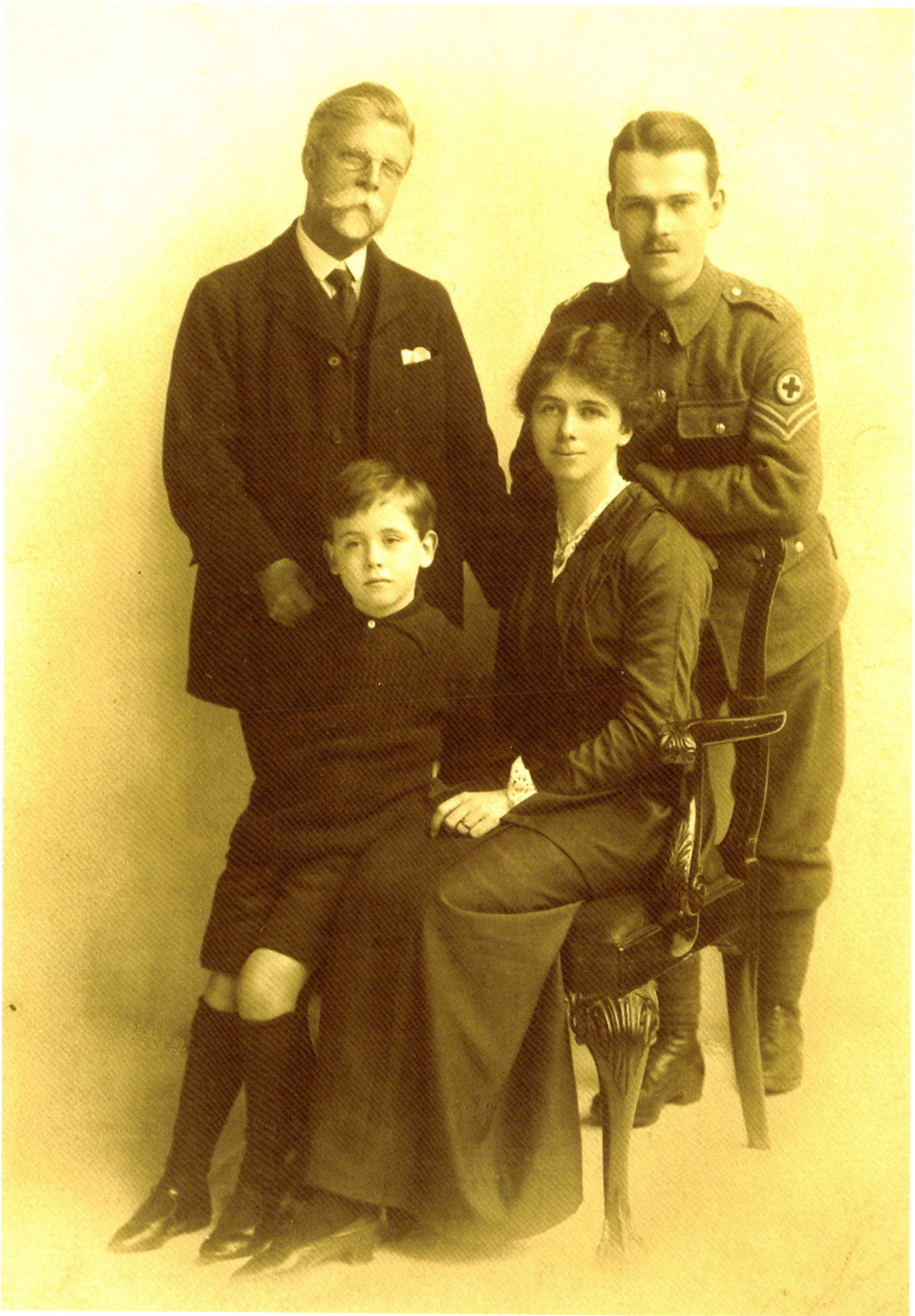

Brethren. As it is well known, the Conscientious Objectors, 'C.Os', or 'conchies' were dealt with very sternly, not only by the army authorities, and their fellow soldiers, but by the British public, encouraged to see the objectors as cowards with pariah status.

The Military Service Act of January 1916 conscripted all single men aged between 18 and 41. A second Act in May 1916 extended this to apply to married men as well. Conscripted men who were unwilling were allowed to appeal to Military Service Tribunals, with the object of receiving a certificate of exemption. In Norwich the tribunal consisted of ten men chosen by Norwich City Council. The tribunal's decisions, and the reasons for them, were published in the *Eastern Daily Press*. Those who defied conscription could, in some cases, be imprisoned.

A number of reasons to be exempted were given, chiefly that an applicant was indispensable in his work place, or that his job was vital for the war effort. Since Norwich was home to many non-conformists, there were also several Conscientious Objectors who appealed on religious grounds. Generally these men were conscripted in non-combative roles.

In a reversal of popular attitudes, there were arguments among the Bible reading Brethren. At the prayer meetings that Skipper attended, other Brethren questioned him for allowing his son to go to the battlefields. Was he contradicting the word of God? Or was George to turn his back on his own son, who was struggling in gore and mud across the channel? Here was a deep crisis of conscience.

Needless to say, it had been a misguided attack on Skipper. For a start, Theo was twenty years old, and was not one of the Brethren. More to the point was the one-sided interpretation and condemnation. The architect, much less busy than usual, felt aggrieved and upset, and began to apply his intellect and knowledge of the scriptures.

George studied the Old Testament pages and took notes. He recorded each instance of the use of the word 'sword', and in the following year issued a private edition that was published and printed by Jarrolds.

Titled, *The Sword: Its Authority in Scripture*, the book appeared to be without an author, but there was an elaborate triangular colophon on what should have been the title page. Almost unreadable under a graphic knot of entwined twigs and leaves, the initials 'GJS' were just visible. The Bible is notoriously open to interpretation, but Skipper had found a way to gainsay the unkind voices at the Meeting House. The Brethren had wished to present

Pl. 139
Sergeant Theo Skipper, RAMC, c.1916

a united front in front of the tribunals and they certainly saw Skipper's publication of *The Sword* as opposition. As was so often the case in Brethren history, there would be a parting of the ways.

Betty Skipper, George's daughter-in-law, speaking in 2019, said that he was "thrown out" of the Brethren, though one suspects the decision was partly George Skipper's. Despite his membership of forty-one years, his blood was up. He felt he was in the right, backed up by the biblical references, and his pride and loyalty to Theo, let alone a sense of patriotism in Britain's time of need. What we do not know is whether George was glad to have parted

Pl. 140
George Skipper,
Title page of book,
The Sword,
1917.

THE SWORD
Its Authority in Scripture

"The Lord . . . is the *sword* of thy excellency."—DEUT. xxxiii. 29.
"I will . . . put *My sword* in his hand."—EZEK. XXX. 24.
"Gird *Thy sword* upon Thy thigh, O most mighty.—Ps. xlv. 3.

JARROLDS
PUBLISHERS (LONDON)
LIMITED

company with the Brethren, or not. It would certainly have made his life easier to be free of them.

For clarification, Betty Skipper added, "Well he certainly didn't go to meetings after he was thrown out". George had parted company with the congregation, but had not lost interest in God, or in the Bible. In future there would be Bible reading in the Skipper's family home, but without Brethren attending.

Aside of this drama, for George Skipper, as for most people, the changes to ordinary life during the war years were fundamental. There were no architectural commissions, no need for new buildings, or anything that took away from the war effort. Most of his staff volunteered, or were conscripted. There were shortages at home, including petrol for his motorcar, which was garaged; he would walk to his office.

Norwich's streets were alive with bustling workers, very many of whom were occupied in the war effort, whether making boots or biplanes. Within a couple of years food rationing was introduced. Once or twice Prisoners of War were seen under guard in the Market Place; Zeppelins flew over Norfolk and bombed coastal towns; the county's hospitals were expanded to accommodate wounded servicemen – these are glimpses of five extraordinary years in Norfolk.

In 1917, shortly after the publication of *The Sword*, George Skipper received a small commission to design a stained glass memorial window in St Augustine's church. The request came from Harry and Alice Pert of Pitt Street in Norwich, who wished to honour their son, Lance Corporal Leonard Harry Pert of the 8th Battalion, Rifle Brigade, killed at the Battle of Arras on 3 May 1917.

Following Skipper's design, the window was made by the esteemed firm of Morris & Co in London, and installed in the south nave aisle of St Augustine's in 1918. Depicting the Virgin Mary and Mary Magdalene as they confront an angel before Christ's sepulchre, the inscription stated, ' He is risen'.

The artist-architect's original drawing in colour, Pre-Raphaelite in style, is held in the RIBA collection. It features an abundance of May blossom on all sides, and included all the Lead cames. This must have been a preliminary design, since the actual window in St Augustine's church was somewhat different, with larger figures, brighter colours and none of the decorative blossom motifs.

What was there to do, during those wartime years, for an architect, unused to not working? George had his library of architectural classics; he wrote letters to Theo, and maintained the house and garden. He had owned a couple of small dogs when Theo was growing up, and possibly had another at this time. By comparison with the grief and loss in many households, the domestic arrangements in Kingsley Villa were pleasant enough.

Then Alice announced that she was pregnant and later, on 8 October 1918, gave birth to a boy, Edward John Goodwin Skipper. The Great War ended a month afterwards. Throughout Britain there were celebrations, homecomings, and hopes and resolutions.

George Skipper had more reasons to be cheerful. Theo had returned, unscathed. Discarding his uniform, he planned to continue with his studies, switching to dentistry and enrolling at one of London's Dental schools, possibly King's College School of Medicine and Dentistry.

There was talk of a new era. The Housing Act passed through Parliament in 1919 gave power to the local authorities to build council houses, referred to by Lloyd George as 'homes for heroes'. Norwich City Council was among the first to put the policy into effect, starting survey and groundwork for the Mile Cross estate in the same year. Here was work for architects and George, with his newly found inclination for town planning, was fully ready. In due course he would be one of four architects for the huge project.

Pl. 141
George Skipper, Architect, 1919, 'The Elms' estate, housing for Caley's chocolate factory, Norwich.

Shortly after the legislation Skipper was asked to supply designs for The Elms, a small estate off the Unthank Road, and not far from his home. The client was Messrs Caley & Son, the chocolate manufacturers at Chapelfield. The design was extended to include a Recreation Association building for employees, and later a pavilion used for sports and social occasions.

In order to give an idea of the working life of an architect, there follows a list of what Skipper might submit for a commission such as this. Ten large plan sheets are held in the National Archives (N/EN/24/150). Three of them, scaled one inch to 32 feet, were disapproved. Another of the same size shows the approved layout and sections for the first block of houses. Then there are elevation drawings of a second block, still dated 1919, and subsequent plans, elevations and sections for a third block, in 1920, all at one inch to eight feet scale.

This was social housing attached to the chocolate factory, rather than Norwich City Council. The blocks were small terraces of five dwellings, with one-and-a-half storeys and two bays each. The small houses display distinctive cross-gables and dormers beneath red tiled roofs, and are in good condition at the time of their centenary. The site is particularly well lit, and raised above Mill Hill Road, where George Skipper and his family lived. Following the successive exodus of Caley, Mackintosh, Rowntree and Nestlé from Norwich, the small estate is no longer connected to the chocolate factory.

The quantity of drawings required for 'The Elms' project prompt the question of whether the architect still had staff at his London Street office, which he had kept open, after a fashion, throughout the war. 'The Elms' estate work was not large by Skipper's standards, but it still required the work of surveyors and draftsmen. Some of his staff had returned from the war and taken up their former employment, and this included his surveyor, Henry Trueman.

Skipper was also occupied in 1919 with other works for rural councils (RDCs) in Norfolk. There were a series in the South-West of the county: those located at Garboldisham, Hopton (five miles S. of Garboldisham, actually in Suffolk) were built and survived until about 1987. A group of them survive in Blo Norton, their clay lump walls rendered over. Another group of the same dwellings, still in their original condition, were sited on a broad crescent in a field on the edge of East Harling. These were large double-dwellers, traditionally East Anglian in appearance, with pantile-clad roofs, dormers, and porches, with a long wooden drip mould running across the elevation. Apart from his designs, the key factors were materials, since the walls were made of clay lump, standing on a brick plinth, presumably with a foundation.

Country Life sent one of their writers, Randal Phillips, up to Norfolk to have a look at Skipper's use of clay lump. In a feature (9 September 1922) he began, 'It is not just a sentiment that attracts us to the old ways of building. It is recognition of the soundness of the work, and its possession of certain qualities that a mechanical age has lost'.

This return to a traditional building material was a reminder of the pre-war Arts and Crafts movement, but the reasons for using clay lump were economic. It was an exceptionally cheap, stable, immovable material for walls, but has been wrongly regarded as primitive, damp or mice-ridden. If made properly and kept dry, walls made of clay lump, which are blocks of moulded and compacted clay-mud, are faultless. The Bishop Bonner Museum in Dereham houses a mould for making clay lump blocks. It is about the size of a small beer crate.

The houses Skipper designed at 1–16 The Crescent, East Harling, were laid out with lots of space between the buildings, and trees that are now large and mature. The appearance of The Crescent equated to the 'Garden city' concept,

Pl. 142 *(facing page)* George Skipper, Architect, 1919, 'The Crescent' East Harling, Norfolk

(i) Similar elevation drawing by GJS in 1919.

(ii) Clay lump construction in 1919.

(iii) 2019 centenary photograph.

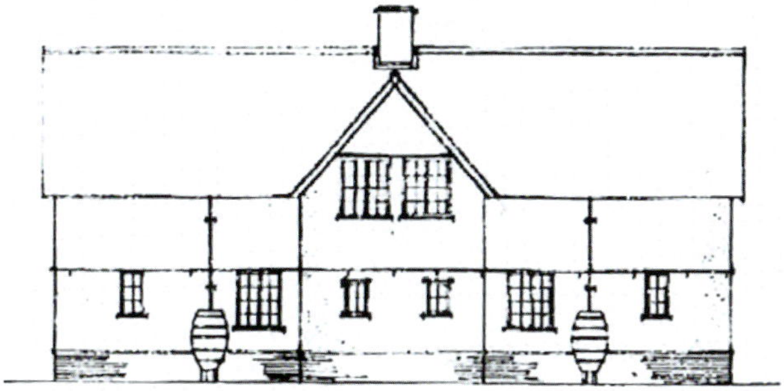

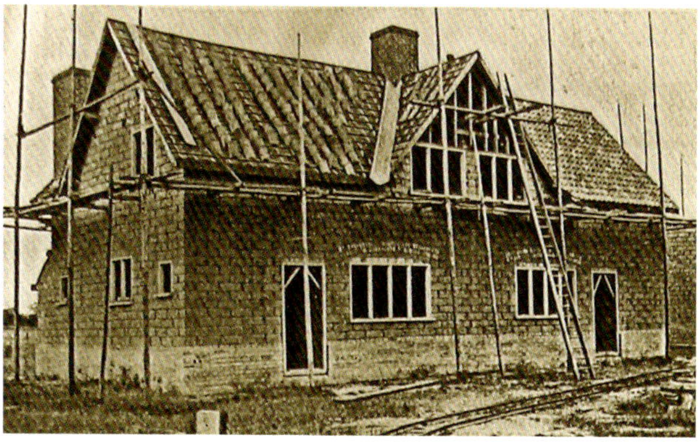

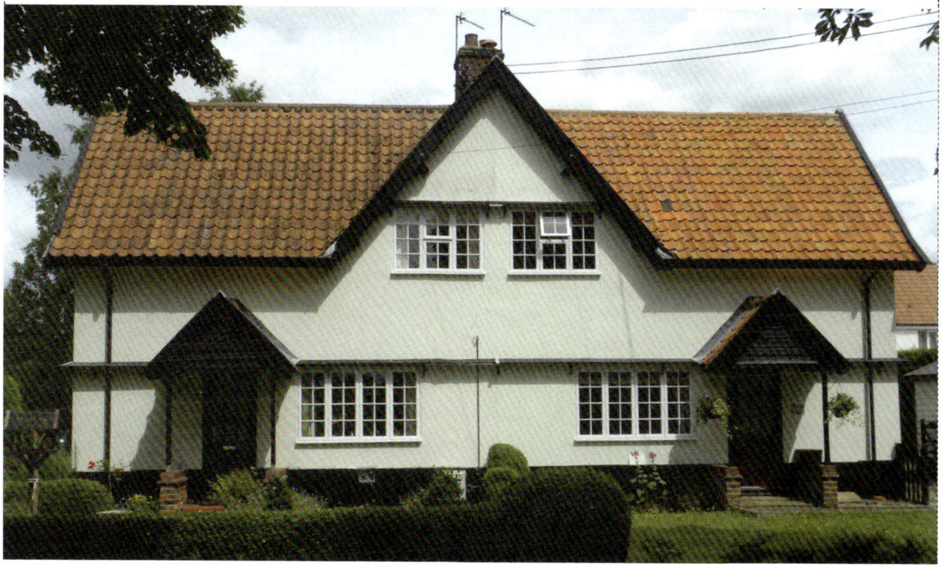

shown in parts of Letchworth, Hertfordshire, or Hampstead Garden suburb in London. More schemes were to follow in other parts of Norfolk. Skipper provided variations at different prices, and had ready-made plans for houses with a parlour, or without one. Blofield RDC, to the East of Norwich ordered four houses without parlours to be built in Reedham.

While in East Harling the architect had been invited to design a house in the village. The plan was delivered in February the following year to the client, a mysterious officer who Skipper referred to as 'Colonel M'. Without a name or a location there is nothing more to tell. For reasons that will be recounted, Skipper's proper records and plans did not survive, and the only references are abbreviations in his notebooks.

In some ways George Skipper was starting again after the First World War. His investments had been unfortunate – some would say unwise. Without much money, he intended to support and provide for his family. Like architects throughout Britain, he was looking at a changed landscape. The great country houses, maintained by servants, were to be a thing of the past. There would be other sorts of work. George, now aged sixty-three, would have to show his ingenuity again.

One category of commission that other architects responded to in 1919 were war memorials, not only uplifting or sombre edifices with panels of dead mens' names, but memorial hospitals, memorial town and village halls. Fundraising, memorial committee decisions, design and construction lasted for another decade. Some architects and sculptors made their reputation with memorials. The sculptor, Henry Fehr, who we remember from Surrey House and Sennowe Park, contributed work to eleven memorials in the next five years. One might have expected a man of George Skipper's outlook and experience to be involved in the memorial process, but he was not.

Chapter seven

1920—1929

George's family brought happiness to him. Firstly Theo, now aged twenty-six and starting his career in dentistry, announced that he had become engaged. His fiancée was Evelyn Madeleine Elizabeth Wright, known to all as Evie. Two years younger than Theo, she came from the S.W London and Surrey area, which was where the marriage took place in an Anglican church at the end of July 1920. Theo and Evie were compatible, and she fitted in with the Skipper family, travelling up from Surrey to see the family in Norwich often in years to come.

Pl. 143
Family portrait at Kingsley Villa, c.1920: *left to right* Edward Skipper (aged one), George Skipper, his wife Alice Skipper, and daughter-in-law, Evie Skipper.

George and Alice had their own delight when Alice again announced a birth to come in the spring of 1921. Happily this was a daughter, Margaret Elizabeth Skipper, born on 8 April 1921. After all the brothers, and George's Theo and Alice's Ralph, here was some balance. His two little children, Edward and Margaret, were further incentive for George Skipper to enact a sort of post-war second phase in his career.

Pls. 144 and 145
George Skipper,
Architect, 1922–26,
Houses for Norwich City Council,
Margaret Paston Avenue,
Mile Cross Estate,
Norwich.

After the First World War the architect had seen a way to continue his practice. If, as stated, his finances were weaker from investing in the East Kent coal mines, he would not be alone. Not just investors, but the nation at large experienced the bite of poverty. In one year, 1920, England's miners went on strike, Sylvia Pankhurst, campaigning for votes for women, was sent to prison, and in parliament the Government of Ireland Act was debated: these three issues dominated political and social life through most of the decade. Britain's exports dropped, unemployment increased and, for many families, the priorities were food and shelter. Skipper's initial way forward was attuned to the families in need, and the new houses to be built for them in Norfolk, and elsewhere.

For two years, following the 1919 Housing Act, a government grant was available to those regional councils that were ready. Norfolk's Rural District Councils (RDCs) could specify what they wanted, and George Skipper had designs available, classified as either 'Type A', or 'Type B', and various others up to 'Type 17' and maybe beyond.

Skipper's designs were taken up by the City Council and the RDCs. Construction at the smaller projects began immediately. Forehoe and Henstead RDC ordered a block of 'Type 9A' semi-detached houses for Browick Lane in Wymondham, and more in Poringland. Built in brick, with hipped pantiled roofs, porches, and a central chimney, these three-bedroomed houses were substantial and in no way sub-standard. A different scheme of 'Type 5B' housing was arranged for the Kerdiston scheme by Aylsham RDC. These were similar in appearance to the East Harling houses at The Crescent, and were also built from clay lump, later replaced by brickwork. They had render over the clay lump, and featured another traditional material, being thatched with Norfolk reed (since clad with pantiles). Another sale of one of Skipper's designs, this time 'Type 17', a block of three houses, went to Brundall and Strumpshaw RDC, to the East of Norwich.

By 1921 Norwich City Council had cleared land to the North of the city. Professor Adshead, the planning administrator of the large scheme at Mile Cross, selected four architects to provide suitable house plans. These were George Skipper, Stanley Wearing, Stanley Livock, and Skipper's father's former apprentice, Augustus Scott. The Mile Cross Estate was held up as an example of Town Planning, and the first houses were referred to as 'architects houses'. They demonstrated good design and were repeatedly shown to other architects, including those from other parts of Britain. The estate eventually covered over 160 acres and would house more than 10,000 people. Apart from the circular street plans around Civic Gardens and Suckling Avenue, the greater scheme was not finished for several years. It included a street of shops and amenities, and a branch library of notable architectural interest, though Skipper did not design this. After the 'first wave' of council house construction, he continued to offer his array of plans and details for another ten years, as we shall see.

Now that Skipper was designing smaller houses, he could be approached for ready-made designs. The Countess of Verulam purchased designs and plans

Pl. 146
George Skipper, Architect, 1922–26, Houses for Norwich City Council, Lubbock Close, Elizabeth Fry Road, Norwich.

in 1922 for a pair of cottages for her estate at Gorhambury Park, St Albans, Hertfordshire. These were low-cost single-storey versions of his 'Type 5Bs' with just a window and door to each dwelling, and a shared double-dormer in the attic, beneath a half-hipped tiled roof. A wooden drip-mould ran across the building above the doorways. The design drawing for the cottages is retained by RIBA (36292), who describe the building as Arts and Crafts in style, and provide a date twenty years earlier.

An interesting commission arrived in 1922 when the architect was approached by Wyman & Sons, printers and bookbinders. They were the biggest employers in Fakenham, which had a history of printing. Like every other expanding printworks, Wyman's had set up printing machines in a variety of sheds and factory buildings. Now they needed an office separated from the noisy machinery, a 'front of house' where they could conduct business with visiting clientele. The proposal was an office facing Whitehorse Street. Skipper's designs were approved and Wyman's office was built later, between 1924–1928.

Pl. 147
George Skipper, Architect, c.1925, Office for Wyman & Sons, Fakenham, Norfolk.

Photo: by courtesy of Fakenham Community Archive.

It was unusual, a small structure with big features that would lend Wyman's and the street a civic air. A cube-shaped building of two-storeys, its brick walls stood on a plinth of Portland Stone blocks, and its corners were prominently marked with alternating Portland and brick quoins. The strongest feature of all was the colossal inverted porch, also in white Portland, rising almost to the eaves. At the ground floor the porch contained a large doorway and above this a large arched window. Outside this was a small balcony and, as if Wyman's was a miniature town hall, a low balustrade supporting a large clock facing the street below.

Another comparison for Wyman's office was that of a Norman keep, the resemblance enhanced by small upper windows with stone architraves. Elevations to either side of the front were plain, with three large casements beneath white keystones at ground floor, and smaller windows above. The roof could not be seen, hidden behind a brick and Portland parapet designed with a hint of Art Deco. A final comparison would be Skipper's Norwich Union Insurance office in Cambridge, the only other of his buildings to feature an oversized and inverted stone portico.

After Wyman's office was built, there were speculative discussions between the directors and the architect: the subject was the provision of library buildings. After the First World War there were amendments to the Public Libraries Act, whereby the provision of the public library service was brought into the control of the county councils, throughout Britain. The discussion ran along the lines that hundreds of new branch libraries would need to be built, and that this could involve Britain's biggest book printers in some way. The diversity of these 1920s and 1930s libraries around the country would be innovative, and of interest to architectural historians. As far as is known, however, these talks between Skipper and Wyman's did not amount to an actual commission.

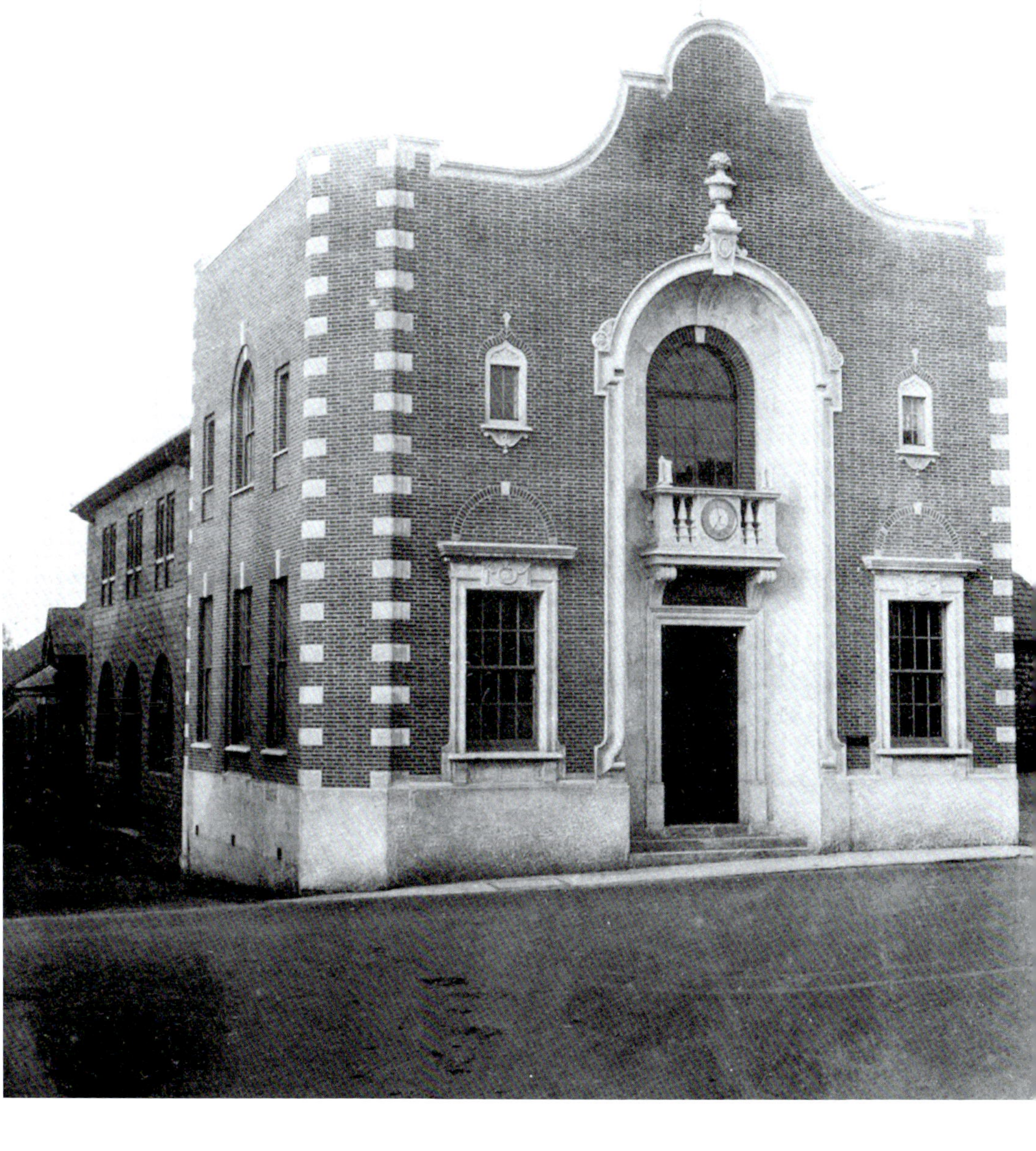

Pls. 147 and 148 Demolition of Wyman & Sons, Printers, (Cox & Wyman's) Fakenham.

1987 Photos: courtesy of Fakenham Community Archive.

Wyman's continued but, in common with other printers, had joined their business with another firm some distance away. Combining with a printer in Reading, Berkshire, the firm became Cox & Wyman's. They, along with very many printers in Britain prevailed as best they could in a fast-changing business, but at moments of crisis, cut assets and shed responsibilities. Shifting all business to Reading, Cox & Wyman closed the Fakenham works in 1982.

What should have happened at this point is that a vigilant citizen should have placed some sort of preservation order on the office. Architecturally the factory buildings to the rear, occupying nearly all the site were of no consequence, but the office could have been nominated for Listing. The entire site was flattened by bulldozers in 1987 to make way for a supermarket and car park. All that remained were memories for men and women in Fakenham, and a photograph. Here was a Skipper building that had been worth saving.

On the subject of saving buildings, it was in the early 1920s that George Skipper encountered a post-war civic disregard for historic buildings and, with others, fought a campaign to preserve one of England's finest Mediaeval buildings, in what might be called 'The Case of Bishops Bridge'.

George Skipper's involvement in Norwich City Council's planning processes was not confined to providing designs for social housing. With his perceived role as a member of the MTPI, George also pored over maps of the city and considered the old roads and streets in view of the new traffic. By 1923 there were 383,525 motorcars on the roads of Britain and at least 100,000 vans and lorries. By 1930 there would be three times those figures, and in the next decade they would double again to 2 million cars and 500,000 commercial vehicles.

The City Council was urged to prepare for arterial roads that would run straight through Norwich. The prevailing view was of narrow streets and dilapidated old buildings: the Council wanted to make changes, to swiften and ease the progress of the motorcar. The problem, of course, was that it was a mediaeval city, with important landmarks and a wealth of historic structures.

It cannot be said if Skipper was 'the whistleblower', who first alerted the public to what would now be referred to as a 'heritage crime'. Norwich City Council found Bishops Bridge over the river Wensun too narrow for the purposes of motorized traffic, and wanted to widen it, or if that was not possible, to demolish it. Work on breaking the parapet had already begun. Help!

The bridge was situated just East of the cathedral. According to Francis Blomefield's eighteenth century *History of Norfolk* the Prior had been given licence for its construction in 1275. The bridge was rebuilt in 1340 and maintained initially by the bishops, who added a large fortified gatehouse on top of the first arch. Four hundred and fifty years later, cracks were found and the defensive tower was taken down in 1791. Perhaps the most important factor is that it was an extremely handsome structure, a three arched bridge of old brick, flint and stone, with a parapet and recesses. For readers of the 2020s, it is almost unbelievable to read about the City Council's attempted demolition of this beautiful bridge.

Pl. 149
Bishop's Bridge.
Norwich.
(1920s postcard).

Faced with the City Council's plan, Skipper and other architects, notably Edward Thomas Boardman, diverse antiquarians and concerned citizens, including the Suffragette Lady Mayoress, Helen Colman, met on 23 March 1923 at Curat House in Norwich's Haymarket. This group of individuals appointed Boardman as Chairman and selected a committee to do whatever it took to save Bishops Bridge. They applied immediately to the Ministry of Works in London to obtain a preservation order under the Ancient Monuments Consolidation and Amendments Act of 1913.

The association, which was to name itself 'The Norwich Society' followed this up with seeking similar Preservation Orders for Norwich's Cathedral Close, Norwich Castle and Norwich Guildhall. (The list of historic buildings protected by Preservation Orders is frequently referred to as 'The List' in these pages).

Beginning in 1923 The Norwich Society was following in the footsteps of The Society for the Protection of Ancient Buildings, founded by William Morris in 1877. It has remained active and done enormous good in safeguarding Elm Hill, Strangers Hall, the Assembly House, Tombland, and several other significant historic buildings in the old city. George Skipper and, later, his son Edward, twice elected chairman, were active members.

In 1925 Skipper had been asked to have a look at Headmaster's House at Harrow school. This was not exclusively the headteacher's residence, but the oldest of the school's twelve boarding houses, housing scholars, including Winston Churchill in the 1890s. It was an old town house in the High Street, dating from about 1660, built in brick, with Dutch gables and other architectural features. There is no record of what alterations Skipper made, or planned. He was also invited to submit a design for a cricket pavilion; again we have no information whether his design was taken up.

It was at about this time that Skipper returned to his work for Jarrold's in Norwich. The work involved adding extra bays to extend down Exchange Street, as described earlier, in combination with his earlier work in the 1900s.

In the years after the First World War, George devoted time to make plans for Hersden, the new village near Canterbury that would service the Chislet coalmine. Readers will doubtless be suspicious about the financial arrangements, remembering that Skipper had already invested and lost badly in the Kentish coalmines almost ten years earlier.

More than a thousand miners, relocated from traditional coalmining areas, were living in Ramsgate and coming to Chislet by railway. When more coal was found and a northern extension was made to the workings, a degree of confidence encouraged the formation of Chislet Colliery Housing Society in 1924. It was the CCHS, partly funded by the government, which made contact with George Skipper. The job was to build three hundred houses at Hersden, though in the end only one hundred and sixty-five were built, along with a pub, 'The Black Horse'. In spite of the financial precariousness of the Kent coalfields, and the state of the economy, the miners' houses at Hersden were built to a decent standard.

Now that Skipper had organized his plans for council houses into 'Types' – type 7A, or 9B etc., it is quite likely that the architect provided the Chislet Colliery Housing Society with designs he had made already. As an available reference, we can look at a low-level aerial photograph of Hersden, taken in 1931. In the centre of the photograph is 'The Black Horse', a large brick and rendered two-storey building with large casements, attic dormers, and two tall chimneystacks. Built in 1929, the inn had a large forecourt, defined by walls, pillars and posts. To the left of the photograph one sees a block of large 'double dwellers', which may have been the homes of senior staff at the adjacent colliery. They had hipped and tiled roofs with gable dormers; the walls had the same arrangement as those of the inn, with brick surfaces rendered and painted at the upper level.

To the right of the photograph were a few streets formed by rows of smaller buildings consisting of pairs of semi-detached houses. These too had hipped and tiled roofs, rear extensions, and front and back gardens. They had electric lighting and contained three bedrooms, bathrooms and internal WCs, which most miners' terraces in Wales did not. Like many housing schemes, progress was ongoing, and the architect would come back to the overall plans and make additions. Skipper did not cease his connection with Hersden until about ten years after the start in 1924. Some of the later additions might, or might not have been designed by him. One uncertainty is the Hersden Methodist Church, which later became the Hersden Community Centre.

Pl. 150
George Skipper, Architect, c.1924–1934, Hersden village near Canterbury, Kent, built for the Chislet Colliery Housing Society.

(1931 aerial photograph during construction).

Pl. 151
George Skipper,
1925 photograph.

Chislet Colliery continued, and was assimilated into the National Coal Board in 1948. Twenty years later, when British Rail changed to diesel power and terminated their contracts to buy coal, the mine ceased to be economic. It closed in 1969. Other Kent collieries continued, even beyond the Miners Strike of 1984; the last one closed in 1989.

As ever George Skipper had several irons in the fire at the same time. At the other end of the social scale he was in contact with His Majesty King George V. Firstly the work at hand concerned the 'Queen Mary Cottages', which were four small bungalow-cottages set close together, with a small sundial to the fore (drawings in RIBA 36293) on the Sandringham estate. How had the King found George Skipper? Did he come by recommendation, or reputation? Perhaps the town hall in nearby Hunstanton advertised his ability.

'Dear old Sandringham, the place I love better than anywhere else in the world', the King had once said. His grandfather had bought it for his father, and now it was his, a private residence, rather than a royal estate, which was why he was obliged to oversee household matters. He wanted a lift to be installed at Sandringham: ordering the machine was one thing, but it would involve a lift-shaft, and lift-head at roof height. George Skipper's second task for the King was to manage the installation, and to hide the ugly lift-head.

George must have visited Sandringham to eye up the job, but there is no account of a meeting. The building was relatively modern, rebuilt 1870–1892 in the neo-Jacobean style, to designs by architects A.J Humbert and R.W Edis. Architectural critics have competed with each other to make the most dismissive comments about the place. The comparison with a golf-hotel at St Andrews is not necessarily unfavourable; shorn grassland and heath make up much of the grounds. Built of brick with limestone details, Sandringham presented a long front of pointed gables and chimneys, and a vast amount of windows (this was before the removal of ninety-one rooms in 1975).

Emerging from the roof above Sandringham was an octagonal stair-tower, capped with a copper dome. Using this existing cupola as a marker, the architect drew plans for the lift shaft to rise nearly twenty feet from a roof overlooking the back of the house. It was encased in Skipper's new brick tower, square in plan, with limestone quoins and mullions; this too was covered by a cupola, to which he gave an ogee-shape and a white ball finial. It was not a complicated job for Skipper, who had designed more than a few turrets with cupolae. Some say the feature was a trademark of his. Apparently the King was pleased: all agreed that the view of Sandringham was improved from all sides by the presence of another tower.

King George V's third request was for a small parish hall, or village hall for the tiny village of Shernbourne, in the middle of the vast estate. George Skipper submitted an attractive design, very Arts and Crafts in nature, which was approved and built. The little parish hall, along with a small kitchen and cloakroom, adjoined an existing village building. The appearance the new hall presented to the road was that of a small cottage, with flint pebbledash walls and brown carrstone quoins, and a notably deep-overhanging and steeply hipped roof, clad with a set of many-toned peg tiles. To the front was a large

Pl. 152
George Skipper, Architect, 1925, Tower at Sandringham House for King George V. (The purpose of the square-section tower, with its ogee shaped cupola, was to hide the head of a new lift shaft).

Pl. 153
George Skipper, Architect, c.1929 Former Parish Hall for Shernbourne village on the Sandringham estate.

window in a flint-faced gable; to the side, a deliberately oversized chimney was raised from the ground with the outline of a bottle, or even a guitar. The lower part of the stack was pierced by two small windows on either side of the hearth. It is said that the little hall utilized recycled materials from Queen Alexandria's storm-lashed beach-house at nearby Hunstanton. The hall, which is in good condition, is no longer used by the parish, and functions as a showroom for a bed manufacturer.

The Royal Institute of British Architects retains an interesting piece of paper (RIBA 36290) with two photo-mechanical transfer images of the parish hall. The floor plan is penned-in below, indicating that the hall is 32ft x 24ft. Between the image and the plan was an example of George Skipper's meticulously hand-drawn lettering (an art deco style piece of lettering in capitals and small capitals, plus extra letter-spacing) with the words, PARISH HALL, SHERNBOURNE / *for* HIS MAJESTY THE KING; next to this was his best handwritten signature:

George J. Skipper F.R.I.B.A
Architect
Norwich & London.

RIBA have correctly captioned the document with the subject date as 1927, and added an image date of 1922, which is definitely wrong. But seeing the document that George presented to H.M The King, with the image of the finished hall and the signature, those handwritten words 'Norwich & London' catch the eye. The architect had not used an ampersand, but an emphatic squiggled + meaning 'and'. George Skipper was telling the King of England that he also practiced in London. And for that reason we can be sure that the true date of the document is later, an after-the-event one as late as 1932, and certainly no earlier than 1929.

It is a shame to explain this anomaly at this point, because it causes Skipper's chronology to run ahead of itself. Nevertheless, the 'spoiler-alert' is that George was going to go back to London, after an absence of fifty years. This would be in the early 1930s in circumstances to be explained later. It was significant then, as it is now, that George added the word 'London'. He did not want to be seen by the King as 'just' a Norfolk architect. He was a man of the world beyond East Anglia and if His Majesty needed any work at Buckingham Palace, (I jest) he would know that George Skipper was in London and ready for work!

Interestingly this aspect of not really being a London architect might be seen as something that took away from Skipper's reputation, as if he was provincial and not up to the mark for London – a false impression indeed. But George was vulnerable: more than seventy years old, he was going back into the fray.

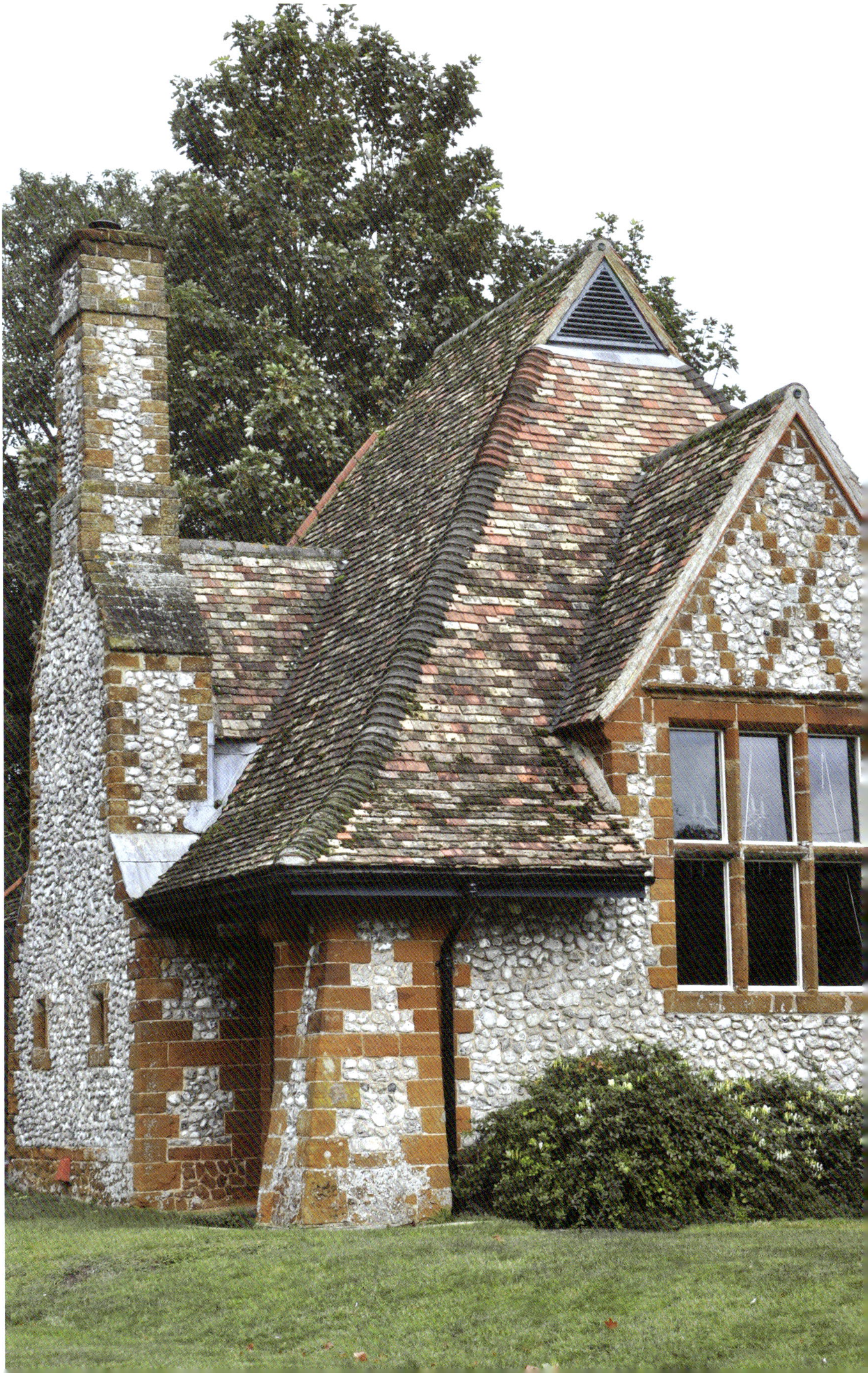

Before this came about, George Skipper went back to unfinished work. Twenty years earlier he had remodelled and extended the University Arms, a landmark of a building in Cambridge. Built in 1834, it was Cambridge's main coaching inn, facing Regent Road, the route from London, and backing onto Parker's Piece, a public parkland area of twenty-five acres.

Skipper had made major alterations to the hotel in 1903, at precisely the same time he had overseen Cambridge's Norwich Union Insurance office. The work comprised an extension to the 19th century structure, doubling its length and stretching towards the town in a more Baroque manner. Skipper's extension in white gault bricks dominated the older building, bringing seven bays including a pair of three-storey bowed bays, and a pair of towers with a cupolae. One of these was situated at the point where Skipper's extension met the original building at the back, overlooking the open space of Parker's Piece.

Pl. 154
George Skipper, Architect, University Arms, Cambridge. 1912 photograph showing first (1903) extension of the hotel.

Pl. 155
The Builder 17 June 1927. George Skipper's proposal for the Reception Hall, University Arms, Cambridge.

More than twenty years later, in 1926–27, George Skipper was invited by the owners to return to the big hotel in Cambridge and to make it even bigger. Skipper repeated the process of the earlier work, using the same materials and the same features to extend the previous extension by another four bays. He moved one of the towers and added another. The three towers with their distinctive balconies, doorways, and bell-shaped green cupolae against the sky, became distinguishing features, recognised by all.

Skipper also drew a design for a Reception Hall, an architectural reverie with details garnered from his fine editions of architectural books. The design was amended and not built, or decorated, to the standard shown in this drawing. The picture was printed in *The Builder* on 17 June 1927. Looking at the image of the interior we see light pouring in from a half-glazed dome above, fitted on a tracery of metalwork. It illuminates the lower part of the rounded ceiling, and falls over paintings and frescoes, rich with patterns and classical scenes, before reaching the ground, where an arched colonnade surrounded a marble floor.

There have been further rebuilds. The University Arms' historical elements are seen best from the back, from Parker's Piece: firstly you see, at its core the late Georgian coaching inn with its gable and dormers, then the early 20th century two-part extensions by Skipper in an Edwardian Baroque style. There are more modern extensions on the other side, by Feilden & Mawson architects, built in two stages in 1965 and *c*.2015, following a fire in 2013. Finally there

Pl. 156
George Skipper, Architect,
1903 and 1927,
University Arms, Cambridge.

2018 photograph showing original building at centre, the two extensions by George Skipper on the right (renovated after fire damage), and modern extensions by Feilden & Mawson on the left.

has been a thorough renovation and 'upgrade' in 2018 by the architect, John Simpson, in a Neo-classical style. The hotel received a new *porte-cochère* at the street front, suitable for limousines.

Skipper was managing a clutch of diverse commissions and projects in the period 1926–27. In between the Kent colliery, the University Arms hotel in Cambridge, and small works for King George V, the architect maintained a flow of sales of his designs for council houses. Most, though not all, were for his home county.

There is a note in his sketchbook, dated 25 October 1926, referring to houses in Norwich to be built on the junction of Burges Road and Margaret Paston Avenue, still in the vicinity of Mile Cross, with all its new roads and houses. Skipper sold one of his designs in both variations, type 'A' and type 'B', that is to say with a parlour, and without one. The houses without a parlour were built for a total of £416 by Norwich City Council. In the following year more of the Skipper's popular type 5 'B' designs were chosen for a cul-de-sac leading off Elizabeth Fry Road in Norwich (numbers 17–32 Lubbock Close). –*See pages 196–197.* A further eight plots were ordered for the Earlham Road estate, for houses without parlours. These large areas on the outskirts of Norwich have been filled in with more council houses, mostly after the Second World War.

Among thousands of dwellings, those built in the 1920s to Skipper's designs stand out, with telling signs of their maker, for instance hood-moulding above windows in some cases, or recessed and chamfered brick doorways, or shared gable-dormers; of course there have been alterations too, following privatisation of many council properties in the 1980s. Norwich, which had a strong City Council and far more council houses than other cities of a similar size, managed to retain a relatively high proportion of them. As a reference to Norwich's council estates of the 1920s, it should be noted that a few, coming from other sources (*i.e* not architects), were constructed of eight inch thick pre-fabricated concrete slabs, for instance the 'Duo-slab', or the 'Winget' house. These non-traditional constructions did not fare well and were gradually replaced.

More of Skipper's plans went to the coast, for a housing scheme to be built on behalf of Erpingham RDC in the village of Cley-next-the-Sea. Others went to Blofield RDC. In all likelihood there were more Skipper designs, not listed here, that were sold to District Councils in other parts of the county, and in Suffolk. One small scheme outside the area was for shops, with flats above them, on the Lindsay Manor Farm estate, at Shepperton-on-Thames, then in Middlesex, now Surrey.

The most sensational commission came in 1927, when he won another architectural competition. It led to the job which would cause more problems than any other in his life, but which also promised the most prestige. The Sutton Estates, freeholders of a whole street in London, wished to develop it and engaged George Skipper. The street was Sackville Street, and the job for the architect, as it was then, was to rebuild both sides of the street.

Pl. 157 *(facing page)* Studio photograph of George Skipper in 1927.

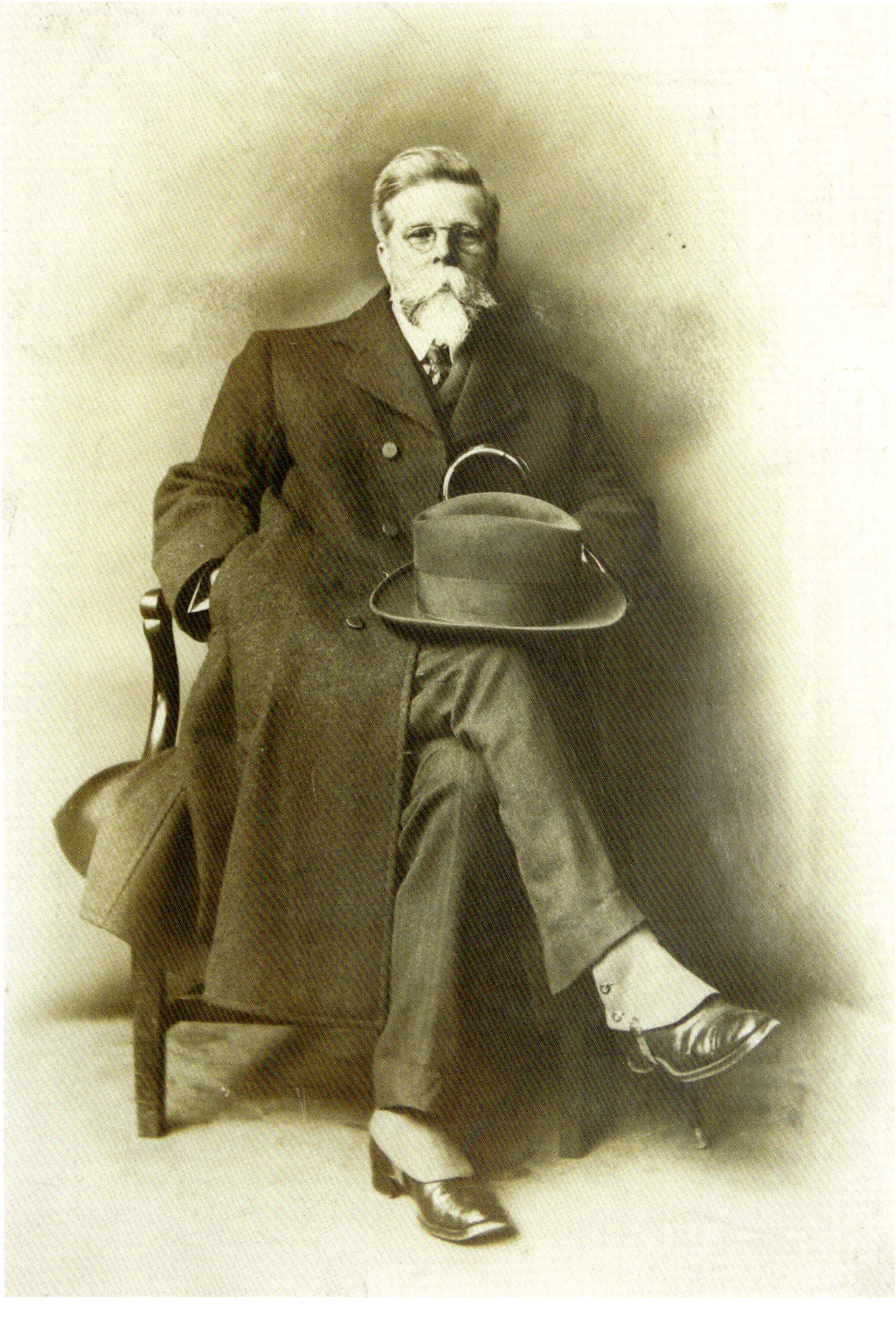

Sackville Street runs North at right angles from the West end of Piccadilly, before meeting the 'T' junction of Vigo Street, itself joining Regent Street. The area touches on Mayfair and St James's, and is the home of more wealth than any part of the United Kingdom. It included Sotheby's auction rooms, the Ritz Hotel, Saville Row, and the Royal Academy of Arts. Sackville Street was in an area that simply exuded wealth and power. For Skipper, so long away from London, there were feasts for the eyes in the form of elegant architecture. RIBA was within walking distance.

Skipper started to sketch the view as it might be, looking up Sackville Street. Time and again he sketched variations of the scheme, seen only in his pocket-sized notebook, and not in proper drawings, except for one well-known illustration, retained at RIBA. The job was not ready to start, as more freeholds were being purchased, and Skipper was given to understand that there was plenty of time to prepare.

For inspiration perhaps, or a holiday of sorts, Skipper decided to take Alice to Paris for a few days in 1928. The only evidence we have of the short sojourn are a few insignificant drawings dated 27 February, seen in one of his trusty pocket books. One page shows individual features quickly sketched in different places. We see a monumental pedestal and plinth at the Château de Courances, a balustrade at the Château de Bizy, some iron posts at St Cloud, some iron railing and an urn at the Château de Fontainebleau, and a fence in the gardens of Les Tuileries. On another day the couple took a trip to Bayeux, doubtless seeing the famous tapestry.

They were back in Kingsley Villa in Norwich a few days later. George was in a state of excitement, his mind fixing on different elements of the great Piccadilly design to come. His two young children, aged ten and seven respectively, got on well with each other and romped around the house. George had bought a 'Little Builders' toy set, with tiny clay bricks, and was intending to give it to Edward for Christmas. He was a kind and gentle father, Edward and Margaret both stated in later life.

He was becoming more flexible too, as another family anecdote relates: one evening, returning from London, he arrived back at Kingsley Villa earlier than usual. He found Alice entertaining three guests in a Bridge party. Previously, as a member of the Brethren, the activity of card playing might have merited disapproval, but on this occasion George made no comment.

The closing decade would be remembered for the stock-market crash in America, which occurred on 24 October 1929. Leaving aside the woes of that nation, the linkage with the international gold standard caused instant repercussions in Britain and its dominions. The country had struggled economically throughout the 1920s. The next decade would begin with what historians later called 'The Great Depression'.

George Skipper read the newspapers, and reflected that he was fortunate to have an important London commission ahead of him. There were obviously going to be hard times ahead.

Chapter eight

1930—1948

For George Skipper, the greater part of the 1930s, the decade leading up to the Second World War, was occupied in trying to see the Sackville Street plan put into effect. In terms of prominence and prestige, none of Skipper's other plans over the years could match it.

The client, Sir Richard Sutton's Settled Estates, owned numerous properties in Mayfair, and had just built what is now the Sheraton Hotel in Park Lane. The trustees and executors of the estates were commercially minded to increase the value of their holdings. One of these was Sackville Street, leading off Piccadilly, and their plan was to demolish both entire sides of the street, irrespective of antiquity and architectural history, and to erect a uniform Neo-classical structure.

Pl. 158
One of several design attempts for Sackville Street. Drawn in his his pocket sketch book on 17 December 1927, it had little resemblamce to the final design.

The street had already been cleared of old houses in 1730 by the owner, William Pulteney, later Earl of Bath. New houses were built within the old leasehold divisions, with about twenty properties on either side of the street, plus seven more at the Piccadilly end, entered from Piccadilly. The street was reasonably wide; most of the Georgian buildings were three-storeyed, built of brick or stone, and many of them had attics and basements. The occupants in the 1740s, described in *The Survey of London*, included 'the minor nobility, the dowager, the member of parliament, the senior army officer and the prosperous medical man', and even the brother of the famous architect, Sir John Vanbrugh. Some of the houses had fine staircases, panelling, and decorative plasterwork.

By the 1920s and 1930s, however, the occupants were less illustrious, leases were expiring and the houses were in various states of repair. The ground landlords, the Sir Richard Sutton Settled Estates, previously headed by a succession of Sutton baronets of Norwood Park in Nottinghamshire, had acquired vast acreages of farmland in the shires and a sizeable chunk of London's West End. Quite why they wished to reorganize Sackville Street is not certain, though the rebuilding was likely to increase the value of the holding, and the rents they would receive.

Following George Skipper's 1927 competition-winning entry plan, both sides of the street would resemble a Palladian mansion between wide-flung projecting wings. The first resistance to Skipper's original plan was reasonable: people claimed the design was ill suited for the purpose of providing façades for shop and offices.

Skipper was asked to revise the plan in July 1931. His new perspective drawing showed the Piccadilly end and the East side of Sackville Street as far as the central feature, where, with clever artistry, the features became less distinct. At both ends of both sides of the street there would be a Neo-classical building of three bays, constructed entirely in Portland stone. They would comprise an arcaded street level in rusticated stonework, with the upper three-storeys recessed behind a tall Ionic columned pseudo-portico. Above this a pediment reached to the skyline.

Other structures, quite similar, would stand at the centre of either side of the street. These were to be be flanked by single-bay buildings, with their upper-storey windows framed in a tall arch. The frontage in between the wings and central features would consist of two house-fronts in grey brickwork. The same drawings showed Skipper's idea of having the East side further recessed to create an area for fountains and formal shrubbery, though this was never pursued. To begin with, however, the 1931 idea was followed.

Work had begun with the demolition of houses on the east side of the south end of Sackville Street and round the corner at number 38–40 Piccadilly. The rebuilding of the important corner started in 1929 and continued at least until 1932. The dominating central feature of the building was the central entablature, three-storeys tall, which was not unlike Skipper's design at Surrey

Pl. 159 *(facing page)* George Skipper, Architect, 1931-38, View of south end of Sackville Street, London. 2020 photograph.

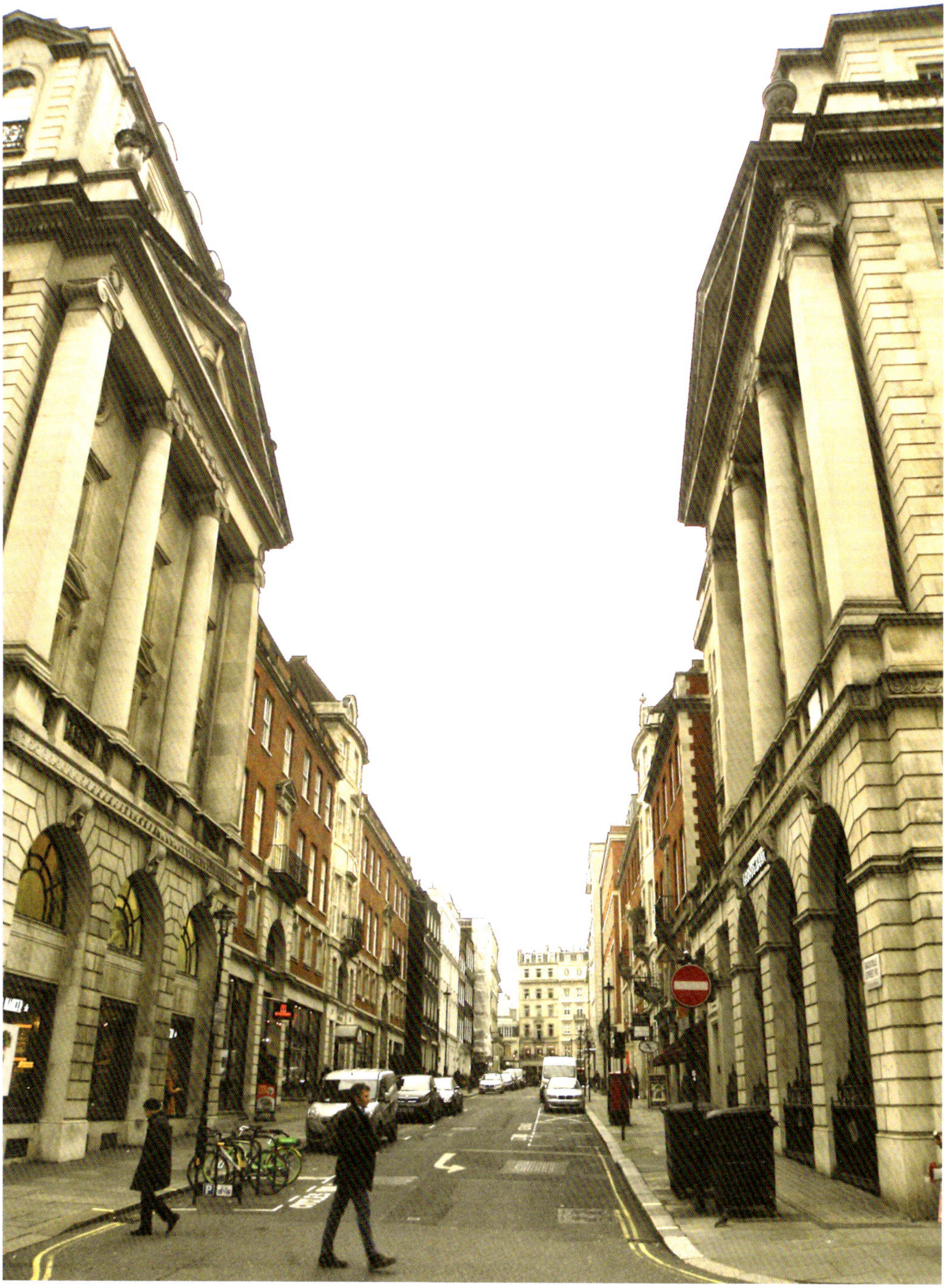

House for Norwich Union three decades earlier. Other details included a Vitruvian key line, a stone balustrade, and oculi beneath the pediment. (An attic was added later).

So far, so good; the Sackville Street scheme was in motion. George was up and down to London, firstly staying and receiving meetings at the former Curzon Hotel in Curzon Street, and then, in order to establish a base, renting a small office in Vigo Street, which actually joined with the north end of Sackville Street. It is from this time that Skipper could, if it mattered, be regarded as a London architect.

From the new office in Vigo Street the architect could summon and address contractors, and answer to the Sutton Estates, and even other clients. Knowing Skipper, he would also have strolled the very short distance to the Piccadilly corner site itself every day, and offered his thoughts to the clerk of works.

Skipper took his thirteen or fourteen year old son to London. Edward recalled, 'Building was well ahead when I was old enough to climb the scaffolding and watch the stonemasons carving the Ionic volutes to the columns'.

Pl. 160 *(facing page)* George Skipper, Architect, 1931-38, Number 38–40 Piccadilly (South end of Sackville Street), London.

The builders and tradesmen were chosen by Sutton Estates. The architect must have remembered his talented team of the 1900s, when Mr Potter's masons had cut and dressed stone in the workshop, before adding details and flourishes. The Sackville Street building on the South-East corner, now Lloyds Bank, had additional decorative wrought and cast-iron screen-work running across the higher part of the street level windows. This feature might have derived from something he saw in Paris.

During this time the Norwich office was still open. Skipper handled the Hersden village site from London, but East Anglian commissions were operated from Norwich.

Down in Kent, the brewers Shepherd Neame, who ran The Black Horse in Hersden, now wanted a hotel to be built in Sturry, halfway between Hersden and Canterbury. There are notes in Skipper's pocketbook stating that the plans were approved. Despite enquiries, there seems to be no hotel in Sturry. It may be the case that Shepherd Neame bought the plans from Skipper with a view to building at another location. Another possibility is that is was destroyed, since Sturry was one of the villages to be repeatedly bombed in WW2, due to its proximity with the cathedral city. These bombings of places of culture and heritage were known as the 'Baedeker Raids', named after the German *Baedeker Guides*, which provided detailed maps of historical sites and places of interest to tourists. Skipper's home city would also experience a severe Baedeker blitz.

Skipper's tasks in Norfolk at the time were divided between private clients and municipal authorities. In the first category was an April 1930 plan for an extension to a 17th century country mansion, 'Humbletoft House', another Dereham property belonging to Colin MacLean (owner of 'The Heath'). The work included the addition of a bay window, said to be in an Arts and Crafts

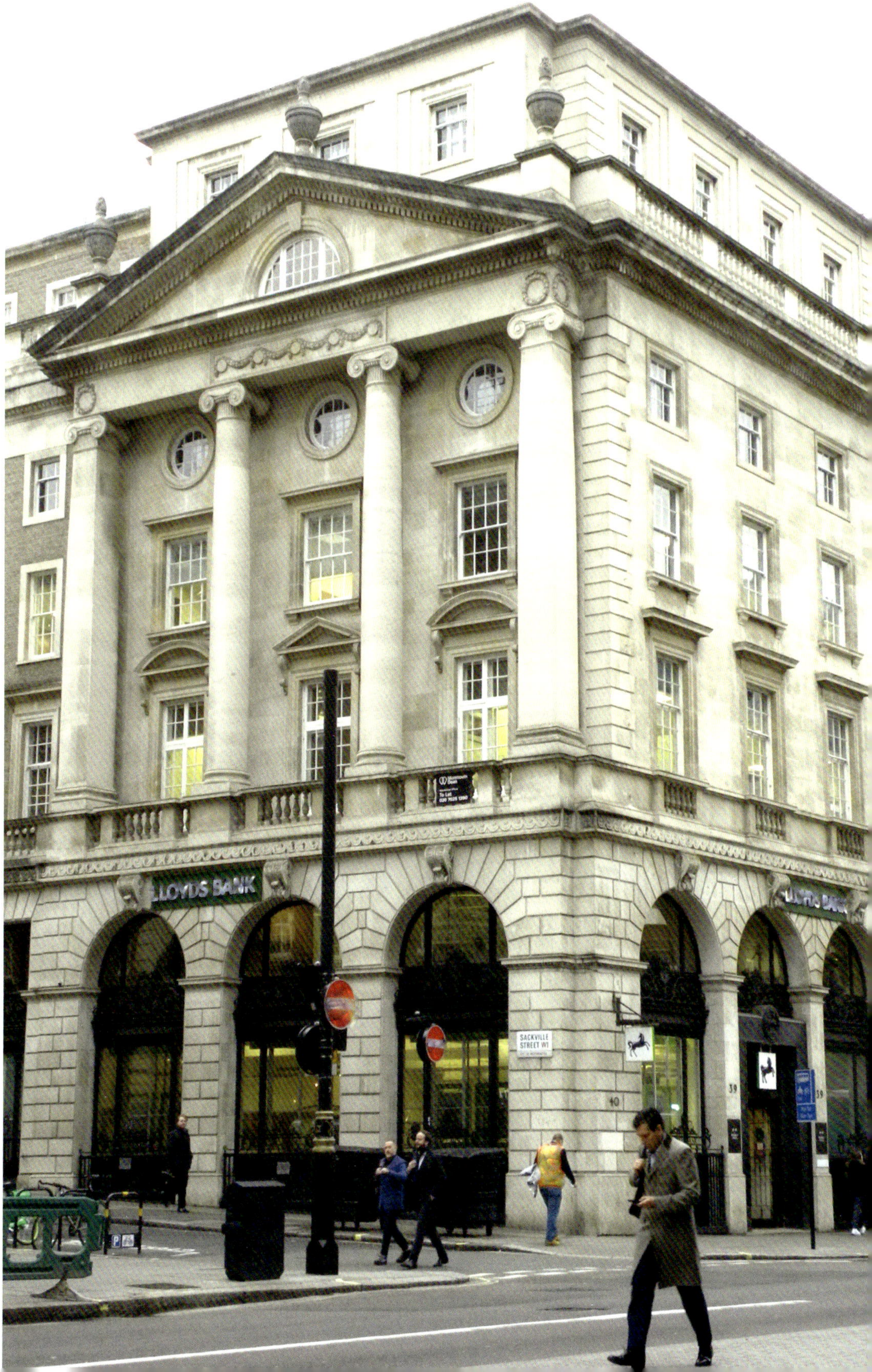
LLOYDS BANK
SACKVILLE
STREET W1
40
39

style. Today, in a diminished form and with some of its grounds taken by new housing, it is a grade II Listed building.

Another private commission in Norfolk, also in 1930, was for Framingham Hall, an old house at Framingham Pigot, five miles South-East of Norwich. The client was Geoffrey Colman, a director of Colman's Mustard in Carrow, Norwich. Colman acquired the building in the previous year and decided to change the name of the hall to 'The Chase'. Skipper's work was in extending the house, and possibly designing some outworks in the well-kept grounds, including a gateway resembling a small 'walk-through' temple, and a rotunda with a wrought-iron pierced dome. After the death, in 1970, of Geoffrey's widow, Lettice Colman, a patron of the Arts, the entire house was demolished in 1973.

In Norwich itself, Skipper provided a design in May 1932 for a Mrs Wyatt, relating to a property at the junction of Recreation Road and The Avenues. In the same year he sold plans to R. Whitmore for three houses in Earlham Road. The actual addresses are hard to decipher from his pocketbooks, but if visiting locations, readers might recognize the signs of Skipper in private housing, for instance arched and recessed doorways, sometimes at the corner, gauged or contrasting brickwork, hood, or label mouldings, and tall chimneystacks.

In the following year the architect drew up ideas for a further extension of Christchurch Road for the landowners, probably the diocese of Norwich; nominally the clients were the Ecclesiastical and Church Estates Commissioners for England. Once the overall plan was approved, the commissioners came back to Skipper in 1934 for designs for a number of small houses to be built in Christchurch Road. Years later, writing in *Celebrating Skipper 100*, Edward Skipper recalled the site. At the time he must have been aged about thirteen, his sister three years younger.

> "My father never lost an opportunity of talking to me about architecture and I soon became aware that it was his ambition that I should follow in his footsteps. My younger sister, Margaret, played hide and seek with me in the partially built houses on my father's supervision visits. Many of these can be singled out in the Christchurch Road area, when my father, acting for the Church Commissioners, completed its link with Earlham Road across their land".

At the same time the architect pored over maps of South Norwich. His task was to supply the City Council with technical drawings of the topography and existing drainage of the area between Unthank Road and Eaton Park, all dropping westwards to the Yare valley. These combinations of new roads, drainage and building plots required a lot of surveying.

George was often on the train between Norwich and London. The Skipper family recounted that on one occasion Alice and the children had travelled on the same train in a Second Class compartment, while George sat elsewhere in

First Class. On another occasion George walked briskly to Norwich station to catch the London train, passing beneath the portico and the large clock; heading for the platform, he suddenly heard a whistle-blast and caught sight of the London train in motion.

"Stop that train", he roared, in the mode of a Sergeant-Major. Surprisingly the guard on the platform signalled to the driver, and the train slowed to a halt. The smartly dressed, white-haired gentleman made a reprimand to the LNER staff for attempting to leave early, then climbed aboard as if nothing was unusual.

It is interesting to note that although the architect had always been enthusiastic about competitions, and won many of them, he did not even enter the competition that had been run in 1931 for the prize of designing Norwich's new City Hall. One reason for him not to have entered the competition was that he would be fully occupied with the London scheme. Attracting one hundred and forty-three entries, the competition was won by architects Charles Holloway and Stephen Rowland Pierce. Construction began in 1936 and was completed by October 1938. It was an impressive Art Deco-Classical-Modern arrangement, described by Pevsner as 'the finest inter-war civic building in Britain'. The appearance of City Hall attracted no comment from Skipper; fanciful perhaps – but I think he would have approved.

Frederick Skipper, aged seventy-five, finally retired in 1935, so ending his working partnership with his son, Eric Hayward Skipper. Eric would continue, of course, work from an office at 55 London Street.

Unlike his brother, there was no retiring for George Skipper. The 1930s were tense and difficult and the nation suffered. The Great Depression, as regards Britain, had befallen a country still not on its feet after the ravages of the 1914–1918 war. Industries were halved, and unemployment was increasing. The Conservatives were blamed and a new Labour government was confronted with economic problems far greater than first thought. Britain limped on: public sector wages were cut, Sterling was dropping, and the North of England and South Wales were experiencing great hardship. One of the very few economic benefits during the Depression was the increase in building of social housing.

However, for a grand building project such as Sackville Street in London's Mayfair, the atmosphere changed. It happened by degrees and came in different forms – as reticence, as criticism, as a change in confidence. Maybe it also came as professional jealousy from younger architects brought in to modify the scheme. These are possible reasons why progress faltered and halted before more than a part of Sackville Street had been completed. 'The vision was never fulfilled', as Pevsner put it in *The Buildings of England: London 6: Westminster*.

Despite the wealth of the landlords, the projected figures no longer added up. The trustees of the Sutton Estates were not greatly inconvenienced, but the process of seeing his grand plan diminished must have been very upsetting for Skipper. Any emotions described here are imagined, as Skipper wrote nothing about the situation. It was not his fault: circumstances were far beyond his control. Was age a factor, not only his own, but the age of such grand expressions of Classical architecture?

The Survey of London observed that late modifications to Skipper's 1931 plan took the form of cancelling the stone piers and columns at street level. There were to be additions of high attics and roofs where Skipper had planned none; the central features were redesigned. The outcome would not be uniform, or even recognizable as a single plan.

Some buildings retained their 18th century frontage. The extent of Skipper's scheme actually completed were both sides of the Piccadilly end of the street, with the two neo-Classical buildings facing each other with identical columns and porticos. Beyond this the mid-street buildings were finished on either side. The fifth property to be raised according to his plan was the dignified building in grey brickwork adjoining the S.E corner. A few other houses on the east side displayed features adapted from the original plan.

Skipper's Sackville Street would have been very much in line with the surrounding architecture, where Portland stone columns of the three orders abound. One comparison would be the magnificent and continuous Neo-classical uniformity of nearby Regent Street, to the design of John Nash (1752–1835). Indeed, one of the most galling aspects of the unfulfilled vision was that it would stand among the greater achievements of other architects. Skipper knew his reputation would suffer.

He had his 80th birthday in 1936, the year in which the old King died and his son abdicated. At some point Skipper probably felt 'past it'. Fate had triumphed over will and Skipper had to accept this. He was an ambitious man and had spent a decade on a scheme that had won him nothing. He decided to return to the Norwich office.

One or two photographs of Skipper at this time show him holding a cigarette. He may have just started at a late age, or taken up the habit a little earlier. Most men smoked in those days. Although an abstainer throughout his life, he was permitted, or even recommended a little whisky, with bread and milk, before bedtime. While he was pouring it, he sometimes feigned a tremble, which increased the measure.

The architect's son Edward, only nineteen at the time of King George VI's Coronation in 1937, had started helping in the Norwich office. Now he went

Pl. 161
George Skipper, Architect, 1931-38, View of East side of Sackville Street, London.

down to join Skipper in the London office, and to help him tie up the ends and quit.

Edward recalled, 'Leaving school in 1937 I became a student at the Royal Institute of British Architecture and spent about eighteen months before the war as an apprentice with my father'. Edward's wife, Betty, described his earlier upbringing. 'George had always wanted his son to follow him into an architectural career. Edward had initially been schooled at Norwich Grammar School, though he had been discreetly asked to leave, as he never bothered to work. He had then attended a small private school, Unthank College, where he became involved with the Sea Scouts and soon became Patrol Leader, but he still had not bothered with schoolwork. His half-brother Ralph was asked to tutor him, which did not please Ralph'.

Ralph, some years older, had also gone to Norwich Grammar School. After leaving he became a Quantity Surveyor, encouraged by George, and worked from the Norwich office in the years when Skipper had been in London. Ralph actually wanted to be a schoolmaster, like his father. He called his stepfather, George, 'Governor'.

Pl. 162
George Skipper, with his son, Edward, and his daughter, Margaret. Photograph c.1936

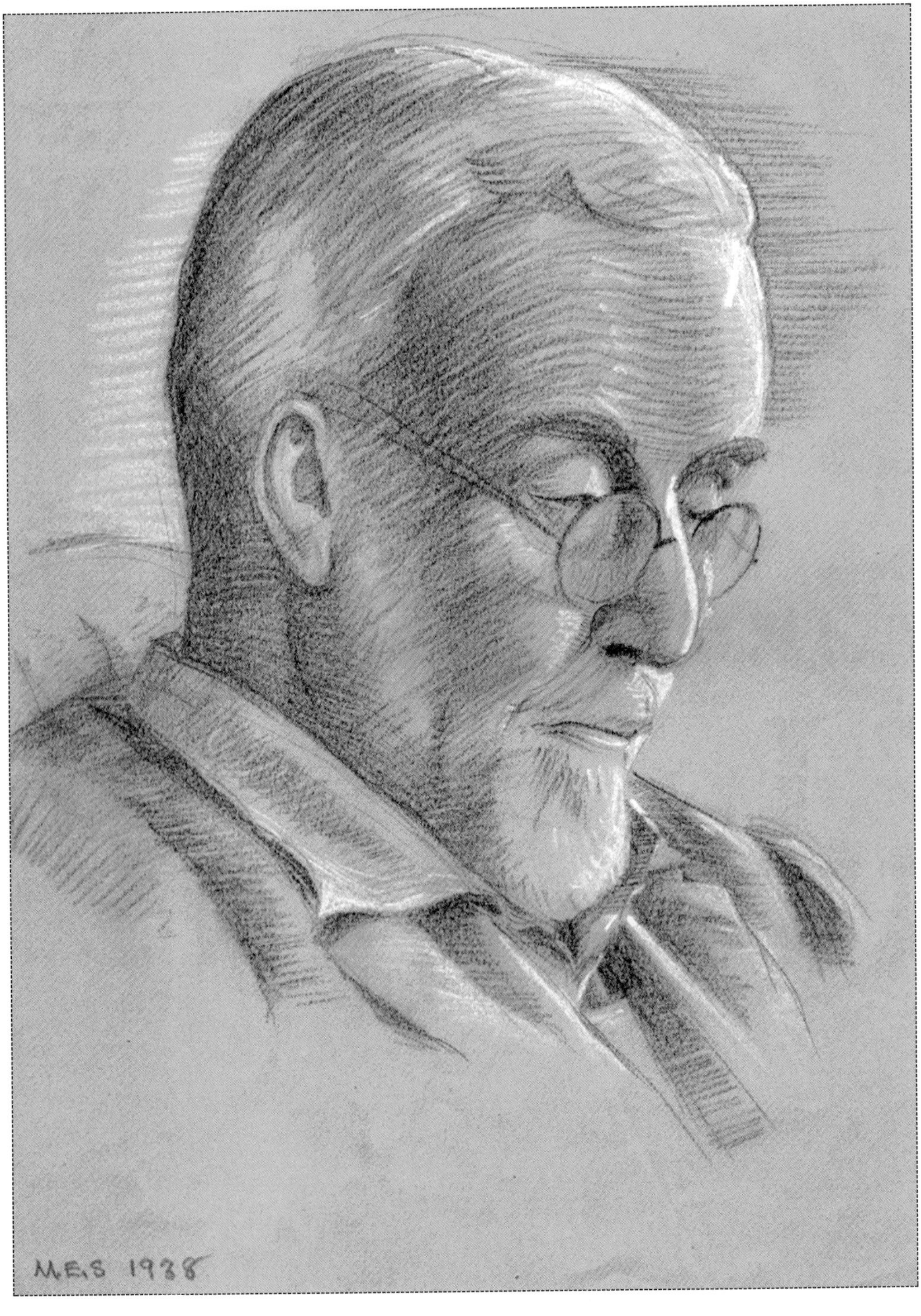
M.E.S 1938

The final move, the closing of the Vigo Street office, and the departure for Norwich, was made in 1938. Skipper did not return to an empty office, or an empty home. Quite apart from his family, there were his books, to which he had added more rare editions purchased in London. Edward described his father as a 'workaholic' whose favourite pastime was to sit by the fire, perusing his fine volumes, whether Colen Campbell's 1731 *Vitruvius Brittanicus*, or J.S Cotman's 1838 folio, *Architectural Antiquities of Norfolk*.

George's daughter, Margaret, had originally wished to study Domestic Science, but she was a very competent artist. (Her 1938 portrait of George, in charcoal and chalk on light-brown paper is shown here). As a water-colourist and landscapist she was, perhaps unsurprisingly, able to paint buildings and make attractive compositions. She was primed to apply for Norwich School of Art, where she enrolled in September 1938.

Readers will be aware, with hindsight, that the Second World War was months away, and that whatever Margaret, Edward, and their parents hoped for would be sidelined by world events. After one year Margaret's art studies were cut short by the outbreak of the war in September 1939, at which point the Art School was closed. Joining the ATS (Auxiliary Territorial Service) she was initially based in Norwich, and then in Bristol, where she would live with half-brother Theo and his wife. Miss Skipper's duties in the ATS were almost architectural, and involved measuring up buildings and copying plans. Buildings in both cities were to be badly affected by bombing.

Edward Skipper enlisted in the corps of the Royal Engineers, and was seconded as an officer to Queen Victoria's Own Madras Sappers and Miners, the 'Quinsaps', in southern India. Like many others, he suffered from dysentery several times, a continuous ill health that prevented him from being sent to Burma in 1945. It seemed to his family, however, that the army was actually the 'making' of Edward, introducing him to responsibility. Margaret and Edward's half-brother, Ralph Charter, worked during the war in the construction of buildings at airfields. Ralph married and lived with his wife and four children in Norwich, later moving to Stafford.

Pl. 163 *(facing page)* Portrait of her father by Margaret Skipper, 1938.

This left George and Alice Skipper living quietly at Mill Hill Road throughout the war. According to Betty Skipper, speaking in 2019, 'George's health was by then going downhill and money was getting short. However, he was determined to keep the office going for Edward's return'. Presumably this was just about possible with the help of his nephew, Eric Skipper. The whole family chipped in with money at various times in order to cover the expenses of retaining the office.

George had always walked the short distance down to the office, passing his creations in St Giles Street, but by the late 1930s he was ageing and so he took the bus. This was a slight embarrassment for the family, as George had decided everyone knew who he was in Norwich, so he would not need to pay his fare. The bus company sent someone round to Kingsley Villa to approach Alice for the money.

But living quietly? As far as Norwich, and George and Alice Skipper, were concerned, the Second World War was a terrifying experience. There had been much talk in the late 1930s of the nightmare vision of aerial bombing and the death and destruction that would be brought to the civilian population. A limited amount of bombing, with relatively little damage in Norfolk, had taken place in 1940–41.

On March 28th 1942 the RAF's Bomber Command sent aircraft across the North Sea to drop incendiaries on the very old town of Lubeck, on Germany's Baltic coast, creating a firestorm. It was an experiment that worked only too well and infuriated the enemy. Steve Snelling, writing in *Norwich: A Shattered City – The story of Hitler's Blitz on Norwich and its people 1942* describes what happened next. 'Hitler, furious at what he regarded as an attack on a defenceless city of no military importance, demanded reprisals'. Goebbels, Nazi Minister of Propaganda, made the policy known. "Like the English, we must attack centres of culture". And so the Baedeker raids began, firstly with Exeter. Four nights later the first raid on Norwich took place. Death and destruction had come to Skipper's city.

Two nights after this, on 29th April, the second blitz, comprising at least three raids, caused even more havoc. Norwich's hospitals, schools, churches and swathes of residential streets were smashed and burnt. The 'other' Norwich Station was destroyed, large stores such as Bond's, and Curl's, and Bunting's (most recently John Lewis, Marks & Spencer, and Debenhams) were hit. The incendiary bombs dropped by the Dorniers and Heinkels fell in groups and the ensuing fires were raged in a wind. Caley's chocolate factory, a vast site presently occupied by the Chapelfield Mall, was engulfed in flames. The smell of burnt chocolate would linger for weeks. There were many losses to life, homelessness, and personal tragedies for almost everyone.

As for George and Alice 'living quietly in Mill Hill Road', the night of the second blitz was unforgettable. A young girl, Judy Swain, recalled standing with her mother in front of her parents' house in Mill Hill Road. 'Four or five houses went up in flames and we stood there wondering if our house was going to escape, because the wind was fanning the flames. We seemed to be surrounded by fire'.

Kingsley Villa was untouched. How helpless George, now aged eighty-six, must have felt in those hours. The view next day, or whenever he was able to venture into the streets, would have distressed a man who knew and loved the buildings of Norwich. There had been two other Baedeker raids in 1942, one in May and the other in June.

Truly remarkable, however, was the escape of 'Skipper's buildings'. There had been fire and destruction on both sides of Surrey Street – maybe the bomb that destroyed the bus-station was intended for Surrey House, which remained unscathed. Just down the hill other bombs had turned St Stephen's Street into rubble. Both Commercial Chambers and the adjacent bank in Red Lion Street were untouched, though the other side of the street was flattened. The same was true for Haymarket Chambers. The Royal Arcade was undamaged. Incredibly all the bombs falling around London Street had missed the terracotta frontage of Skipper's office and Jarrold's corner. A short distance away, the ancient Guildhall had survived. Bombs landing nearby had affected the building next to Number 7 St Giles Street, but the Carraraware exterior was hardly touched. Skipper's sublime Baroque palazzo further down St Giles's was safe too.

Pl. 164
St Stephen's Street in the Norwich blitz. 19 April 1942.

The only destroyed building connected to George Skipper was the elegant Friends' Meeting House in Gildencroft, where he had made adjustments many years earlier. The full list of architectural losses, for instance the silk mills in Oak Street, the Victorian College, Clarke's Shoe factory (not connected to Clark's of Somerset), was extensive. While not on the scale of London, or Liverpool, or Coventry, the old city of Norwich had endured its own blitz. Although Skipper and his family were safe, and so were 'his' buildings, there were indirect losses to come.

The wartime ARP, or Air Raid Precautions organisations, manned by salaried wardens and tens of thousands of volunteers, had been renamed the Civil Defence Service. One of their chief functions was to check that offices and houses conformed to the Blackout, so that no light could guide aircraft to a target. Inspecting Skipper's office in the heart of the city, Civil Defence gave stern warnings. They saw an old man surrounded by paper. The maps and charts pinned to the wall, the scrolls of elevation drawings, the plan chest full of large plans and waxed paper — these were a fire risk, especially in a barrage of incendiary bombs. Skipper was ordered to remove them.

And so it was that the elderly architect, helped by his nephew, Eric Skipper, packed and took away the large quantity of documents and drawings. I imagine George picking out a drawing of some scheme from sixty years earlier, and remembering events and faces from long ago. The papers were very probably carried to George's home, the bulk to be thrown away or, in the case of a few drawings, retained. Some years later George's son, by then a practicing architect in his own right, donated the retained papers to RIBA, including all the pocketbooks covering most years from 1873 to 1936.

In 1971, after asking Edward Skipper about the quality of the paperwork, Faith Shaw commented:

> 'The earliest basic sketch plans submitted to the City Engineers were usually on waxed tracing paper, by then ageing and crumbling. From 1900 onwards the drawings were all done by hand on Waterman's polished linen paper, with fine black ink, and coloured ink shading. The draftsmanship and lettering was of a consistently high standard, and GJS was always insistent that the foremost qualification of a young assistant was a fine hand'.

The plans to Surrey House were retained, the preparatory watercolour for Sennowe Hall, the charming watercolour of Haymarket Chambers, the perspective drawings of the first Sackville Street scheme — all of these would eventually be lodged with RIBA. In the view of architectural historians, the loss of all the other drawings and plans was incalculable.

Two years later Skipper's daughter Margaret married a young architect, Peter Foster (1919–2010), who had read Architecture at Cambridge, graduating in 1940. Commissioned into the Royal Engineers, Foster served with the Norfolk division and the Guards Armoured Division in France and Germany. The wedding took place at the Holy Trinity church, just off Unthank Road in Norwich, on 5 May 1944, only a few days before D-Day.

After the war ended Peter Foster went back to Cambridge to complete his studies, subsequently joining the architectural practice of Marshall Sisson RA, (1897–1978). He and Margaret would have two children, Elizabeth and Philip. In years to come Foster became Surveyor of Westminster Abbey, a highly prestigious appointment, for which he was honoured with an O.B.E in 1990.

Skipper, despite the rest of his family urging him to let go, had held on to London Street, largely due to the presence of his nephew, Eric. Then, when Edward returned from India, he was able to persuade his father to finally relinquish the office in 1946–47, after fifty years of occupation. Eric Skipper who had spent the wartime in Scotland, returned to Norwich and opened a new office in Theatre Street, which he kept open until Edward qualified.

George's health was waning. A photograph was taken of Edward and his father at the time of Margaret's wedding in May 1944. Edward wears a suit and looks to the camera. There is a curious expression on his face, as if to say, 'This is how we are'. His hand is hooked under his father's arm, supporting him. Slightly stooped, George looks directly, without his spectacles, at the unknown photographer. He is wearing a Homburg hat, a suit and tie, and over this a thick double-breasted serge overcoat. He is cleanly shaven, with only his life-long moustache. He has a carnation buttonhole on his lapel and carries a spray of honeysuckle in his hand. His other hand grips a walking stick.

Pl. 165
George Skipper and his son, Edward Skipper. May 1944.

Before long Alice could no longer manage George's welfare. He went to live in a residential home, Heigham Hall, which is where he died on 1 August 1948, five days before what would have been his 92nd birthday. The cause of death was noted as senile decay. Administration of his will made probate to his wife Alice, and his son, Edward.

George had stated that he wished to be buried in the grave of his first wife in Norwich (Earlham) cemetery (grave M61 in block L). His gravestone is inscribed:

IN LOVING MEMORY OF ELIZABETH TILLS SKIPPER THE DEARLY BELOVED WIFE OF GEORGE JOHN SKIPPER WHO DEPARTED THIS LIFE APR 17 1890 TO BE WITH CHRIST ALSO OF GEORGE BELOVED HUSBAND OF THE ABOVE WHO DIED 1 AUG 1948 AGED 93. (*Ed:– he was, of course, just shy of 92*).

The loss was felt by Alice and his children, now adult and confronting a new era. Edward completed his studies at Norwich School of Art, which conducted a shortened course in the evenings for ex-serviceman. George's wife, Alice had remained in Kingsley Villa, initially with Edward, but then in a separate part of the house when Edward married. Subsequently Alice went to live in Hemingford Grey, near Huntingdon, the same village as her daughter.

In 1953 Edward Skipper married Elizabeth Farlie, known as Betty, whose reminiscences have been so helpful to this text. Although they met in Norwich, Betty had lived in India, and she and Edward shared fond memories of warm climes. They took over the house in Mill Hill Road, where twins Catherine and Jonathan and, later, Robert and Rosemary, were born.

In common with other architects in Norwich, Edward Skipper was required to come up with various schemes to fill those gaps made by bombing. Although he did not follow his father, either in character, or in architectural style, Edward did engage as an active member, and was twice chairman, of The Norwich Society, which continued its very necessary role as guardian of Norwich's built environment.

Edward Skipper was commissioned by Norwich Union to make certain additions to the back of Surrey House, firstly in 1969, and again in the 1970s. Among others these involved adding a third-storey connection to the adjacent 1960s office block, and converting the Law Room into a kitchen. Edward Skipper's work was mostly in Norwich and included improvements to Carlton Terrace and Carlton Gardens in Surrey Street, the St Benedict's Street revitalization, renovations at Eaton Old Hall and at St Michael at Pleas church. In Great Yarmouth Skipper Associates made plans for improvements to the Market Gates area, and to Church Plain and Priory Plain.

Edward decided to disperse his father's library of architectural books, a very fine selection which included many 17th and early 18th century editions. One of these, *A New Book of Architecture Set Forth by Robert Pricke* printed by J.Darby in 1669 was described by the auctioneers, Sotheby & Co, as 'very rare'.

There were only three copies in existence. The auction took place in London on the 29th and 30th January 1970 at Hodgson's Rooms in Chancery Lane. George's son-in-law, Peter Foster attended, and was able to bid for some of the items, for instance paying forty-eight guineas for a large folio in red-morocco backed cloth, *The Temples of Jupiter Panhellenius at Aegina, and of Apollo Epicurius at Bassae* by C.R Cockerell.

Edward Skipper was consulted by David Jolley of Norwich Art School, in preparation for the *Architect Exuberant* exhibition in 1975. It was this, and the subsequent publication of *Celebrating Skipper: 100 Years of Architecture 1880–1980*, co-authored by Jolley and Edward Skipper, which started the process of 'Skipper Studies'. Sadly, David Jolley died before the publication appeared. He had been inspired by Faith Shaw's 1971 primary research.

George's daughter, Margaret, although married to an architect, did not join the profession, but she had undoubtedly inherited her father's ability to draw or paint a building. As a very competent amateur, she painted landscapes and buildings in Scotland, England and Wales, and also in Italy, Brittany, Bavaria, and Corfu. After she died in 2009 some of her paintings were gathered into a book, *The Art of Margaret Foster*.

When their subjects die, writers typically wish to sum up. Here, with an assessment of Skipper's life and works, a question is posed: was he a provincial prodigy, or an architect deserving national recognition? This will remain unanswered, though he was both.

For a start, it is inevitable that George Skipper's place in British architecture is entwined with world history. His life spanned a period from the Crimean War to the Second World War, from slums to council houses, from gothic revivalism to 'modernism', from horses and first railways to aviation and nuclear energy. Skipper was at work for at least sixty-five years, much longer than most architects. By 1946, when his son Edward was taking over, George's portfolio appeared Victorian, or Edwardian, certainly historic in comparison with new and bland post-war structures, whose way had been cleared by wartime bombing.

Stephen Thomas, whose 2005 dissertation on Skipper has been a constant inspiration, put it this way: 'Thus the talent of an architect who had so successfully extolled the virtues of classicism, rich decoration and fun, was lost on the immediate post-war generation. It is only now with a further half century of hindsight that we can look back on his work with perspective'.

Skipper's portfolio stretched over decades. It contained highly original and playful works such as Number 7 St Giles Street or Commercial Chambers in Norwich. It encompassed magnificent buildings such as Surrey House, or St Giles Hotel in the same city, either of which compare with the grandest Classical or Baroque buildings anywhere. It included Arts and Crafts creations, from the Yacht Club in Lowestoft to social housing. As for materials, Skipper used the full palette of unfired clay lump to terracotta ornament, bricks and glazed wall-tiles, from stained glass to wrought iron, from the finest building stone of Clipsham, Portland and Doulting to rough lumps of Lias and 'gingerbread' Carrstone, from green slates to Brindley's exotic marbles. Such diversity is a problem for critics, searching for category and classification: they might construe this variety of styles, purposes and materials as inconsistency.

Steven Thomas continued:

> 'Maybe he was too eclectic ... ... making it harder to relate all his buildings to one designer. This may be a problem of wishing to comfortably assign Skipper to an architectural category, something that in the past architectural historians were too concerned about. What we need to remember is that for all his eclecticism Skipper was, above anything else, an architect in the classical tradition, someone who appreciated that all buildings demand a precedent'.

A small digression: if thinking of George Skipper's legacy, we must remember his urns. No 20th century architect was responsible for as many of them. As it happens, Skipper had made contact with the Mr Potter, the monumental mason who had 'shiploads of Portland Stone' and electrically powered machinery, at the same time as Norwich welcomed a new statue in 1905. This was the tricentennial memorial figure of Sir Thomas Browne (1605–1682), seated on a tall urn-shaped plinth in the Haymarket, opposite his old house, which was next to Skipper's Haymarket Chambers. Browne was a physician who had studied in Italy and followed an interest in urns by writing *Hydrotaphia: Urne-buriall, or A Discourse of the Sepulchrall Urnes lately found in Norfolk.*

Skipper could hardly have missed Browne's statue and the increased interest. It would have enhanced his appreciation of classical urns, revived as 18th century ornament by English architects. It is known that there was a 1728 first edition of *A Book of Architecture containing Designs of Buildings and Ornaments* by James Gibbs in his private library. At the risk of repetition, George Skipper's numerous urns, to be seen at Surrey House, St Giles House, Sennowe Hall, and Jarrolds were significant. Carefully designed, as seen in several drawings in his pocket-sketchbooks, Skipper's urns were made in at least four variations. Without these architectural ornaments the buildings would have had less impact.

For the more academic architectural historian, the search for Skipper has been made more difficult by the loss of design information. We will never know precisely what was removed from Skipper's office in the time of the blitz – the lists and addresses, the quantities of plans, the elevation and perspective drawings. Some commissions resulting in actual houses, for instance for 'Colonel M', or Dr Legge-Paulley, cannot even be located. We know nothing of designs submitted by Skipper that were not taken up by clients, like Gostwyck Grange, which only existed on plan. We know nothing of other works, unmentioned so far, for instance Skipper's amendments to Tostock Place, a grand house mostly demolished, near Bury St Edmunds.

More mystery, unmentioned so far, is the total absence of any written material, or any drawings, even a single sketch, from his three years in London from 1873 until 1876. His sketchbooks begin with the trip to Belgium and jump to his return to Dereham three years later. There is no possibility that George did not draw, paint or sketch in this period. We must assume that the sketchbooks from those years were lost, or even, conceivably, retained by his erstwhile master, John Lee.

Another factor were the gaps in the street. The Grand Hotel and the Metropole Hotel were demolished. No photographs of the Metropole's seaward façade exist. The dignified office of Wyman's in Fakenham was crushed and removed before it could be preserved. The Cambridge office of Norwich Union, which emanated architectural quality, was felled and the site cleared, to be replaced by a building of no quality, though it faced Emmanuel College, of 16th century origin. Although the architect's commercial properties in Norwich are listed buildings, even they have been altered in ways that cannot be reversed. Skipper's rural council houses at Hopton and Garboldisham were pulled down, though they could have been retained. It is only through Listing and enforceable preservation, wisely arranged in the 1970s (after the destruction mentioned above) that there remains a corpus of works for us to see.

Very likely the main reason why George Skipper and his works were left in the shade (until David Jolley, John Betjeman, Ian Nairn, Gavin Stamp and others began to take notice of him) was the post-war desire to look to a future: this was conflated with modernism. A key element of modernist attitude was the disregard shown to the art and architecture of the 19th century. George Skipper's death came at a time when this outlook prevailed, and so his death was not particularly noted at the time.

If we are to search for other reasons why Skipper's reputation might have been levelled, there are other questions. Could architectural writers have decided that he was not original in his designs, whether this was true or not? His Neo-vernacular work in Somerset was derivative, so were his Cromer hotels, so were his two banks in Norwich and maybe the present day St Giles Hotel (very grandly so), and so too was the Sackville Street scheme. But for other works, for instance the Castle Street entrance of the Royal Arcade, Haymarket Chambers, the newspaper building at Number 7 St Giles, or Commercial Chambers, or even Jarrold's façade, and his own office – any derivations are delightfully combined in a clearly original way. Skipper was no mere copyist.

For David Jolley the borrowings were not important.

> 'For whatever architectural language he was engaged in, the buildings are recognizably his: the borrowings are not the crux of the matter – the inexhaustibly inventive use of them is'.

Skipper seemed to do best when trusted and left to his own devices, particularly at the yacht club in Lowestoft, and at Sennowe Park, where Skipper and his remarkably talented team were left in charge while Albert Cook was abroad.

Stephen Thomas echoed the conclusions of Jolley and others:

'... ... there is evidence of a free eclectic approach, of an architect who blended styles into an overall harmony, with originality, which is why those who have studied his work recognise his inventiveness, exuberance and style'.

Should George Skipper be compared with Richard Norman Shaw (1831–1912), Alfred Waterhouse RA (1830–1905), Charles Voysey (1857–1941), or even Edwin Lutyens (1869–1944) who were all approximately contemporary? In one sense, the boat has already sailed, and Skipper's name is not associated. Or should he be ranked with other impressive, but less commonly known figures such as the Arts and Crafts architect William Bidlake, or Halsey Ricardo (1854–1928), who worked with ceramic artist, William de Morgan? Frankly the business of ranking and grouping artists' careers and reputations is clumsy and liable to mislead. George Skipper is never going to fit into a single category.

Skipper's great-nephew, Colin Geoffrey Skipper FRICS, (1929–) offered this assessment, made by another architect:

'George Skipper's interwar career marked a prolonged anticlimax to a sparkling late Victorian and Edwardian period which put him briefly in the front rank of national architects, and enabled him to delight in and realize his own vision of the individualistic gentleman-architectural-artist before his unremitting, somewhat embittered, and irascible later years'.

Another appraisal of Skipper's character and status was written by Faith Shaw in her 1971 thesis, *An Introductory Study to the Life and Work of George J. Skipper,* the earliest instance of 'Skipper Studies'. Writing fifty years ago, Shaw was able to discuss Skipper with people such as Skipper's Surveyor, Henry Trueman, and William Spear, formerly of Norwich City Council, both of whom had known GJS in person. Through Edward Skipper, Shaw even had access to George's wife, Alice.

'One of the clearest facts to emerge from even a brief study of George Skipper and his work is that first and foremost he was an artist. He continued to draw for interest and his work was exhibited in the Royal Academy.
Those who knew GJS say that he relied on his builders and surveyor to correct constructional mistakes, or even insert constructional detail, but they had to be very careful not to alter any of GJS's ideas. As can be seen from the notes and correspondence associated with architectural

plans, he often contravened bye-laws. In spite of this his staff were usually devoted to him and admired his flair and enthusiasm even while they struggled to convert a beautiful sketch of a front elevation into a constructable building.

He was considered to be difficult and self-opinionated, a martinet in some ways, yet generous, affectionate, and even sentimental. Although his family often held different views from him, they were proud of his dignity, his achievements and his integrity'.

The question remains: was he a national architectural figure, despite the concentration of work in East Anglia? Having provided a few motives for architectural historians to neglect him, there are two convincing reasons why Skipper will not disappear.

One of these is the list of artists, artisans and specialists of high repute with whom Skipper is linked. With Minns and Gunton's, with Neatby and Doulton, or with Brindley's Italians carving Potter's stonework, the architect was matchless, not just in Britain in the Edwardian era. To those names are added sculptors Fehr, Chavalliaud, Young and others still to be named. The professional craft skills on display at Surrey House, Sennowe Park and 'Telephone House' – now St Giles Hotel – have ensured these buildings will not go unnoticed.

The other is heritage Listing, guaranteeing preservation and upkeep, and drawing the attention of Pevsner and a number of writers ever since. The 'rediscovery' of George Skipper began forty-five years ago with David Jolley's exhibition at Norwich School of Art. The new interest encouraged the gradual heritage Listing of almost all of George's work, not only in the eastern counties, but whole streets in Doulting and Street in Somerset. Importantly, Skipper's Surrey House for Norwich Union (Aviva PLC) is Listed grade I, and this means that his name endures.

Skipper's reputation is still rising. When the Bank of England wanted an image of a visual artist to be printed on the back of the new £20 note in 2015, George Skipper's portrait was proposed (a Scottish economist was chosen, but the English architect would have served very well). It is gratifying, nonetheless, that he can be listed as a visual artist, as well as an architect of high repute. These days there are guided tours to Skipper sites in Norwich, there are informative booklets dedicated to him, there are references, for instance David Summers's text on Skipper in Kathryn Ferry's *Powerhouses of Provincial Architecture*. It seems that 'Skipper Studies' are of increasing interest to the public, many of whom have personal relationships with some of his buildings. These studies will not end here.

Bibliography

ALLTHORPE-GUYTON, M (1982) *A Happy Eye: A School of Art in Norwich 1845 –1982*, Norwich, Jarrold.
ASH, MARY & BURALL, PAUL (2019) *Social Housing – A History of Norwich Leadership*, The Norwich Society.
ARNOTT, K (1987) *Hunstanton – The Story of a Small Norfolk Seaside Resort*, Kings Lynn Borough Council
AVERY, D (2003) *Victorian and Edwardian Architecture,* London, Chaucer Press Architecture Library.
BAILLIE SCOTT, M H, ed (1995) *Houses and Gardens: Arts and Crafts Interiors*, Woodbridge, Antiques Collectors Club. First published in 1906 by George Newnes Ltd. Bradley.
BOOKER, JOHN (1991) *Temples of Mammon: Architecture of Banks*, Edinburgh University Press.
BRODIE A; FULSTEAD, A; FRANKLIN, J; PINFIELD, L & J OLDFIELD (2001) *Directory of British Architects 1834 -1914*, London and New York, Continuum.
BROWN, J (1989) *The Art and Architecture of English Gardens*, New York, Rizzoli Int Publications Inc.
BURGESS, E & W, (1904 reprint 2014) *Men Who have Made Norwich*, Norfolk Industrial Archaeology Society.
BUSSEY, D & MARTIN, E (2012) *The Architects of Norwich: George John Skipper, 1856–1948*. Norwich Society.
CLARKE, PENNY(2013) *What has the Norwich Society done for Us? A Record of 90 Years*, Norwich Society.
COCKE, RICHARD (2013) *Public Sculpture of Norfolk and Suffolk*, (Public Sculpture of Britain Series Vol 16) Public Monuments and Sculpture Association / Liverpool University Press.
COLVIN, H (1995 3rd edtn.) *Biographical Dictionary of British Architects 1600 –1840*, London, Yale U.P.
CRUICKSHANK, D (2002) *The Story of Britain's Best Buildings*, London, BBC Worldwide Ltd.
CUMMING, E & KAPLAN, W (1991) *The Arts and Crafts Movement*, London, Thames and Hudson.
CURL, JAMES STEVENS and WILSON, SUSAN (2016) *The Oxford Dictionary of Architecture*, Oxford, O.U.P
DARLEY, G & MCKIE, D (2013) *Ian Nairn: Words in Place*, London, Five Leaves Publications
DAY, J.H (1879) *Report of the Shepton Mallet District Hospital and Dispensary for the year 1879*, Shepton Mallet Library ref: T.362.1
DEAN, D (1983) *The Thirties: Recalling the English Architectural Scene*, London, Trefoil Books.
DIXON, R & MUTHESIUS, S (1997 2nd ed. reprint) *Victorian Architecture*, London, Thames and Hudson.
FRAMPTON, K (1997) *Modern Architecture: A Critical History*, 3rd edtn, London, Thames & Hudson.
GOODRUM, PETER (2020) *Jarrold 250 Years: A History,* Norwich, Jarrold.
GOODRUM, PETER (2014) *Five Norwich Lives*, Norwich, Mousehold Press.
HAIGH, D (1995) *Baillie Scott: The Artistic House*, London, Academy Editions.
LONG, H (1993) *The Edwardian House*, Manchester University Press.
MANSELL HATERSLEY, R (2004) *The Edwardians*, London, Little & Brown.
HITCHMOUGH, W (1997) *C.F.A Voysey,* London, Phaidon.
JOLLEY, D (1975) *Architect Exuberant*, Norwich School of Art and Design.
JOLLEY, D & SKIPPER, E (1980) *Celebrating Skipper: 100 years of Architecture 1880 -1980*, Norwich.
McGARVIE, M (1986) *Guide to Historic Street ~ A History of Street as shown in its Buildings*, Unpublished –Street Library, Somerset.
MUTHESIUS, S (1990 4th edtn.) *The English Terraced House*, New Haven & London, Yale University Press.
NEWMAN, J (1983 3rd edtn.) *The Buildings of England. North East and East Kent*, London, Penguin.
PEVSNER, N (1970) *The Buildings of England: Cambridgeshire*, London, Penguin Books.
PEVSNER, N revised by RADCLIFFE, E (2002) *The Buildings of England. Suffolk,* New Haven & London, Yale University Press.
PEVSNER, N & WILSON, B (1998 reprint of 2nd ed.) *The Buildings of England. Norfolk Vol. I: Norwich and the North-East,* London, Penguin Group.
PEVSNER, N & WILSON, B (1999 2nd ed.) *The Buildings of England. Norfolk Vol. 2: North-West and South*, London, Penguin Group.
RICHARDSON, M (1983) *Architects of the Arts and Crafts Movement*. London, Trefoil Books.
SERVICE, A (1977) *Edwardian Architecture: A handbook to building design in Britain 1890 -1914*, London, Thames & Hudson.
SNELLING, S (2012) *Norwich – A Shattered City: The story of Hitler's blitz on Norwich and its people, 1942*. Wellington, Halsgrove Publishing.
SUMMERS, DAVID (2009) 'George John Skipper: Norfolk architect', in: FERRY, KATHERINE, *Powerhouses of Provincial Architecture, 1837-1914*. London: Victorian Society.
STAMP, G (2001) *Edwin Lutyens Country Houses*, London, Aurum Press
STUART GRAY, A (1985) *Edwardian Architecture: A Biographical Dictionary*, London, Duckworth & Co Ltd.
VAN LEMMEN, H (2002) *Architectural Ceramics*, Princes Risborough, Shire Publications.

Journals / Features / Reports

ASLET, C (1981) Sennowe Park, Norfolk -I. *Country Life*, 24 December 1981 Vol. 170, pps 2242–2245.
ASLET, C (1981) Sennowe Park, Norfolk -II. *Country Life*, 31 December 1981 Vol. 170, pps 2298–2301.
COOK, N (1987) *Eclectic Excellence ~ A study of Norwich Union Life Insurance Society's Head Office at No.8 Surrey House, Norwich, 1901–05*, unpublished BA dissertation in Aviva PLC Archives.
DARLEY, G (1976) Town of the Shoemakers ~ Street, Somerset. *Country Life*, I July 1976, Vol.160, pps 42–44.
GIROUARD, M (1971) Days of Victorian Glory: Cromer, Norfolk. *Country Life*, 26 Aug 1971, Vol.150, 502–505
MACARTNEY, M (1908) Surrey House. *Architectural Review, Vol. XXIII*, January–June 1908.
MUTHESIUS, S (1972) *The Marble Hall: George Skipper and the Norwich Union*. University of East Anglia Bulletin, January 1972, pps 15–18.
NAA (Norfolk Association of Architects) (1976) *Celebrating Skipper, Norfolk Association of Architects Broadsheet*, Issue No. 18, 1976.
SHAW, FAITH (1971) *An Introductory Study to the Life and Work of George J. Skipper, Architect of Edwardian Norwich and Norfolk* (unpublished Master's degree thesis, University of East Anglia).
KNIGHTS, ANTHONY, (1999) *George John Skipper 1856-1948: Architectural Chameleon*, (unpublished Dissertation, University of East Anglia).
THOMAS, STEVEN (2005) *The Architecture of George John Skipper (1856–1948) ~ A Norfolk Architect Worthy of Esteem* (unpublished Dissertation submitted to the College of Estate Management).
WILSON, B of Wilson Compton Associates (2004) *Surrey House (Marble Hall) Record and Analysis Survey Vol. I - Text*, Norwich (unpublished report held by Aviva PLC).

Archives

RIBA Collections
RIBA PA25 1/1
RIBA PA25 I 13
RIBA PA 251/1-15
RIBA PA 256/28
RIBA PB486/2
RIBA PB486/6
RIBA PB486/12
RIBA PB486/7(1-2)
RIBA PA 256/1-6 & 23-34
RIBA SKG 1-2
RIBA SKB 322 1st sketchbook.
RIBA SKB/323/1
RIBA SKB 323/2
RIBA SKB 325/1
RIBA SKB 326/5
RIBA SKB 328

Lowestoft Record Office LRO
LRO Display Boards
LRO 540/34/4/14
LRO 540/40/4/15

Norfolk Record Office NRO
NRO BR35/2/96/2
NRO BR35/21701 Ifl
NRO BUL 4/259
NRO N/EN 31 Register of Norwich building 1893 -1899.
NRO Drawings Collection including images of University Arms Hotel, Cambridge, and Sackville Street, London. (Illustration of Norfolk & Norwich Savings Bank in Boardman archive).

George Skipper
Royal Academy Summer Exhibitions.

1903 No.1481: Commercial Chambers, Red Lion St, Norwich.
1903 No.1590: Design for a Savings Bank.
1904 No.1633: Norwich Union Life Assurance new Head Office.
1905 No.1406: Norwich & London Accident Assurance, 41-43 St Giles Street, Norwich.
1906 No.1516: Norwich Union new Headquarters – interior.
1910 No.1640: Sennowe Park, entrance to the stable courtyard.
1910 No.1674: The Red House, Cromer.
1916 No.1661: Sennowe Park, Ryburgh Gates.
1917 No.1389: Drawing Room, Framingham Hall, Norfolk.
1925 No.1061: Chislet Colliery Village, Kent – Village Green.
1932 No.1208: House at Great Missenden, Buckinghamshire.
1932 No.1247: Rebuilding of Sackville Street, London.

ARCHITECTS

Bidlake, William   232
Boardman, Edward   48, 73, 132–133, 202
Bond, John Owen   62
Buckler, John   54
Burton, Decimus   157, 168
Campbell, Colen   107
Cockrill, John 'Concrete'   97, 98
Cockrill, Ralph   98
Colcutt, Thomas   97
Edis, R.E   205
Feilden & Mawson   209
Foster, Peter (George's son-in-law)   226
Fowke, Francis   21
Gaudi, Antoni   93, 94
Gibbs, James   107, 230
Godwin, George   27
Hall, Henry   29
Havers, Albert   154
Hill, William   22
Holloway, Charles   219
Hollyer Evans, E   125
Humbert, A.J   205
Jobson, F.J   22
Lane, Richard   22
Lee, John Thomas   20, 22, 162
Lutyens, Edwin   73, 122, 232
Mendelsohn, Erich   134
Nash, John   220
Nesfield, William Eden   21, 162
Nesfield, WIlliam Andrews   21
Palladio, Andrea   119, 121
Palmer, Frederick Charles   156
Peruzzi, Baldassare   130
Pearce, J.B   48
Pierce, Stephen Rowland   219
Ratcliffe, George   40
Reynolds William   44
Ricardo, Halsey   232
Scott, Augustus Frederic   23, 73, 81
Scott, Sir George Gilbert   103, 153
Shaw, Richard Norman   21, 232
Simpson, John   210
Soane, Sir John   107
Statham, H.H   48
Sulley, Henry   22
Voysey, Charles   134, 232
Waterhouse, Alfred   20, 103, 232
Williams-Ellis, Clough   94
Worthington, Thomas   22
Webb, Philip   137
Wren, Christopher   126

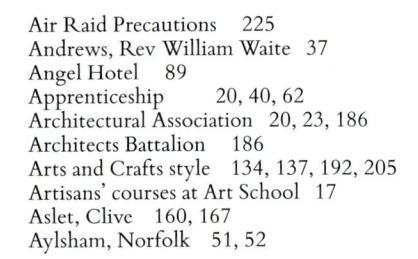

Air Raid Precautions   225
Andrews, Rev William Waite   37
Angel Hotel   89
Apprenticeship   20, 40, 62
Architectural Association   20, 23, 186
Architects Battalion   186
Arts and Crafts style   134, 137, 192, 205
Artisans' courses at Art School   17
Aslet, Clive   160, 167
Aylsham, Norfolk   51, 52

Back, Lt Col Philip Edward   56
Banks, designs for   156
Baines, Elizabeth Tills   36, 228
Barcelona   93, 94
Bareham, Rachel   51, 85
Barwell, John   16
Barrett, Sir Francis Leyland   73
Baedeker Raids   216, 224
Bayes, Gilbert   125
Belgium, visit to   19,20
Bell, John   16
Betjeman, John   93, 94
Bignold, Sir Samuel   116
Bishop's Bridge, plan to demolish   201–02
Blitz, Norwich – bombardment   224–25
Boathouse   **177**, 178
Boer War   89, 99
Borrow, George   9, 138
Brethren   22, 51, 126, 182, 188, 212
Bracondale School   11,12, 15
Bricks   13, 168
Brickmaking   10, 12, 13
Bridge design   **179, 180**
Brindley, William   **103**, 104, 105, 110, 113, 115, 153, 158, 167, 171
Browne, Sir Thomas   230
Bruton   30, 31
Builder, The (weekly magazine)   **26**, 27, 30, 34, 64, 178, 209
Bulwer, William Earle Gascoyne Lytton   49
Burmantofts Pottery   88
Burr, Arthur   183
Bussey, David   119, 130
Butleigh Hospital, Somerset   28, 29

Cabell, Benjamin Bond   63, 64, 65
Caley & Sons, Chocolate makers   191, 224
Canterbury House, Norwich   148, **149**, 150
'Carraraware'   94, 97, 98, 121, 126
Carriage yard, Sennowe Park   **173–175**
Caxton, William   94
Charter, James Ord   182–83

INDEX

Charter, Ralph (stepson)   182, 221, 223
Chavalliaud, Léon Joseph   115
Chislet Colliery   184, 202-204
City Hall, Norwich   94
Clark, W.S (C. & J. Clark Shoes)   36, 41, 42, 44, 47
Clay lump   192
Cliff Hotel, Gorleston-on-Sea   60
Clock Tower and Bell Tower   44, **45**, 175-**76**
Cobden, Richard   46
Cochrane, Robert   16
Cockrill-Doulton Patent Tiles   **97**
Cole, Henry   16
College Road, Norwich   52
Collins, Arthur, City Engineer   125
Commercial Chambers, Norwich   85, 97, 118, **120, 121, 122, 123, 124**, 125, 224
Conan Doyle, Arthur   184
Conscientious Objectors   188
Cook, Thomas Albert   157–58, 160, 170, 172, 179
'Cosseyware' – See Costessey ware
Costessey (near Norwich)   10
Costessey Hall   54
Costessey ware terracotta   49, 52–56, 58, 59, **70**, 73, 75, 80, 82, 84, 86, 87
Cottage Hospitals   29, 38
County School   14, 159, 177
Country Life Magazine   160, 192
Cringleford Bridge incident   93, 101
Crispin Hall, Street, Somerset   **40, 41**, 42
Cromer, Norfolk   62 –75, 79
Cromer Town Hall   **64**, 65, 70
Cromer Pier   77
Curl, James Stevens   167

Defoe, Daniel   94
Demolition of Skipper's buildings   231
De La Warr Pavilion, Bexhill-on-Sea   134
Dereham (East Dereham)   9–10, 13–14, 23, 24, 28, 36, 53, 61, 138, 159, 177, 185, 192, 216
Doulton & Co, /Royal Doulton   87, 88, 90, 92–94, 97, 98, 121, 125, 126, 127, 130, 173
Doulting (Somerset)   25, 32, **33**, 34, 35, 36
Dover   184
Drawing   15, 16, 17, 98, 212
Drinking Fountain   63, **175**

Eastern Daily Press   125, 188
East Harling, Norfolk   **192**, 194
Ecclesiastical Estates Commissioners   218
Elms Estate, Norwich   **191**, 192

Faience   88, 94 – also see Carraraware
Fakenham   198, 200
Farmer & Brindley   21, 103 – see Brindley
Fehr, Henry Charles   113, 125, **171**, 194
Framingham Hall / The Chase   218

Garboldisham, Norfolk   192
'Garden City' concept   137, 192
Gatehouses   158, 160, 162
Gauged brickwork   168
Gildencroft Chapel   53, 225
Gill, Thomas, builder   141, 143
George V, H.M The King   204–206
Government Schools of Art   15, 16
Gostwyck Grange, Australia   140–141, 230
Grand Hotel, Cromer   65, **66, 67**
'Great Depression' (1930)   212
Gunton, George – see Costessey ware

Halesworth, Suffolk   29
Halsey House, Cromer   **73**, 137
Harrow School   202
Haymarket Chambers, Norwich   97, 127, **128, 129**, 130, **131, 224**
Hersden, Kent   202, **203**, 216
Hethersett, Norfolk   37
Heydon Hall   48, 148
Heydon well-house   48–50
Hippodrome, Gt Yarmouth   98
Historic England   32, 92
Homeopathic remedy   144
'Homes for Heroes'   191
Hospital ventilation   30
Hotel de Paris, Cromer   **74, 75, 76**, 77
Housing and Town Planning Act (1909)   184
Housing Act (1919)   191
Humbletoft House   216
Hunstanton church   **37**, 38
Hunstanton Town Hall   77, **78, 79**, 204

Jarrold   60, 82, 141, **142–43**, 144, **145–46**, 147, 202
Jarrold Publishing   147
Jerningham, Sir George   54
Jolley, David   93, 179, 180, 229, 232
Jubilee Clock Tower, Street, Somerset   44–**45**
Jubilee Memorial Well-house, (Heydon, Norfolk)   48, **49**, 50

Kemp, Sir Kenneth 66, 88, **89**, 100, 130, 150
Kent, Ivan 40
Kent Coal Company 183, 184, 202
King, Miss 144

Larking, Charles 124, 125, 126
Lee, John Thomas – see Architects
Legge-Paulley, Dr Job Nathaniel 56
Le Strange, Hamon 77
Lift-head (Sandringham) 205
Listed Building – see Historic England
London & Provincial Bank, Norwich **154–55**
Lowestoft 50, 56, 59, 132–138,

Maltings 61, 138–140
Mancroft Towers 56, **57**, **58**, **59**
Market Place, Norwich 146
Martyn & Co, H.H 115
McLean, Colin 185, 186, 216
Metropole Hotel, Cromer 68, 93, 231
Mile Cross estate, Norwich 197, 210
Military Service Act 188
Millfield House, Street **47**, 48
Minns, James Benjamin Shingles 59, 82, **86**, 87, 113
Morris, William 137, 138, 190, 202
Munnings, Alfred 58, 129
Murray, George 113

Nairn, Ian 150
Neatby, William James **88**, 90, 92, 113, 121, 124, 125, 130, 158, 232
Norfolk, Duke of 101
Norfolk Daily Standard 93, 94, **95**, 96, 97
Norwich Argus 96
Norwich Mercury 182
Norwich Art School 15–19, 86, 113, 223, 229
Norwich City Council 185, 188, 191, 196, 197, 201, 210, 218, 232
Norwich City Hall 219
Norwich School of Artists 15
Norwich Society 202
Norwich & London Accident Insurance 150
Norwich Union Insurance office (also see Surrey House) 99–102, **104–118**, 171, 175, 224, 228, 233
Norwich Union Insurance in Cambridge 126, **127**, 156, 198
Norwich Savings Bank 118

Oulton Broad 56–59, 138, 139

Paget, Richard Horner 25, 28, 31, 32, 36
Palazzo Massimo alle Colonne, Rome 130
Palazzo Thiene, Vicenza 119
Paris 212
Patrick Stead Hospital 29
Pavilion **172**
Pert, Leonard Harry 190
Peto, Samuel Morton 133
Pevsner (N. Pevsner Series: *The Buildings of England*) 23, 74, 93, 99, 101, 121, 150, 154, 156, 172, 219, 233
Piccirilli brothers, sculptors 116
Polychrome 130
'Poppyland' 63
Potter, E.W.D, Monumental Mason **104**, 105, 107, 108, 137, 148, 150, 153, 172
Public Libraries Act 198
Putti 121
Queen Alexandria's beach-house 206
Queen Mary Cottages, Sandringham 204

Railways (G.E.R) 13, 14, 77, 159, 177, 219
Read, Benedict 153
Rebus 58
'Red House', Bexleyheath 137
Red Lion Street, Norwich 118–125
RIBA (Royal Institute of British Architects) 23, 38, 48, 103, 126, 129, 141, 198, 204, 206, 212, 221, 226
Rochester Infectious Diseases Hospital **29**, 30
Royal Academy 16, 73
Royal Arcade 89, **90**, **91**, **92**, 93, 97
Royal Army Medical Corps 186
Royal Norfolk and Suffolk Yacht Club-house **132–137**, 138
Rural District Councils 192, 210

Sackville Street, Piccadilly, London 212, 213, 214, **215**, 216, **217**, 219, **220**
Sandringham Estate 204–206
Savoy Hotel, London 97
Scott, Clement 62
Sennowe Hall, Sennowe Park **157**, **158**, **159**, **161**, **162**, **163**, **164**, **165**, **166**, **168**, **172**, **173** 170, 171, **174**, 175, **176**, **177**, **179**, **180**
Sewell, Anna 147
Sexey's School, Bruton 30, 31, **31**
Shaw, Faith 84, 181, 229, 232

Shepherd Neame   216
Shepton Mallet   25, 28, 32
Sherborne Minster, Dorset   38, **39**
Shernbourne, Parish hall, Norfolk   205–**207**
Singer, J.W & Sons   116
Sketchbooks   19, 38, 231
Stained glass design   190
The Sword – Its Authority in Scripture
188, **189**, 190

SKIPPER, GEORGE
   Birth   9
   Schooling   11
   At Art School in Norwich   16–19
   Apprenticeship in London   20–22
   Assisting his father's practice   23–24
   First office in Bank Plain   27, 28
   Second office in Opie Street   48, 62
   Third office in London Street   82, **83, 84, 85,** 86, **87,** 101, 219, 220
   London office (c.1930–38)   216, 221, 223
   Marriage to Alice Skipper (Charter)   183
   Previous marriages   36, 51, 61, 147
   Private Library   121, 223, 228–229
   Towers and turrets   142–143, 205
   Town Planning 132, 184–85, 191, 197, 200
Skipper, Alice (Elizabeth Alice Charter — wife)   182, 228
Skipper, Betty (daughter-in-law)   189, 221, 223, 228
Skipper, Colin Geoffrey   118, 150, 232
Skipper, Edward John Goodwin (son) 181, 190, 195, 216, 218, 220, **221, 223, 226,** 228, 232
Skipper, Eric Hayward   62, 181, 186, 219, 226
Skipper, Elizabeth (mother)   9, 10
Skipper, Frederick Wilemer (brother) 10, 23, 48, 60, 99, 126, 141, 181, 186
Skipper, John Henry   10, 183
Skipper, (Foster) Margaret Elizabeth (daughter)   195, 218, **221,** 223, 226, 229
Skipper, other Skipper families 9, 12, 18, 19
Skipper, Rachel   51, 85, 99, 147
Skipper, Robert (brother) 10, 23, 28, 48, 99, 183
Skipper, Robert (father) 9, **11,** 12, 15, 22, 23, 147
Skipper, Theodore ('Theo')   62, 147, 148, 182, 186, 190
Smith's, J.S, builders   74, 121, 126
Snettisham, Norfolk   98
Soman, Philip / Soman Wherry Press 96–97
South Kensington System 16, 17, 19
Southwold   130, 132
St Augustine's Church Memorial window 190
St Giles Street, Norwich   94, 97, 121
St Giles Hotel, formerly Telephone House 150, **151, 152, 153,** 154, 224, 233
Stables   173, 174
Stamp, Gavin   122, 231

STONE
   Bath stone   150, 153, 154
   Carrstone   77, 79, 205
   Clipsham Stone   104, 108
   Doulting limestone   36
   Lias limestone   44
   Knapped flint   72, 80
   Marble   103, 110, 111
   Portland Stone   104, 115, 150, 153, 154, 172, 198
Street, Somerset   **40–48**
Strode, William   43
Surrey House – see Norwich Union Life Insurance
Sutton Settled Estates, London   213, 219
Swonnell's Maltings   138–140
Sykes, Godfrey   87

Talbot, William   115
Terracotta – see Costessey ware and 87–88, 125
Thomas, Steven   156, 229, 230
Thun Stadtkirche tower, Switzerland   44
Tinworth, George   88
Tostock Place, Suffolk   230
Town Planning Institute   185, 200
Trueman, Henry   84, 192, 232

University Arms, Cambridge 126, **208–209**
Urns   117, 152, 172, 230

Verulam, Countess   197
Victoria Hotel, Lowestoft   59, **60**

Wells-next-the-Sea   139, 159
Westminster Cathedral   103
Whinburgh Chapel   24, 51
Windham, Maria, Countess of Listowel   63
Winter Garden   170–171
Withers, John Showell   11
Wyman's & Sons, printers, Fakenham 198, **199, 200,** 231

Yarmouth, Great   60, 98
Young, Arthur Stanley, sculptor   117
Young, James (Young's builders)   50, 58, 65, 79, 104, 117

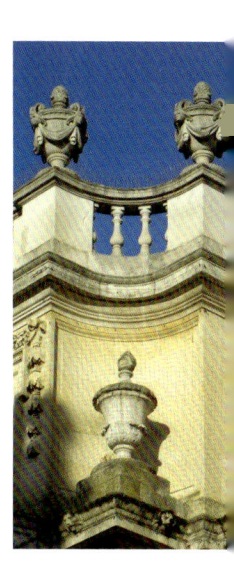

Glossary of Architectural Terms used in this book

Acanthus: classical ornamental leaf shape.
Antefixae: upright ornament punctuating cornice or parapet.
Architrave: moulded frame of window, or door.
Ashlar: blocks of stone cut to provide flat faces and square edges.
Balustrade: Series of vertical supports at edge of balcony, or bridge.
Bay window: either canted (straight fronted), or bowed (curved).
Bellcote: usually small gabled or roofed bell-house.
Campanile: free-standing bell-tower.
Capital: head of a column or pilaster (Doric, Corinthian, Ionic).
Cartouche: framed tablet, usually decorated.
Caryatid: female figurative sculpture supporting balcony or roof.
Chamfer: rounded profile made by smoothing sharp edge or corner.
Coping: protective upper course of bricks to cap a wall.
Corbel: Projecting feature to support something else above it.
Cornice: horizontal moulded ledge on top of building or entablature.
Cupola: small dome, usually made of copper.
Dentilation: display of brickwork with projecting headers.
Dormer: projecting window on sloping roof.
Entablature: horizontal arrangement of cornice, frieze and architrave.
Frieze: middle part of entablature, often decorated.
Gauged brickwork: bricks cut and rubbed smooth to a uniform surface.
Hood-mould, dripstone or label: moulding over window etc., to dispel rain.
Keystone: central stone over an arch.
Label-stop: end of hood-mould.
Loggia: open arcaded or colonnaded gallery.
Lunette: semi-circular window, also Diocletian window.
Mansard: roof with four sloping sides becoming steeper halfway down.
Mathematical tiles: facing tiles simulating brickwork.
Mullion: vertical bar between window lights.
Ogee: 'S' or reverse 'S' shaped outline.
Oriel: bow window seated on corbels or brackets above ground level.
Overthrow: fixed arch over gateway, usually wrought iron.
Pediment: triangular classical profile on gables, and above doors and windows.
– Broken pediment: peak of triangle is absent.
– Open pediment: base of triangle is not continuous.
– Segmental pediment: convex curved upper part instead of triangular.
Pilaster: flattened classical column attached to wall.
Quoin: sturdy blocks of masonry reinforcing corners of building.
Rustication: surface of masonry roughed, or channeled to give effect.
Spandrel: triangular area in upper corner of arches and doorways.
Stringcourse: noticeable horizontal course of decorated bricks/stones.
Tourelle: small turret sitting on corbels against wall.
Transom: horizontal bar between window lights.
Vitruvian scroll: ornamental wavy line running horizontally across elevation.
Volute: spiral scroll on Ionic capital of column.
Voussoirs: wedge-shaped stones on either side of keystone.